NEIL PATRICK HARRIS

CHOOSE YOUR OWN AUTOBIOGRAPHY

NEIL PATRICK HARRIS

CHOOSE YOUR OWN AUTOBIOGRAPHY

BY NEIL PATRICK HARRIS

AS UNSHREDDED AND PASTED BACK TOGETHER BY
DAVID JAVERBAUM

CROWN
ARCHETYPE
NEW YORK

Library of Congress Cataloging-in-Publication Data is
available.

ISBN 978-0-385-34699-3
eBook ISBN 978-0-385-34700-6

PRINTED IN THE UNITED STATES OF AMERICA

Photograph and source credits appear on page 292.
Book design by Elizabeth Rendfleisch
Illustrations by Antony Hare, P.I.
Jacket design by Michael Nagin
Jacket illustration by John Defreest

10 9 8 7 6 5 4 3 2 1

First Edition

My very first job was working in a bookstore. It was there that I discovered the Choose Your Own Adventure books. I'd spend hours lost in those novels—I loved the idea that I could write my own story, or at least try to figure out which path was the winning one. When it came time to write my memoir, I couldn't think of a better way to depict my twisty-turny life, so I decided to adapt the Choose Your Own Adventure concept (albeit as a relative parody). If you're familiar with the series, then welcome; make yourself at home. If not, by all means rush to your nearest bookshoperie, seek out Choose Your Own Adventure books, and enjoy. They are awesome.

To David: I couldn't be happier that my many paths and choices have traveled to you.

To Gideon and Harper: May your lives have countless chapters, and may those chapters be filled with laughter, adventure, and great good times.

WARNING! ! !

This self-serving celebrity autobiography is different from other self-serving celebrity autobiographies.

Because this is a **choose-your-own autobiography** . . . and YOU AND YOU ALONE will be responsible for living the life of Neil Patrick Harris.

Throughout this book, you will be presented with choices. Choose wisely and you will end up happy, successful, and married to the man of your dreams. Choose poorly and you will end up fat, balding, and slicing turkey behind the counter at a Schlotzsky's. Either way, at some point you'll be spending a few months working with Anne Heche on Broadway. (Have fun!)

If you want to make it through these memoirs in one piece, you will have to rely entirely on your wits, instincts, and ability to turn to specifically numbered pages.

Good luck.

And remember, the decisions you make won't just be affecting you.

From this point on, Neil Patrick Harris's life . . . is in your hands.

Thanks for purchasing the latest in our three-name-choose-your-own-autobiography series!

1. GEORGE BERNARD SHAW
2. BILLY BOB THORNTON
3. SALT 'N' PEPA
4. MARY ELIZABETH MASTRANTONIO
5. DAVID HYDE PIERCE
6. DAVID AFTER DENTIST
7. CEDRIC THE ENTERTAINER
8. JOHN WILKES BOOTH
9. NEIL PATRICK HARRIS

You, Neil Patrick Harris, are born in Albuquerque, New Mexico, on June 15, 1973, at what you're pretty sure is St. Joseph's Hospital, although it's hard to be certain as the whole experience leaves you a little blurry.

The first person you encounter is, not surprisingly, your mother, Sheila Scott Harris. As the years go by you will come to learn she is a truly remarkable woman filled with love, kindness, fragility, selflessness, intelligence, wisdom, and humor. The kind of mom who will talk to you like a person and treat you with respect from the age of two. The kind of mom who will hold you in her lap for an entire four-hour car ride, lightly scratching your back. The kind of mom who teaches you the rules of Twenty Questions and then lets you guess the "right" answer even though it wasn't what she was thinking, but does it subtly enough to keep you from realizing that's what she's doing. The kind of mom traditional enough to sing in the Episcopal church choir every week but hip enough to improvise a horrific death for a character in the bedtime story she's reading you just to make sure you're paying attention. The kind of mom who sews your Halloween costumes and plays the flute and loves to laugh and encourages you to pursue your passions and at one point trains to become a Jazzercise instructor and at another decides to go back to law school in her thirties and commute four hours each way every weekend for three solid years to make sure she spends enough time with you.

Yeah, you luck out, mom-wise. But at this *particular* moment she isn't any of those things so much as a grunting, sweating, shrieking woman in pain.

As she reaches over to hold you for the first time, you notice a man smiling at you. This is your father, Ronald Gene Harris. As the years go by you will come to learn he is strong, stoic, and wise, an amazing husband, lawyer, logical thinker, and fixer of problems. The kind of dad who sometimes trades his legal services for old furniture, which he then spends months refinishing to its pristine, antique glory. The kind of dad who helps you craft winning Soap Box Derby cars while he builds his dream house in the mountains. The kind of dad who, claiming "emergency law work," begs off a weekend trip to Albuquerque to celebrate your seventh birthday, causing you great disappointment . . . until you get home to realize he's actually spent the entire time building you a tree house, complete with a sandbox, rope ladder, secret trapdoor, and zip line. The kind of dad who plays folk songs on the guitar, teaches himself the banjo, and shows you how to sing. And, perhaps most important, the kind of dad who's *funny*. Not "Dad funny" (i.e., not funny) but *actually* funny. He looks like a serious conservative thinker, but he is blessed with a dry and untiring sense of humor. He owns every Smothers Brothers and Kingston Trio and Brothers Four LP and plays them constantly. And he is the master of repetition comedy. From the time you are fifteen years old, whenever he is handed the phone to talk to you he will stage-whisper, "No, I don't want to talk to him, I don't want to . . . oh, HI, Neil! How are YOU??" *Every time.* And you will do the same. *Every time.* And then the two of you will cackle about how funny you are. *Every time.*

But again, none of these things are immediately apparent to you right now, seeing as how you're crying, covered in viscous afterbirth, and zero years old.

. . .

You come in weighing a very average, very sexy seven pounds, seven ounces. As it happens, that is also the *exact* weight of an Emmy Award. Coincidence? Yes . . . but true fact? No.

After your cord is cut for your convenience, you're immediately whisked away for tests, measurements, and the embedding of the electronic neural microchip secretly implanted in all American babies born after 1953. Exhausted from your nine-month ordeal, you ask for and receive permission to spend the night in a comfy bed in the hospital's maternity ward. You request a single instead of a twin, because you are not a twin.

The next morning you deem yourself ready to go home.

Upon arriving at your new *ex utero* digs you meet the third member of your immediate family. Your brother, Brian Christopher Harris, is three years older than you at the time of your birth and, as it turns out, will remain so throughout your life. He is the kind of brother who is brilliant and imaginative, a rebel who will spend much of your childhood insisting to you and your parents that he is a Russian prince who somehow ended up in this family under mysterious circumstances he is not at liberty to discuss. The kind of brother who is the family's designated boundary-tester and who prides himself on being smart and wily enough to survive on wit. The kind of brother who will often confide in you about his secret trips to the numerous abandoned mine shafts dotting the New Mexico landscape whose perpetual status on the brink of sudden collapse are a terror for you but an exhilaration for him—"Neil, I'm going into a mine. If I don't come back, here's my location. Don't tell Mom and Dad unless I'm really truly missing. Bye." The kind of brother who is paradoxically both an outsider and very popular, who runs for elementary school student-body president with posters reading "SEX!!! . . . Now that I've got your attention, vote Brian Harris for Student Body President." The kind of brother who will throw parties when your parents are out of town and be kind enough to include you, and to whom you will owe your first beer, your first wine cooler, and your first (and only) make-out session with two girls at the same time.

He will be your hero.

*If you would like to experience a happy childhood,
turn to page 8.*

*If you would prefer to experience a miserable childhood
that later in life you can claim to have heroically overcome,
turn to page 5.*

You, Neil Patrick Harris, are born in Albuquerque, New Mexico, on June 15, 1973. You're pretty sure it's in the backseat of a taxicab, but you can't be certain because maggots have eaten the upholstery.

Your mother, Cruella Bathory Harris, is the kind of mom who drinks alcohol and smokes crack a lot because she is an alcoholic crack addict. The kind of mom who slaps you for waking up, punches you for brushing your teeth, and smacks you with a brand-new belt "to weatherize the leather." The kind of mom who gives you and your siblings nicknames based on the diseases she hopes you come down with later in life. (Your nickname is "Emphysema." Your youngest sister's is "Non-Hodgkin's Lymphoma.") The kind of mom it takes multiple lifetimes to overcome.

As for your father, he is the kind of dad who could have been any one of the five starting players for the 1973 University of New Mexico basketball team. (They're called the Lobos, and for good reason.)

But your childhood has one saving grace: Grandmapa. Grandmapa is one of your mom's parents, although due to his/her appearance you never figure out which one. But it doesn't matter. Grandmapa is there to comfort and inspire you. S/he believes in you. S/he also believes in goblins and banshees and that the Martians killed Kennedy, but that's not the point.

One particularly brutal evening, after a day spent hosing out the abandoned coal car you call your home, you find yourself alone and crying deep in the mine shaft you call your community. It's pitch-black. Below, you hear the flapping of bats' wings. Above, you hear the screech of the 8:05 freight train bringing yet another shipment of fresh bats. Suddenly you hear Grandmapa's familiar clopping gait.

"What's the matter, Neil?"

"Oh, Grandmapa, life is hopeless. I'm unloved, I have webbed feet, and I just don't think I'll ever amount to anything in this lousy world."

That's when Grandmapa slaps you hard across the face and says, "Don't you ever talk that way, young lady!"

"Actually, I'm a b—"

"Now you listen here, girl. You are going to rise from this muck because you are destined for great things. You are destined for fame and fortune. You are destined to be a Broadway star. You are destined to have not one, but two long-term television roles. You are destined to host numerous awards shows. You are destined to have a fairly impressive film career, although you will still be looking for that one great dramatic role that will put you in the elite echelon of, say, future Brad Pitt. You are destined to be president of the Magic Castle. You are destined to have a bizarre encounter with celebrity son Scott Caan outside an LA nightclub. You are destined to have a long inner journey of sexual self-discovery culminating in a lifetime partnership with the man of your dreams. And above all, Nell—"

"Neil."

"—you are destined to tell your heartbreaking, coal-miner'sdaughtery, but ultimately triumphant tale of overcoming adversity to the world, so that others can draw strength from your superhuman resilience and determination!"

And that's when the bats get her/him.

If you would like to experience a more wholesome childhood, turn to page 8.

If you are eager to meet your own children, skip ahead thirty years and turn to page 276.

Your parents live in Ruidoso, a beautiful mountain town of around five thousand people perched over a mile up in the Sierra Blanca range of south-central New Mexico. It looks like an idyllic place to spend a childhood, so after careful consideration you choose to grow up there.

You're a normal, happy, outgoing kid. You worship your big brother and think there's nothing cooler than when he lets you hang out with him and his friends, or when he treats you as his confidant and partner on their various adventures. You dig out little tunnels and caves in the dirt by your driveway and play army with the little soldiers you bought at Ben Franklin's (the local version of Walmart), making them swim across enormous "rivers" trickling from garden hoses. You occasionally take firecrackers and blow up Star Wars action figures, which your parents disapprove of, although not as much as Brian likes to imagine they do. Sometimes after school the bus drops you both off downtown at your dad's office. A half block away there's an unfinished building with an exposed basement. You and Brian call it "the Dungeon," and you love going there and exploring its depths, playing pretend war games and rescuing princesses from phantom dragons.

From early boyhood you are drawn to musical theater. Your parents sometimes play LPs of Broadway cast recordings, and you come to know every note of *Annie* and *The Best Lit-*

tle Whorehouse in Texas, which is not nearly as R-rated as the name suggests. When you're eight they take you to Albuquerque to see a touring company of *Annie,* and you love it so much you teach your brother and all your friends the choreography to "It's the Hard-Knock Life" and act it out with brooms and show it to parents and neighbors. Admission is free, and worth every penny.

Your first-ever stage role comes in 1983, when thirteen-year-old Brian and his friends audition to be Munchkins in Tularosa High School's production of *The Wizard of Oz.* You tag along, and when they see you they ask if you're interested in playing the role of Toto, the dog.

"Bark!" you respond.

You love it. Love, love, *love* it. Everything about it. The makeup, for example: you love watching your transfiguration in the mirror, enthralled by the way a few skillfully applied dabs of gelatinous, alchemical-like substances can transform you from human to canine. You love removing it too, with the Noxzema cold cream and its bracing menthol smell, rubbing it sensuously on your skin and watching that carefully painted dog face falling apart and the colors bleeding into each other until you end up looking like a clown from the 1880s.

For the first time, the glorious illusion of performance, the way the experience is simultaneously real *and* fake, exerts its primal pull on you. It thrills your soul. It also engages your mind. It raises all kinds of existential dilemmas. Why is it, for instance, that when you're onstage as Toto you're on all fours, but when you're making your way down the yellow brick road, which winds its way through the rows of the audience, you're on your "hind legs"? The director feels there's no other practical choice, so it's okay. You don't. You consider it a gross inconsistency that besmirches the meticulous realism of the rest of the high school production of *The Wizard of Oz.*

From that moment on, you never have to be persuaded to do anything that might result in a bunch of strangers applauding you. You quickly build up an impressive résumé in roles at both elementary and middle school and the Cree Meadows Country Club, the home of Ruidoso's Little Theater, a haven for that group of locals who were—you will realize in hindsight many years later—if not closeted, at the very least not big football fans. You play Amahl in *Amahl and the Night Visitors*. You play John Darling in *Peter Pan*. You play Winthrop ("Gary, Indiana") Paroo in *The Music Man*.

Then in middle school you're lucky enough to come under the wing of a wonderful drama teacher named Churchill Cook who, sensing your talent and enthusiasm, begins delegating to you a lot of the musical arrangement and direction of the school plays and musicals. He helps create the highlight of your prepubescent thespian career: your work as narrator and quasi-director of *How the West Was* Really *Won*. (How? Hint: it involves hacky puns and box-step choreography.) It's a comedy revue about the Old West narrated by an old guy with a corncob pipe. You play the role of Old Guy with a Corncob Pipe. Man, do you ham it up. You put on fake old-man wrinkles using the Tom Savini book on proper makeup application, but it's your own idea to put baby powder in the pipe so that when you pretend to smoke, a little puff of powder comes out. Neil Patrick Harris, you are a genius!

You seek out other avenues for performance. You sing in choirs. You even join the public-speaking circuit. At the age of thirteen you enter a contest sponsored by the Optimist Club, a huge international organization with a positive attitude when it comes to semifilled glasses of liquid. Their assignment: deliver a speech on the subject of optimism. You and your mother (a/k/a Optimom) conceive and write the speech together. At the competition you deliver it with the masterly studied casualness of a young man who spent *waaaay* too many hours practicing it in the bathroom mirror. You win the regional finals and its prize . . . a $1,000 college scholarship.

You will never get to use it.

If you want to begin exploring the world of theater, turn to page 14.

If you want to start learning magic, turn to page 21.

If you want to spend waaaaay *too many hours practicing the Optimist Club speech in front of a bathroom mirror, go to the bathroom, go on to the next page, and start reciting.*

Optimism: A Way of Life
An Award-Winning Speech by Neil Patrick Harris, Age 13

"Oh great, another optimism speech. I hate optimism, it's so happy and energetic ... eh, at least I don't have to give one."

Those words came out of the mouth of Scott Jensen. Scott was a thirteen-year-old pessimist. Well, he wasn't really a pessimist, he just definitely wasn't an optimist. His appearance was okay, but the main thing that made him a pessimist was his attitude. He was always too bored. He looked down on things. He looked down on life.

The child who was speaking sat down, and Mr. Maddox, Scott's teacher, grabbed a piece of chalk and went to the blackboard. Now there, he drew a square with a cross in the middle. Scott shook his head and laid it back down on the desk thinking, Now, what does that have to do with optimism? Mr. Maddox quickly turned to him and said, "I know what you're thinking, what does that have to do with optimism? Well, that is a window which represents optimism. You can open that window and have a gateway to a happier life. If you are in a room that's dismal and lonely, you could sit and feel sorry for yourself, or you can go to a window, open it up, stick your head out and smell the fresh air. You can look in the distance and see a rainbow."

Next, Mr. Maddox drew a squiggly line and said, "Now, this isn't just a squiggly line, it's a worm. And it isn't just any old worm either, it's a caterpillar. And a caterpillar is one of the most optimistic creatures I can think of. He believes in himself, and he believes in the future. He knows that he's more than just a funny-looking caterpillar, and that someday he'll become a beautiful butterfly. That's optimism, think about that."

The bell rang and all the kids trampled out of the class, except Scott. He was still sitting, deep in thought. His posture had improved a little, and he was smiling. There was a glisten in his eye that gave him a "happy look."

That afternoon Scott went home and up to his room, and let me tell you, his room was the room of a pessimist. However, on this day, he cleaned it up, made his bed, took a shower, then sat down and began drawing on pieces of paper.

At bedtime, Scott's parents looked in and said, "What are those crazy pictures you've hung on the wall?" Scott smiled and said, "This is a window, and this is a worm."

Throughout the next week, Scott's classmates gave their speeches. On Friday, Mr. Maddox stood up to announce the winners. But before anyone received an award, Scott raised his hand and said, "Mr. Maddox, may I give an optimism speech?"

Mr. Maddox was astonished. He held out his hand, and Scott walked to the front of the class.

"You know, for the last five or so years, I've had a bad outlook on life. I'd get on the school bus, and everyone seemed to be picking on me and disliking me. When I got to school, the students and the teachers seemed to be avoiding me. The trees were glaring at me, and the grass never looked green. I always wished I could change things, but I never quite knew how. After Mr. Maddox spoke to us, I decided to give optimism a try. And hey, it worked. I felt better, and so I decided to continue trying. Over the last week, things have begun to change. No one is really avoiding me, the trees are welcoming me, and the grass is growing greener on my side of the fence. And I just want you to know that I'm trying, and I need a few friends."

Boy, Mr. Maddox smiled the biggest smile he had smiled in a long time. And no, Scott didn't win an award for his speech, but he won something much, much more valuable. He won an optimistic outlook that changed his entire life.

And maybe—just maybe—it could change yours too.

If, having practiced this speech to within an inch of your/its life, you feel ready to begin exploring the world of acting, go on to the next page.

If, having practiced this speech to within an inch of your/its life, you feel ready to audition for your first movie role, turn to page 33.

If, having practiced this speech to within an inch of your/its life, you feel ready to host a major televised awards show, turn to page 211.

If, having practiced this speech to within an inch of your/its life, you are so imbued with optimism you are ready to stare down a crazed young actor outside a Los Angeles nightclub, turn to page 62.

*A*nnie is great. *The Best Little Whorehouse in Texas* is great. But it's *Les Misérables* that first opens up your adolescent soul to the glorious alternate universe that is theater.

You become acquainted with the show at the age of thirteen, when a friend from camp plays a cassette tape of the London cast recording. (Cassette tapes, of course, being the cool way to buy and record music that will never go out of style.) On initial hearing it doesn't sound like much more than nonsense gibberish insanity. An opera, in other words. It's your friend's explanation of the theatrics of it all—here's where the barricades go up, here's where so-and-so kisses so-and-so, here's where this detective dude commits suicide—that you find really interesting. You can picture it unfolding in your mind . . . and if you do say so yourself, your mental stagecraft is awesome.

You buy the cast album and play it an infinite number of times. Soon you're forcing your poor mother to listen to Fantine's dying song, but only after providing her with enough schmaltzy context to make sure she's crying by the end. *Les Miz* enters your psychic landscape, permanently solidifying its place early on in your career when you lose an audition to an actor named Braden Danner, whose principal credit is as Gavroche in the original Broadway production. *Oh, no wonder he got the part,* you think. *I'm just some small-town rube from the Mountain Time Zone, and he's done friggin' Gavroche on Broadway, and man, if I could just be in that show. . . .*

A year later you get your first big misérable break when you and your family visit New York for the first time. You see a great deal of the city and discover the reports are true: it is, indeed, a helluva town. But more important, you get to take in some Broadway shows, and even importantlier, you get to see *Les Miz,* and wow. Wow wow wow. It is a phenomenal, transcendent experience. You are used to the Ruidoso style of stagecraft, the kind where theaters have fold-out metal chairs and basketball hoops hanging from the ceiling. So to watch a show in which an *actual workable mid-nineteenth-century-style barricade* appears in the middle of everything just blows your mind and drops your jaw. Literally: when the lights come on at the end of Act 1—whose climax, "One Day More," features a giant French flag waving and the full cast singing in glorious harmony creating a heavenly wall of sound—you actually have to make a conscious effort to shut your mouth. You are utterly overwhelmed.*

Your love for theater never subsides. After *Doogie Howser* takes off you have the financial means to go to New York during shooting breaks, so you take weeklong trips and see up to a dozen shows—two a day, whenever possible. The experience remains enthralling, but now that you're a working thespian it's also educational. By watching carefully you can gain valuable insights about your craft. "That actor's speaking too slowly. That actress is mugging too much. That guy is drunk and possibly high on coke." Instructive, instructive stuff.

You're particularly drawn to musicals with big giant sets and visual wizardry. *City of Angels,* for example. That's a show that goes from color to black-and-white before your eyes. You sit in the audience and marvel, "Where did the set just go? How do the lights do that? How did they move backward? How did everything

---

* Even your brother is impressed. He had felt that the seventy dollars per ticket would in his case have been better spent on a sweater, but afterward he reluctantly admits, "That was better than a sweater," which is not only a noble admission but an internally rhyming one.

go from color to black-and-white in two sec— Wait, now it's back in color?!?" Then you go backstage and get a tour, and this to you is truly the coolest thing in the world. You're shown the set and the lights and the costumes and learn another variation on the same basic lesson about showbiz you will learn over and over again—it's all, fundamentally, just a bunch of crap glued together and spray-painted over. But the wonderful paradox is that knowing this does not detract from the experience of watching it a second time. On the contrary: it makes it that much more miraculous.

One night you visit with Keith Carradine backstage after watching him kick historico-satirical ass in *The Will Rogers Follies*. You have a pleasant conversation, then watch him put on a cap and jacket, open up the stage door, and disappear into the New York street. The image will stick with you forever. For two hours he was a conjurer summoning up the spirit of a beloved American icon; now, once again, he's just one of the crowd. Heralded, then anonymous. *That's* performing.

To begin pursuing your love of acting in a way that might just possibly lead to your big break, go on to the next page.

To finally get your chance to star onstage in a major production, turn to page 76.

You know, a lot of young boys who are into theater turn out to be . . . umm . . . you know, why don't you just turn to page 27.

It's the spring of 1986. In the wake of your star turn in *How the West Was Really Won*, your budding love of performance is in full bloom. Mr. Cook, the choir and acting teacher, is impressed by your ability and initiative. So is Danny Flores, your band director. You're the middle school drum major, but you also play the xylophone, French horn, and pretty much whatever he needs someone to play for a particular song. A little oboe here, a little bassoon there, a dash of tuba. You're a jack of all instruments, and a master of none.

As the end of middle school approaches, both teachers suggest you consider relocating to a performing arts high school. It's a nice thought, but not realistic. What, you're going to move away from your friends and family for four years to pursue, like, modern *dance* or something? Nuh-uh. You know what that scene's like. You've seen *Fame*. You like drama, but not with all that . . . drama.

So your teachers are kind enough to investigate other options for you. They learn about a weeklong theater camp for high school students held on the campus of New Mexico State University in Las Cruces. You'll have to persuade the directors to stretch the rules to let you enroll, since you're not entering high school until the fall, and physically you are thirteen going on nine; you and puberty have yet to make each other's acquaintance. But none of this bothers you, because your parents are into it, you've always preferred the company of older kids (see "big brother, your"), and besides, *theater camp*! A week of scene writing, costume building, improv games, cold-reading audition classes, and lots of other grown-up thespian-type stuff alongside high schoolers with similar interests? You can't wait!

Best of all, the camp even has its own celebrity—illustrious and prolific playwright Mark Medoff. He's won a Tony Award for his play *Children of a Lesser God*, which will be coming out as a movie later this year. He's the head of the Theater Department at NMSU, and he's heavily involved in the camp. As small-town New Mexicans go, he's a superstar.

Summer doesn't seem to come fast enough, but finally Mom and Dad drop you off, bright-eyed and bushy-tailed,* at NMSU. The week proves every bit as fun and engaging as you'd hoped. There are many different theater-based activities, all of which culminate in a showcase of scenes written, directed by, and starring the students. You write a comedy about a couple on an airplane involved in a case of mistaken identity. It goes on to win the Pulitzer Tony Oscar Prize for Outstanding Excellence®, an award bestowed sporadically by the Academy of Imaginary People in Your Head.

As for Medoff, he really is the camp's big kahuna. When he walks around or attends lectures or classes it feels very godly. His role is largely supervisory, but he also teaches one of the seminars in cold-reading auditions. He is one of two teachers. On the first or second day of camp you and the other kids line up for the auditions class. Half of you go to the room on the left. Half of you go to the room on the right.

If you go to the room on the left, turn to page 33.

If you go to the room on the right, go on to the next page.

---

* Not really. You're prepubescent, so no bush.

"I said *smoked* turkey, not regular turkey, jackass!!!" The customer's angry shout jerks you back from fantasy to reality.

"Yes, sir. Sorry, sir."

"Quite the incompetent boob, aren't you . . . '*Neil*,'" he says, squinting at your Schlotzsky's name tag.

As you re-turkey the sub you reflect on the shambles that is your life. The bankruptcy. The hoarding. The four failed marriages (two straight, two gay). And worst of all, the utter anonymity. No one knows you; no one talks to you; never in your life has anyone seen you on the street and said, "Hey, it's Neil Patrick Harris!" No one could care less. Every year when the Tonys or Emmys are on, you feel some instinctive tug, like you're supposed to be involved in them in some way . . . but you're not.

Where did it all go wrong? you wonder as you squeegee industrial-strength mayonnaise over the bun. You are haunted by a nagging sense of what might have been, the lingering suspicion that everything could have worked out far better, had you just made a single choice differently at some point earlier in your life. But when? Which decision?

You stare at the long line of customers. Half of them are in one line, half in the other. Something about the tableau fires a long-neglected synapse. Something about drama camp. Something about auditions. Wait, now you remember. You were thirteen and about to auditi—

"Hey, I want that sandwich *today*, moron!"

Just as suddenly the flash is gone, and you are back to your life of sleep, sandwich making, compulsive masturbation, and TV.

Maybe tonight you will watch a rerun of your favorite show, *How I Met Your Mother*. That Barney Stinson character is hilarious. Sometimes you like to pretend you are him. Or at least the actor playing him. But you're not.

No, you're not Dustin Diamond.

THE END

You are five years old. You are hanging out with your mom's dad, your beloved Grandpa Scott. He hands you a match, a cork, a needle, a clear plastic cup, and a comb, and challenges you to make the match move on its own.

Wait, which, *what*? How is that possible? That's not possible, Grandpa Scott.

Grandpa Scott sticks the needle upright into the cork, and then balances the match sideways on the tip of the needle—like a compass needle. Then he rubs the comb against his head for static electricity and holds it against the cup. The match begins to swing up and back, as if it's being turned.

Holy crap, that's cool!

It is magic. Magic in its purest form: ordinary items being manipulated by someone with more knowledge than you for the benevolent purpose of creating amazement. And you're instantly hooked. You go to the local library and check out every book on magic you can find. Before long you are gathering friends and family for impromptu and fairly awful magic shows that teach you three important things about yourself: (1) you love performing in front of an audience, (2) you must have a very loving, indulgent family if they're sitting through some of the crap you're making them watch, and (3) you love knowing secrets. It's a fundamental part of your nature. You love to be in on secrets. Not gossipy secrets; *actual* secrets, secrets of information, of mechanics, of science. It's a blissful rush you will pursue your entire life, whether the secrets concern theater set design,

Cirque du Soleil tricks, food preparation, cruise-ship logistics, or casinos. But no profession is more explicitly about secrecy than magic.

You often travel from Ruidoso to Albuquerque on weekends to visit your grandparents, and whenever you do they take you on a trip to a shop on the outskirts of the Winrock Shopping Center called Fool's Paradise. It's a mecca of magic, everything a kid could dream of: row after row of practical jokes, optical illusions, sight gags, and every kind of trick or effect you can imagine, along with many more you can't. You love how the illusionist behind the counter teases you with trick after trick that he refuses to teach you . . . unless you buy the items, naturally. The world of magic is a bottomless well of sheer *knowledge.* Palming coins, for instance: there are front palms and back palms and finger palms and others, and learning them all requires practice and subtlety. You invariably leave with a large bag of tricks and practice in the back seat with them all the way home. Once there you continue practicing while popping in a VHS tape of a magician on Johnny Carson or Merv Griffin, or a David Copperfield or Doug Henning special, or the latest *Magic of the Network Stars.**

It's a weird profession, magic. Literally anyone with around $20,000 can go to a store like Fool's Paradise, buy an entire act's worth of illusions, make up a business card, and call himself a magician. And people in fact do this all the time. That's why there are so many bad magicians. They're just doing the same acts they've seen other people do, and not as well, and without any showmanship. But magic is like pizza: even when it's bad, it's pretty good. When you watch your cousin do a card trick at Thanksgiving, you're still blown away by it, even though he's got no flair and he smells funny. And so when you grow up, you want to be a magician. In fact, why wait that long?

---

* Not a real show, but dammit, it should have been.

So at age eleven you decide to turn pro. You perform at the seventh birthday party of a girl from your Episcopal church congregation. You buy a cape and top hat, stuff some tricks into a paper bag, and on the day of the party set off to seek your fame and fortune.

Everything goes great. The rope trick kills. The coin tricks destroy. Even the zombie ball works, and you *hate* the zombie ball. Then it comes time for the amazing finger chopper. You put the birthday girl's index finger in a mini-guillotine, lower the blade, and "sever" her finger without injury. And this is the moment you discover there is more to magic than merely performing the trick. There is also the little matter of understanding your audience. For the birthday girl's little sister has witnessed your sleight of finger, and is at an age where she has not yet grasped the basic premise that magic is illusion. To her, you are genuinely dismembering her big sister.

And so when the blade comes down she begins to scream. And then another girl screams. And then four more. And soon every girl in the party is in full-bore freak-out mode, and the birthday girl's mother, your employer, bounds in to see what is going on. The image greeting her is that of a rail-thin blond-scarecrowy seventh-grade boy dressed in black, one hand holding her daughter's finger, the other having seemingly just removed it, standing amid a tableau of girlish terror.

Appropriately—and yet ironically—you don't get a tip.

If you would like to pursue magic as a hobby despite this fiasco, turn to page 39.

If you would like to pursue magic as a career despite this fiasco, turn to page 30.

If you'd like to perform an actual magic trick right here right now, turn to page 40.

If you're entirely through with magic and would rather focus on acting, turn to page 46.

And now a word from your friend . . .

PENN JILLETTE

Sorry, girls—it's my fault. I'm the one who ruined your hetero dreams. I'm the one who turned Neil Patrick Harris into a gay.

I've heard many women, including my wife (and my wife is a woman; I'm not the gay one in this particular story), curse the fact that you are gay gay gay. You're the perfect man for them, you know, except for that gay thing. "Why? Why? Why?" they all scream (not in unison), looking upward and shaking their fists. "Why?" Well, the answer is me, Penn Jillette. I turned you, the sexy, gentle, smart, charming, understanding, talented Neil Patrick Harris, gay as a three-dollar bill. Sorry.

It was sometime late last century. I had this movie night thing in New York City every Friday night (now we have it in Vegas every Tuesday night) where a bunch of people, mostly show folk (but we had a police officer and a dentist who joined us), sat around the Times Square Howard Johnson's, hung out a bit, then went to watch a midnight movie. There was a lot of talking before, during, and after. It was like the Algonquin Round Table without the wit. We'd say stuff to one another like "Fuck you," and then go to a movie and say things like "Fuck you" to the screen, and then afterward, say "Fuck you" again and leave. It was always a fun night.

In this century you're a big fancy-ass who's president of the big fancy-ass gay Magic Castle, but back then you were Doogie, a normal child who loved magic as a hobby and made millions of dollars on television. You wanted to meet me because I was a big fancy-ass magician on gay Broadway and you'd heard about me. We never let minors into our movie night for obvious reasons, but I knew you were way famous. So your parents, undoubtedly hoping you wouldn't wish them into the cornfield, brought you to join us one Friday night. (I don't know what year this was or how old you were at the time. If you want information, you need to go to a different chapter—that's part of your book's big gay gimmick.)

You attended a few movie nights. Then you and I finally decided to hang out on a non-movie night . . . parentless. I didn't have children back then, and I knew nothing about boys. I hadn't been around a boy since I was a boy, but we went to my apartment to hang out. It was awkward. Yeah, you were smart enough to memorize child doctor words on TV, but I still had a boy in my apartment and that was creepy. My apartment was an NYC bachelor pad. I had all the things women love a single man to have: tons of porn, Three Stooges DVDs, and a DDD silicone breast implant that I would caress, hold, and squeeze while I was relaxing, if you know what I mean. I didn't really know what to say to a boy. I just knew this evening could lead to jail for something. I had a boy in my apartment and I was a big gay Broadway star so the next stop was incarceration.

At first things went well. You picked up the breast implant and carried it around my loft. You said it felt great. You were right. But then you started looking at the porn DVDs. There you were, a child, in my apartment without your parents, holding a silicone implant, and perusing my porn. I realized I was this close to being sent to prison and getting my name on a permanent watch list. All I needed was a hot tub and some champagne with bubbles that would tickle your little nose.

I panicked. I'm not a prison kind of guy. I led you away from *Busty Enema Nurses III*, without even stopping at the Stooges, and took you right to my music CD shelf. I figured that would be safe. I started talking to you about Sondheim's *Assassins* (a show you would star in fifteen years later, way after I made you gay). I told you it was my favorite musical and one of my favorite Broadway shows. I raved about the show and its brilliant, touching, surprising ideas. I had an attractive young boy in my apartment in NYC and we were talking Broadway musicals. Oh dear.

And then . . . I played some of the *Assassins* CD for you.

Some say gay is a choice. Well, that night I made that gay choice for you. Why oh why oh why didn't I reach for the Stooges?

Sorry, girls.

If you're feeling magical now that Penn Jillette is your friend, turn to page 86.

If you're feeling horny now that Penn Jillette has made you gay, turn to page 78.

If you're feeling musical theatery now that Penn Jillette has played Sondheim for you, turn to page 76.

From early in life you are drawn to guys in a tingly kind of way. In elementary school you have a crush (if one could call it that) on the trumpet player in the middle school band. You watch him too much, and when he drinks at the water fountain you go to drink directly after, hoping to taste him in the water.

Paging Dr. Freud.

But for most of your life the prefix that for you most aptly goes before "sexual" is neither hetero- nor homo-, but a-. You are not a very sexual person. When puberty strikes, and the time comes for every patriotic American male to do his duty and start wanking up a storm, you can barely sustain a drizzle. You do hump your pillows a bit, but the chafing and relatively low thread count don't do much for your sexual confidence.

As childhood gives way to adolescence you are interested in girls, but in a confused, quasi-perfunctory way. It's what's expected of you. Boys in high school date girls, and so you do too, but it's awkward. As it happens two of your teenage girlfriends are both quite prudish, so you sit on the couch or lie on the bed and make out for hours until finally, glacially, your hand creeps upstairs to cop a feel of training-brassiered boob, and they recoil and say, "What are you doing?!?" or "I'm not a slut!" And you backpedal and stammer something stupid like "No, no, I thought you . . . had an itch there." But you never wind up with a girlfriend who's viscerally excited by your advances or into your touch, and the fact that you don't is probably not a coincidence.

So why bother? In the back of your mind, are you worried that everyone suspects you're gay and no one's saying anything? Are you succumbing to unspoken social pressure? Or are you just gayanoid? Hard to say; hard to know; hard to talk about. But in 1986 you open up to your mom during a late-night conversation.

"Mom," you say, "I'm afraid I'm gay."

She tells you that a lot of kids your age have those feelings, that they may not be permanent, and that even if you are gay it doesn't make any difference in terms of how much she and your dad love you. All of which is true. But moms are moms, and later in life she will tell you that deep down she always had a strong suspicion.* After all, she was a teenager once. She knows what it's like to have crushes. And she sees that even though you date some really nice girls through your high school years, it's the cute new boy in your class or on set who really gets under your skin and thrills you and spurs your imagination and prompts you to rush home and ask her with badly feigned composure, "Did he happen to call?" Mom knows the deal, even if you don't. Or won't.

Some would say you were in a closet. Some would say you didn't even know you were in a house. The "truth" about a person's sexual preference is often revealed through a long journey of tiny steps, and acceptance is one of the last ones. It's an individual story for every person. There are unique personal prejudices in everyone, created by our families, our social circles, and mostly by ourselves. It's tough to confront those things that you are afraid of in yourself. In your case it will take time. Time, and

---

* "You almost had to have a board slapped against your head not to know he was interested in men, not women." –Your mother, January 21, 2014

experience. Looking around and witnessing others living their lives. Interacting with free spirits more comfortable with themselves than you are.

But you will get there.

To get famous, turn to page 46.

To get laid, turn to page 78.

"And now I, Neil the Magnificent, shall attempt the most amazing trick ever conceived in the history of prestidigitation!"

You are Neil Patrick Harris, the world's greatest magician. You have dedicated your life to mastering the art of illusion, casting aside all other professional ambitions. You do not act. You do not host awards shows. You do not appear in online mini-musicals written and directed by Joss Whedon. You are entirely devoted to magic, 24/7/365. 24/7/366 in leap years.

And now, on a Las Vegas stage, you prepare to debut your greatest trick yet, an escape that would put Houdini to shame. As the capacity crowd watches, you are handcuffed, straitjacketed, and blindfolded. You are then taped down to a chair. The chair is taped down to a larger chair. The larger chair is in turn Krazy-Glued to a sofa. A giant straitjacket is placed around the sofa. The straitjacketed sofa, with you somewhere inside it, is placed inside a vacuum-sealed airless steel trunk filled with venomous snakes, which is then hoisted fifty feet in the air over a giant tank filled with sulfuric acid, suspended only by a single burning rope.

You wait inside, milking the suspense. You know the crowd is absolutely sure you are about to die, and you chuckle at their terror, knowing full well the simple, unguessable secret that will allow you to miraculously appear in your freshly steamed tuxedo in a seat in the front of the balcony ten seconds from now.

Suddenly, out of nowhere, you hear a woman's voice.

"Enjoying yourself, Neil?"

This is *not* part of the trick.

"What the . . ."

"Befuddled, are you? I'm not surprised," says the unseen woman. "I wouldn't expect you to recognize my voice after so many years have passed. Perhaps this will jog your memory."

She lets loose with a pitiful, anguished wail. It sounds like a five-year-old waking up from a nightmare. It's unbearable.

"Ring a bell, Neil?"

"No . . . who are you?!?"

"Who am I? Oh, just a woman who was once a little girl. A naïve, trusting little girl who lived in Ruidoso, New Mexico, in 1984 and watched a certain young magician seem to chop off her big sister's finger at a birthday party."

The memory you have repressed for thirty years comes flooding back. Your first professional gig . . . the one and only time you left a crowd unsatisfied . . . the children, weeping in horror at what they thought you'd just done to a child's hand.

"You!" you scream in horror.

"Yes . . . me. I was that traumatized little sister. You took my innocence, Neil. From that day on I've had an uncontrollable fear of losing my fingers. I constantly wear gloves and keep my hands in my pockets. As a result I'm unable to do things normal people do, like type, play Chopin's *Études*, or give people the finger. I live the life of a recluse. And ever since that moment, I swore one day I would get revenge. It's taken me thirty years, but now I've done it. I've infiltrated your latest, 'greatest' trick. You're about to be a lot more than Neil Patrick Embarrassed. You're about to be Neil Patrick *Dead*."

Your discovery of the hidden speaker attached to your blindfold is simultaneous with the rush of pain from the dozen venomous snakes gnawing on your extremities. You scream, but the sound is muffled by the straitjacket, and the loud snap of a rope breaking.

"Don't worry, Neil. You're sure to make quite a 'splash!'" cackles the demon voice, just as you land in the sulfuric acid.

When they drain the tank an hour later all they find are two wisdom teeth.

THE END

You are a thirteen-year-old boy at a summer theater camp in Las Cruces, New Mexico. You are starting a class in cold-reading auditions, and your teacher is renowned playwright Mark Medoff.

From the beginning he takes a shine to you. The entire conceit of the class is that when auditioning you need to be good *immediately*, without any preparation, and this is one of your strengths: you've always had a knack for picking things up and figuring them out quickly, or at least figuring out how to *appear* to have picked them up quickly. And Mark notices this. His two daughters also attend the camp, and it doesn't hurt your standing that you make them laugh a lot.

Well, it turns out Mark is in the process of adapting an acclaimed novel as a screenplay. The novel is Joseph Olshan's *Clara's Heart*, about the relationship between a Jamaican housekeeper and a family in Baltimore. One of the main characters is the family's young son, David. When acting camp is over, Mark mentions this to your parents, and says he thinks you might be a good choice for the role. Your parents think he's just blowing smoke, but they ask him to "send us the script." (In the years to come, you will realize your parents instinctively struck upon *exactly* the right thing to say.) Sure enough, within a week Warner Friggin' Bros. sends a major-motion-picture script to your dad's law office. After picking their mouths up from the floor, your parents proceed to relate to you all the exciting, unlikely events of this paragraph.

You and your mom drive back down to Las Cruces to meet with Mark, who works with you on a few scenes. Then you go to the AV room at NMSU and shoot them into a video camera. Mark and his daughter read the offstage parts. You do a few takes, head home, and then boom, the tape is off to Hollywood. The whole thing feels disconnected from reality.

But the unreality of the audition is nothing compared to that of being told by Mark soon afterward that you—young, pasty-faced, rural New Mexican, gentile-but-bar-mitzvah-aged-anyway you—are going to star in a major motion picture. Your mom and dad are excited and overwhelmed. You feel like a fish out of water; a deer in the headlights; even, in your wildest moments, like a fish in the headlights.

And so you and your parents are flown out (because when you're in a movie they pay for your airfare! Like, *round trip*!!!) to Maryland for six weeks, with a teacher from Ruidoso in tow to be your tutor.* The first half of the shoot takes place in a small Chesapeake fishing town called St. Michaels; the last three weeks are in Baltimore.

You are awed. Moderately awed. You're struck by how artful and procedural and mechanical everything is. Dolly tracks, for example. They're actual tracks, like a train, that lock together to support a camera along with massive rigging. They're like some futuristic mini-version of the transcontinental railroad. Who thought of them? How were they built? How do they work? Oh, *that's* how they work?!? Amazing!

The crew is intense. The silence during production is *silent*. This is serious business, not the Ruidoso Little Theater. But you take to it pretty fast. Granted, unlike everyone else on set you have to go straight from shooting fifteen takes of a scene to learning chemistry or geometry in your trailer, and that's a bit tough.† But you feel no swell of insecurity, no sinking "I don't

---

* And they're paying *his* airfare too! Dude, this is crazy.
† Get used to it, future Doogie.

belong here" sensation. You enjoy and intuitively understand the process: the line memorization, the rehearsals, the blocking, the discussions of camera angles, the whole thing. It's new, and it's different, and it's exciting, but it's not something you can't handle. You belong here.

And it's a stroke of luck for your emotional well-being that the movie's star, Whoopi Goldberg, is the first genuine superstar you ever meet, because she provides a great example of the right way to be famous. She's incredibly gracious and professional, and she treats you like a regular person, a peer. She shows you how to hit the t-marks at your feet, how to adjust your body to "find the camera," and dozens of other tricks of the trade. Best of all, she always has a mischievous twinkle in her eye. You love her for that.

The entire month and a half feels like an out-of-body experience, the professional equivalent of first love. You are filled with enchantment. There's a small restaurant you can get to only by boat where you order soft-shell crabs and they deliver them in a giant shovel and just dump them on your paper-covered table. Bibs tied and mallets raised, you all whack your steamy dinner into delicious submission. Nothing could be fresher than this. Nothing could make you feel more alive than this.

But like first love, it ends. And you go back to high school. And you learn chemistry the normal way, at a desk, with other ninth graders. And you wait for a maddeningly long time while the director and editor and the other craftspeople involved in the mysterious process known as "post" do their work and put the individual jigsaw pieces you helped construct into one coherent puzzle. Almost a year later you finally have the bizarre, ungraspable experience of sitting in a theater and, for the first time in your life—and who knows if it will also be the last one—watching a giant-sized celluloid two-dimensional version of a person who, it cannot be denied, is you. It's tough to watch yourself performing, mainly because of how you look physically. There's a scene where you're in a Speedo, and the image sears itself in your mind, becoming for many years your pudgy, gangly mental avatar of how you look to the outside world.

There is one final mini–shit sandwich awaiting you at the end of *Clara's Heart*: the reviews. The teenage years are a time of experimentation, but a thirteen-year-old's first tentative foray into, say, lacrosse or French-kissing are not generally praised or panned on newspapers and television. That's not true for your big-screen debut, and while many reviewers like your work and the movie in general, others do not, including the most prominent film critic of all, Roger Ebert:

> *Meanwhile, Clara the maid labors away to bring warmth and understanding into the life of David, the young boy. But even here the movie has problems, having miscast Neil Patrick Harris in the role. Harris . . . is unable to project much more than an overwhelming sense of neediness.*

Well, that kind of sucks.

It's a decidedly strange thing to spend so many months doing all these wonderful, innocent, magical things and then, almost a year later, to see the end result be reduced into little more than an indifferent statement by a film critic. All that work distilled into a "thumbs sideways." It's hard for a kid to wrap his brain around that.

But your brain-wrapping skills will improve.

To bask a little more in the happiness of making Clara's Heart—*and to hear from an old friend—go on to the next page.*

To star in your next movie, this one receiving a cavalcade of negative reviews both unanimous and deserved, turn to page 42.

And now a word from your friend . . .

WHOOPI GOLDBERG

Once upon a time, way back in the day, when I was a big ol' movie star, I had been offered a film called *Clara's Heart* that was to be directed by Robert Mulligan (who directed *To Kill a Mockingbird*, so you know I wanted to make this movie!). The focus of the movie is a little boy who was to be played by you (be it, a much shorter version of you). And the very first time we met, what I saw was a little boy with gigantic glasses, but bigger than the glasses was a boy with a phenomenal heart.

Now, you and I talked about all kinds of things while we were on the set . . . girls, kissing, singing and dancing, and "eww, what are those people doing in the bushes?" Kissing, you definitely want to do. Girls? Who knows. Folks in the bushes, "STOP looking in that direction!"

And through the years as I watched you grow into an amazing actor, there was no surprise to me you nailed everything you wanted to do. Now, there is nothing worse than older people talking about "you" in the old days, but it's been such an honor to be able to watch and say out loud and in a braggy way, "I know that man, I did his first movie!" It's exciting and you, my dear—are exciting.

For a less happy memory from the following year, turn to page 42.

To meet your own two cute kids, turn to page 276.

This marks the end of your professional magic career. But your passion for magic never wanes, and when you achieve fame, and the LA club scene rapidly disillusions you, it is the world of magic that provides the much needed re-illusioning. Stephen Dorff introduces you to Ed Alonzo, a comedy magician who later becomes your best friend. When you start hanging out with him, you learn that he shares a warehouse with Gallagher. As in sledgehammering-watermelons Gallagher. So you spend a lot of time playing hooky from nightclubs with Ed and his wife, tinkering with his magic props and playing with the giant bowling pins, Trojan horse made out of oil barrels, and twenty-foot-long trampolining enormo-couch Gallagher uses in his act.

Being Doogie opens a few magic doors. You get to hang out with mega-magicians Penn and Teller in New York after a show. They are on their Refrigerator Tour, and it's an epiphany to see magic performed so irreverently and bullshit-free. One time Penn even invites you back to his apartment to see all his cool toys.* He has a pickle light: an actual light that uses electric currents, and you stick an actual pickle on it and the pickle glows and lights up. How cool is that? Very, is the answer.

To spend more time in Penn Jillette's apartment, turn to page 24.

If you're not ready for that kind of intimacy with Penn Jillette, go on to the next page.

* Not a euphemism.

Alas, your acting career doesn't leave you with the time or focus to practice magic enough to actively perform it. Your performances end up relegated mostly to talk-show appearances. But you remain an avid fan and aficionado. You never stop studying it, and you're pretty confident no one loves it more than you do. And fortuitously, an opportunity to be of great service to the magic community arises . . . that doesn't require another ill-fated attempt at going pro.

If you would like to pursue this cunningly teased opportunity,
turn to page 159.

If you would like to take part in another life-changing magic trick,
turn to page 162.

And now, in a never-before-attempted bit of meta-metaphysical wizardry, the real Neil Patrick Harris will reappear to bedazzle you with a magic trick. And by "you," we mean you, you. And by "we," we mean me, Neil Patrick Harris. *

I'm going to perform a card trick for you. It will take a little bit of imagination, but if you're willing to help, I'm willing to amaze you.

First, get an ordinary deck of cards. Go ahead, get 'em. I'll wait here, at the period at the end of this sentence. Got 'em? Good. Now shuffle them. Shuffle them as much as you like. When you're done, turn the deck face up in your hands and choose the card facing you at the top. Now of course I can't possibly know what the card is because you're reading this in a book, and I'm not in the room with you. I mean, I'm good, but I'm not *that* good.

Now we're going to "spell" your card, in a manner of speaking. Begin by spelling its name. For example, if you picked an ace, deal the cards face up onto the table, one card atop of the previous one, as you spell the word "ace." If you picked a 7, you'd spell "s . . . e . . . v . . . e . . . n . . . ," dealing one card face up, then another, then another, for each letter. Do that now. Spell the name of your card.

---

* And by "me, Neil Patrick Harris," I really mean with the help of master magical thinker Jim Steinmeyer, who has compiled all the effects for this book. But who are you/me to gaze at the man behind the curtain? *Gah!* Stop reading this. . . .

You now have a pile of face-up cards on the table, right? Good. Drop the rest of the deck on top of those cards, and pick up the whole deck again.

Of course, the name of your card actually has three words. You've just spelled the first. The second is "of," so I want you to spell "o . . . f . . . ," dealing two cards onto the table, one on top of the other one. Then drop the rest of the deck on top and pick them all up again.

Now a little switch, just to confuse you. *Turn the whole deck over in your hands, so it's face down.* Now, with the cards face down, spell the *last* word of your card's name, its suit. It's either "clubs," "diamonds," "spades," or "hearts." Spell the whole name, including the "s" at the end, dealing one face-down card for each letter.

You've got another little pile of face-down cards on the table, right? Good. Drop the rest of the deck on top of *those* cards and pick up the whole deck again.

Since I don't know what card you picked, I can't know how you mixed them. I can't know where it is in the deck. (Did I really need to explain that?) But we're going to find it. Together.

Turn the deck face up again. Look at the bottom card. That's *not* your card. Deal it onto the table.

Now look at the next face-up card, on the top of the deck. That's *not* it either. Deal that card off, onto the table.

But the next card, the card that's showing in your hand, *is* your card.

Isn't it?

If I were there with you now, you'd see me bowing.

If you'd like to take part in another magic trick, turn to page 86.

If not, turn to page 46.

It's 1988, and you are in the director's trailer on the set of a film based on the old novelty song "Purple People Eater" starring you, Ned Beatty, Little Richard, and a profoundly unhappy Shelley Winters, who spends most of her days moaning about back pain and droning, "Where's my pillow? Where's my pillow?"

Clara's Heart has just come out to decent reviews, but the only follow-up project you have lined up is a summer job working the sandwich counter of a Schlotzsky's Deli in a Ruidoso strip mall. You've only been slicing roast beef for a few weeks when your agent calls and asks if you're interested in making a fun, happy family movie called *Purple People Eater* with puppets and hot-air balloons. Farewell, slicing roast beef; hello, pre-sliced craft-services roast beef!

So your brother Brian comes along with you to Hollywood and proudly watches the cameras record your second movie: the story of a dreamy twelve-year-old who plays an old Sheb Wooley LP on his turntable only to find—oh my goodness—its eponymous one-eyed, one-horned flying monster has come to life! To be your friend! And help prevent your elderly grandparents from being evicted by a greedy landlord! And sing a bunch of vintage-era rock 'n' roll songs! And cause Little Richard to appear in a cameo! And maybe, just maybe, melt a few hearts along the way!

Oh dear lord is it a horrible movie. Just . . . yeah. And it requires you to work with two of the more unpleasant people you will ever encounter in show business. One is costar Dustin Diamond. Dustin, playing the role of Big Z (?!?), goes out of his way to offend pretty much every person he comes across, both individually and as a member of a weight class. Decades later, when he is better known to the public as that curly-haired guy who used to play Screech in *Saved by the Bell,* he will publish an autobiography implying that you had some kind of love affair with your best friend Ed Alonzo, who is (a) straight, (b) married, and (c) not even going to meet you for another four years. It's a completely false story that propagates a vicious lie to the grand total of twenty-three people who buy his book, presumably ironically.

The second less-than-pleasant person is the one you have been summoned to talk to in the trailer. She is Linda Shayne, the writer/director/auteur of this visionary sci-fi classic, and she has called you in during this final week of the four-week shoot explicitly to tell you that, based on the handful of times she has observed your attention slightly wandering over the course of the last month, you are an awful actor to work with, and your bad behavior, inability to focus, and overall lack of talent will most likely doom this movie to failure.

She is totally wrong. Also, you are fifteen years old.

You run out sobbing, thinking what an awful thing that is to say to a child you're directing in a movie with only four days left of shooting, particularly when that movie is called *Purple People Eater.* She may be having a bad day. She may be under stress from the transition of going from actress (Bootsie Goodhead in 1983's *Screwballs,* Bank Teller in 1987's *Big Bad Mama II*) to director. But as the years go by, the memory of her outburst will grow in your mind as a textbook example of how not to treat other people of any age, much less children.

And so you return to your own trailer, where the tears dry, then crust into rage; and you begin fantasizing about the day—far, far in the future—when you will enact karmic literary revenge against Linda Shayne.

It would appear that day has come.

If you're ready to appear in a creatively and commercially successful piece of entertainment, turn to page 46.

If you're ready to appear in a better class of kids' movie, turn to page 233.

If you're ready for a vacation, age twenty years and turn to page 121. (Warning: You will take it with your male partner, because by then you will be gay.)

HOW I WET YOUR MOTHER

Whenever you need to relax after a long day of acting, awards-show hosting, or playing starting point guard for the Sacramento Kings, you like to relax with a fine bespoke cocktail. Here's one of your favorites—an original recipe by your friend, the successful mixologist Adam Frager. This unusual concoction blends together two of your favorite drinks, the Manhattan and the Old-Fashioned, combining the dry spiciness of the former with the slightly sweet, fruitier essence of the latter. (And to add an extra twist, it uses a couple drops of the very *spicy Hellfire Habanero Shrub, uniting the whole mixture with a nice New Mexican kick.)*

2 ounces Templeton Rye whiskey

½ ounce Carpano Antica vermouth

½ ounce Pierre Ferrand Dry Curacao

¼ ounce Luxardo Maraschino Liqueur

¼ ounce Averna Amaro

2 drops of Bittermens Hellfire Habanero Shrub

2 dashes of Angostura bitters

Lemon twist

Mix all ingredients except the lemon in a shaker full of ice. Stir and strain into a small coupe. Garnish with a twist of lemon.

Return to the page from which you came.

Although now that you've had the cocktail, it's a little bit harder to find it. What number was it? Did it start with a "g," maybe? Ah, screw it, let's keep the party going by turning to page 59!

After your first film role and a few supporting parts on TV shows, you are utterly addicted to acting. It's something you want to do as much as you possibly can. So you approach your parents with the idea of trying out for a recurring role in a series. They know that would mean moving to Los Angeles, at least temporarily, and they're pretty dead set against it. Not so much for their sake but for yours: the prospect of plunking their beloved fifteen-year-old down in the middle of La-La Land fills them with terror. (The older you get, the more you will realize their terror was absolutely justified.) They offer you only the slightest glimmer of hope by saying, "We would only even *consider* letting you work in TV if it was for a Steven Bochco show." Bochco is the genius behind their two favorite series, *Hill Street Blues* and *L.A. Law,* and they feel the hypothetical chance to work with him would be too incredible to pass up, albeit too unlikely to ever happen.

There then follows a series of strokes of astounding good fortune. Amazingly enough, Steven Bochco is launching another show. Amazingly enough, that show is about a sixteen-year-old child prodigy with a medical degree. And amazingly enough, your then agent's assistant's boyfriend is head of casting for ABC, and he not only tips you off to this information, but sends you the script, and gets you in for an audition with Steven Bochco. It's a set of circumstances so implausible and far from reality it would be completely out of place in a script written by Steven Bochco. But somehow, it is what happens.

You fly to LA and have a great audition. Then you wait for

months. You are one of the very first people to try out for the part, possibly *the* first, and naturally the producers are keen to see hundreds of other potential Doogii.* But your name stays with them, and at the end of the process they fly you back out to LA for one last reading in front of the studio execs.

The casting had taken so long that a few weeks later, when you arrive on the set for your first day of shooting, the entire crew is wearing "I'll Be Doogie" T-shirts as a joke. But it's over. You are Doogie Howser, M.D., and you will remain officially so for four years, and unofficially so, to some extent, for the rest of your natural life.

You and your parents move into a rental apartment near the 20th Century–Fox studio. From the very beginning they're right there with you every time you go in to shoot. Not only do they want to be, they *have* to be. California state law requires that one or both parents be no more than one hundred yards from a working child actor at all times. It's like an anti-restraining order. It cannot be emphasized enough that *your parents have moved away from home solely to support you.* They're putting their careers on hold; it's not like they're licensed to practice law in California. Even worse, you soon come to realize they are ostracized on the set—not for anything they do or say, but simply because they're your parents and having *anyone's* parents on a Hollywood set is awkward. So no one talks to them and they wind up spending all day sitting in folding chairs being ignored. No matter how old you get, you will never forget the image of them sitting in those folding chairs. It will remain your personal image of what unconditional love looks like.

Doogie Howser is a big show. There's a fair amount of comedy, which is what you're naturally most comfortable with, but the dialogue can also be very intense, and the scenes of Doogie's per-

---

* That is the correct plural.

sonal life are often filled with turbulent emotions and conflict. He fights with his family, regularly faces moral and ethical crises, and his love life is a roller coaster. You spend many hours every week learning your lines, not just because you're a professional but because Steven Bochco writes fantastic dialogue, and he's earned the right to expect you to perform it flawlessly.

There's also the medical aspect of the show, the one that frequently involves you running into emergency rooms rattling off medicines and performing procedures. There's a medical advisor on staff and you're always questioning her not only about proper pronunciations but the actual details of real-life operations. You do your best to memorize these lines too, but sometimes when there's a heavy-duty medical scene you just take the relevant script sides, insert them into the medical folders and charts you're holding, and read them off the page. Or if you're doing surgery, you just stuff them into the wounds. This doesn't really hurt the "patients" that much, since they're usually just chicken breasts opened up with fake blood all around them.*

Every week brings a fun new set of challenges. In one episode you have to speak a few sentences of fluent Japanese, so you spend some time learning dialogue from a native instructor. The line is: お会いできて光栄です。あなたが将来的に必要なものがあれば、私に知らせてください。 It means "It's a pleasure to meet you. If there's anything you need in the future, please let me know." The words, along with the pressure and embarrassment you feel having to utter them in front of an actual Japanese person, sear themselves permanently into your brain. In "The Adventures of Sherlock Howser" episode you play an old-school version of Sherlock Holmes, complete with deerstalker hat, stiff-upper-lip British accent, and prosthetic nose. In "Doo-

---

* Mmm . . . wounds.

gie, Can You Hear Me?" you date a hearing-impaired girl whom you're trying to persuade to get a cochlear implant. For that one you spend a month studying ASL, and you will remain forever thankful to have learned something as beautiful and elegant as sign language. In still another episode you and Lisa Dean Ryan, who plays your love interest Wanda Plenn, do a shot-for-shot re-creation of the pottery scene in *Ghost*. (For six months you and Lisa have a torrid but short-lived behind-the-scenes kissing affair. Why not? You're Doogie, she's Wanda, and she's got fantastic lips.)*

You meet dozens of guest stars, some of whom will go on to bigger things: Vince Vaughn, Denise Richards, Jada Pinkett Smith. One of your favorites is Julius Erving, a/k/a Dr. J. He's really nice and professional and frankly a far more qualified doctor than you'll ever be. Not that that's saying much. Television doctoring just ain't the same as regular doctoring. Obstetrics, for example. You deliver quite a few TV babies. How do you deliver a TV baby?

1. Have a casting director find a brand-new mother who thinks her week-old infant is destined for stardom.
2. Cover it in cream cheese and strawberry preserves.
3. Load it between the legs of a shrieking actress.
4. Wait for the director to yell "Action!"
5. Lift the delicious bagel-baby up toward the camera, smile, and wink.

Just like in real life!

---

* If only your face were so flawless. You're sporadically riddled with acne throughout the entire run of the show. You're stuck in an epidermal vicious cycle: you get zits, which the makeup artist covers with makeup, which causes more zits, which leads you to apply Accutane, which makes your lips peel and blister. Evidently dermatology is not Doogie's specialty.

Here's a little-known fun fact: By law, newborn babies can only work twenty minutes at a time. (The Baby Union controls Hollywood.) So it's common for the "baby" to actually be twins or triplets. One day the mother of triplets is on set watching all three of her offspring get the cheese 'n' jam treatment in rapid succession. You politely ask her why she is comfortable allowing her weeks-old infants to be used in this way. She turns to you and says, "I don't know, they just really seem to enjoy it."

Ah, show biz.

And sandwiched in between all of this is school. Yes, you go to school, five days a week. It's the law. Along with the keep-your-parents-with-you-at-all-times provision, California mandates that all on-set children must attend school three hours a day. They also limit your workday as a sixteen-year-old to 9½ hours, *including* the three reserved for school and another one for lunch. That leaves only 5½ hours for shooting. And one more thing: the three hours of school cannot be broken up into increments smaller than twenty minutes.

You have a dedicated school trailer on set, along with a really great tutor/child-welfare professional named Rhona Gordon-Jepsen. Her job is to stay in touch with your high school back in New Mexico, find out what your classmates are studying, and then teach it to you. You take the exact same tests everybody else does. You're not sure if you're learning the full breadth of, say, biology that your peers are, but at the very least you learn what you need to know to pass the test. Is it anything like school? Not really. A typical scenario: You enter the tutor trailer at, say, 10:35:23. At *exactly* 10:55:23, the second assistant director, who's been waiting outside the door with a stopwatch, knocks on the door to get you for the master shot rehearsal. You rehearse, then go back to the trailer. Twenty minutes and zero seconds later, *knock knock!* Time to film the master shot. School. *Knock knock!*

Close-up shots. School. *Knock knock!* Coverage shots. A lot of your time and energy during your first two seasons on the show are spent compartmentalizing yourself into these weird little fragments of school, work, rehearse, school, lunch, school, rehearse, film, school.*

From the day after the first episode premieres, cries of "Doogie!" follow you as you walk down the street. It becomes the single word you hear more than any other, easily eclipsing the previous number one, "the." If you had known people would be calling you by your character name for the next twenty years, you might have asked for a different one. Thunderbolt Howser, say, or Dr. Feelgood, or Baron von Sexy Ass. But no, you're Doogie, and your costar Max Casella is Vinnie, and man, does it get weird when you try to hang out with him. Not that you don't want to—he's a lovely guy and a fantastic actor, in your opinion the secret ingredient behind the show's success. But it's impossible to be with him socially because you find out pretty early on that when people see you together outside the show it provokes mass metaphysical crises. The one time you try to eat lunch together at a mall food court you jeopardize public health. Dozens of passersby start gawking and freaking out and taking pictures and shouting "Vinnie and Doogie!" A handful disappear into the space-time wormhole separating reality from TV reality, never to return.

But being Doogie in particular isn't nearly as uncomfortable as being, or being told to be, a teen star in general. You don't

---

* Another little-known fact: To save time, the producers sometimes use a body double to shoot over your shoulder. The double moves his head slightly while *another* actor sits just below him reading your lines. As it happens, that other actor is Marc Buckland, who a quarter century later will be a major Hollywood producer, no doubt due entirely to the valuable show biz lessons he learned reciting off-camera lines toward your costars' crotches.

consider yourself a teen, or a star, but the undeniable fact remains that you are both, and as a sixteen-year-old who thinks of himself as a gawky ragamuffin with awkward features and an undulating Adam's apple, posing for glamour photos is demoralizing and surreal. You may never feel as out of place in your whole life as you do at the *Teen Beat* photo shoot. All these publicists and photographers and network reps are there asking you to pose as if you think girls would want to have your poster on their wall. Would they *really*? You don't know, and don't want to, but you do know it's a disarming experience to get groomed and then have some random shutterbug stare at you like a pile of fresh produce at the supermarket. "You're doing great! Now same thing, but smile bigger . . . smile smaller. . . . Now look thoughtful . . . raise one eyebrow . . . turn the shoulder. . . ." When you get older you will come to feel much more comfortable in front of still cameras, but right now it's an ordeal.

And yet can any aspect of starring in a high-quality, well-paying network show truly be considered an ordeal? No. The inconvenience of spending an hour at a photo shoot, or the psychological angst caused by being known as your character, amounts to one-half of an anthill of a third of jack-all squat compared to the totality of the *Doogie* experience. You spend four years working with creative, friendly people on a show you feel honored to be a part of. You learn thousands of lessons about collaboration and creativity and production that will stand you in good stead for the rest of your life. And dozens of years later, on those semiannual occasions when you flip channels and suddenly come across a white-robed vision of your teenage self demanding "thirty ccs of penicillin stat!" you will be beyond proud to see that your work, and the show, lives on.

And most of all, you will be happy for Doogie, who, after conquering a twenty-year Valium addiction, now spends his days working with Dr. Drew on *Celebrity Rehab*, and his nights kicking back in the mansion in Valencia he bought with the proceeds of his successful XXX-rated series, *Do Me Now Sir, DP: Volumes 1–35.*

To attempt to enjoy the perks of being a child star, only to discover yourself pretty much constitutionally incapable of doing so, turn to page 59.

To do more TV acting, turn to page 89.

To hear from the creator of Doogie Howser, go to the next page.

And now a word from your friend . . .

STEVEN BOCHCO

In 1988, when I made a long-term, ten-series overall deal with ABC and 20th Century–Fox Television, the first show I elected to make was a half-hour series about a sixteen-year-old doctor named Doogie Howser whose prodigious intellectual gifts had been fixated on medicine since an early-life struggle with childhood leukemia.

You were one of the very first actors I met when we started casting for Doogie. You were a young actor of enormous talent and sensitivity who had already made a name for himself in several well-received films. Though you were in fact sixteen, you looked younger, making the contrast between your youth and the character's accomplishments even more dramatic. From the moment I met you, it was a foregone conclusion—for me, at least—that you were the only actor who could properly portray the character.

By the time I told ABC I wanted to cast you in the role, they were already having some misgivings about the concept. They had envisioned a broadly comedic, joke-heavy, three-camera comedy, whereas I was presenting a far more realistic portrayal of a young man caught in an almost schizophrenic dilemma: on the one hand, Doogie is a sixteen-year-old, living at home like any other kid, obsessing about girls and cars and chafing at parental supervision; on the other hand, he is a gifted medical professional entrusted with the enormous, life-and-death responsibilities of caring for the sick and dying. Not necessarily a laugh riot, to be sure. So, when I proposed casting you as Doogie, the executives at ABC balked, concerned that your sensitivity, coupled with your lack of an obvious comedic persona, would doom the show.

In the tug-of-war that ensued, I finally prevailed, and Neil Patrick Harris, all of sixteen, became the star of *Doogie Howser, M.D.* The show premiered in the fall of 1989, and became, much to ABC's surprise and delight, an immediate success. It lasted for four years, as America watched you grow from a small, cute kid into a tall, handsome, and self-assured young adult. I believe now, twenty-five years later, as I did then, that you were the only actor who could have played the role. Your genuine wit and intelligence, your youthful sensitivity, and your enormous talent all combined to make a potentially unbelievable premise completely credible. You, for better or worse, *were* Doogie Howser, M.D.

Television schedules are rough—long days, often twelve hours or more, week in and week out—pretty grueling for anyone, let alone a sixteen-year-old boy. You had a caring, close-knit family, and I felt a keen responsibility not only to you, but to your parents as well, to provide a professional environment that was as nurturing in its own way as your real family's was. And so I determined that both in front of and behind the camera, I would surround you with caring, stable, and supportive crew and costars, including James Sikking and Belinda Montgomery (Doogie's parents), Max Casella (Doogie's best friend and neighbor, who looked sixteen but was twenty-two and used to sneak outside to smoke cigarettes), and Larry Pressman and Kathryn Layng (his colleagues at work). They became your onstage surrogate family, and took care of you as if you were indeed a favored son and colleague.

When *Doogie Howser, M.D.*, finished its run (about a year prematurely, I always thought), you were twenty, but in the years since we'd started, you had gone from being a kid to being a man. I had always envisioned that the last year of *Doogie* would dramatize that transition, but ABC, in its infinite wisdom, pulled the plug on us after four seasons. Shockingly, it's been twenty years since *Doogie* ended, though in a sense it never will, living on, as these shows do, in the never-ending world of TV syndication.

As I've watched you grow up and evolve, from near and then afar, I have often been struck by the long road you've traveled with such grace, and no small amount of courage. You have become a role model for a great many people over the last number of years. There's a reason the social and cultural shift toward acceptance of and comfort with gay marriage has had such a rapid rise, and you are very much a part of that welcome phenomenon. Not that being gay is your defining characteristic; but it, and the grace with which you have communicated that aspect of your life to the public, is certainly part and parcel of who you are, and is an inspiration to many.

I had hoped this little chapter would be more "fun," perhaps breezier, more anecdotal. But this opportunity to share my thoughts and memories of you remind me that, for all your charm, good humor, and preoccupation with magic, you were a serious and gifted young man who, at sixteen, was better cast as Doogie Howser than any of us ever realized.

Last thought: in my body of work, *Doogie* was, and will always remain, one of my favorite shows. It was sweet, it was funny, it was on occasion melancholy, but it was always true to itself. It was always *about something*. It never, as they say, jumped the shark. And as you go on to enjoy the full measure of success you've earned as an actor, a host, a musical performer, and—ultimately, I am sure—a director, I hope you remain as fond of Doogie and the values his character promulgated as I am.

Go on to the next page.

At the end of every episode of Doogie Howser, M.D., *Doogie types a few sentences into the journal he keeps on his computer. Most of the time the entries are poignant and insightful. Some, like the ones reprinted here, are less so.*

PERSONAL JOURNAL OF DOOGIE HOWSER, M.D.

Sometimes as a doctor, the best treatment is no treatment at all. But today was definitely not one of those times. RIP, van full of senior citizens. Next time I'll use medicine.

It isn't always easy being a good son. Especially since I'm much, much smarter than my parents. But even if I weren't so smart I'd be smarter than them, 'cuz they're stupid.

My favorite color is orange. It used to be purple but then at a certain point it became orange. Maybe by next year it will be yellow. It is impossible to know.

Boobs are amazing.

Friendship is a lot like surgery. It's complicated and bloody and can kill you. Plus it costs a lot of money and the government is very reluctant to pay for it.

Is it normal that sometimes when I see a pretty
girl my pee-pee grows? I have a medical degree so I
suppose I should know, but I must have missed that
class or something.

Parents are people. People with children. When
parents were little, they used to be kids, like some of
you, but then they grew, and now parents are people.

Sometimes I wish I could just go away to a different
place where I don't have to be Doogie Howser
anymore. I'm specifically thinking of page 67.

Other times I wish I weren't such a nice guy. Instead
of being a nice doctor, I'd like to be an evil, horrible
doctor, somewhere far away, like page 181.

And other times I wish I could hang out with Katy
Perry at the Super Bowl, but I'll never get to do that,
because that's in Indianapolis and to get there I
would have to travel all the way to page 255.

There comes a moment in every young actor's life when he is no longer a child. And according to the laws of California, that moment falls *exactly* on your seventeenth birthday.

With the show on hiatus you spend the first half of the year as a senior at La Cueva High in Albuquerque engaging in wholesome acts of tepid teenage rebellion. But when shooting starts you return to Hollywoodland alone and engage in far less wholesome acts. Legally liberated from the need for parents, tutors, or being in any particular place at any particular time, you decide to settle into your new life as a demi-star. You rent your own place in Sherman Oaks. You gradually get less self-conscious about using phrases like "I've rented my own place in Sherman Oaks." And you shell out five hundred dollars for a high-quality fake ID and begin, in both senses, forging your identity.

You and your then buddies Stephen Dorff, Matt Levin, and Jayson Rome dress up, meet up, and go out, your car blasting whatever current song is most likely to make you feel cool for blasting it. (Toad the Wet Sprocket, anyone?) You make the LA club circuit: Tuesday is Skybar night, Thursday the Roxbury, Saturday the Viper Room. Upon arrival you navigate your way through the hundreds of people hanging outside. You work your way past the bouncers by using Stephen Dorff's celebrity, discovering along the way that when necessary you can be the kind of person who pulls that kind of move. You stay till the bars close at 1:30, then go to Canter's or Damiano's for pizza, stagger home, and sleep until noon. Then at 5:00 or 6:00 p.m. you go out and have dinner and begin the pattern again.

It's the circle, the circle of nightlife.

Future centuries will remember the early-1990s child-actor party scene as the cultural and intellectual high point of human civilization, with the possible exception of the mid-eighties Brat Pack era. It's a time and place when even B-list celebrities—C-list, to be honest—feel empowered to get away with some pretty remarkable behavior. Shannen Doherty, for example. She's trouble. Like, soap opera trouble. And she loves living out that role. Once you watch her get into a fistfight at the Roxbury with another young star of the era. (You will never remember the other star's identity; for purposes of completion, let's say Soleil Moon Frye.) On several occasions you witness Shannen get upset when another pseudo-celeb gets too close to "her" section of a bar, then react with her standard public ritual of shouting, glass-throwing, and storming out. These incidents then become fodder for gossip columnists and are used as fuel for subsequent shouting/glass-throwing/out-storming sessions.

Shannen embodies this era. You, alas, do not. For one thing the scene is fueled primarily by alcohol, and you are—by biochemical nature—a dull and crappy drunk. Yes, alcohol loosens your inhibitions, but your habit of self-observation is too deeply ingrained for you to ever do anything tabloid-worthy. Screaming in public, taking your shirt off, belittling valets—all fun and rewarding things for celebutante drinkers to do, no question about it. But your dreams of partaking in such amusing sport are invariably nipped in the bud by imagining yourself being the jackass doing them. (You can, however, more than hold your own against anyone when it comes to morning-after puking, shivering, and wishing you were dead, so at least there's that.)

Cocaine and heroin are two other drugs of choice running rampant in that scene, and they don't remotely appeal to you. They're way too hard-core, too destructive. A few years ago there were those two cheerleader girls back at your high school in Albuquerque who you found out were cokeheads. Once you knew that, you couldn't stop looking at them and thinking, *Cokeheads cokeheads cokeheads cokeheads.* You'd watch them laugh too loud and roll their eyes and just generally act self-impressed and pretentious. Good for them, but there's no doubt in your mind that if *you* were ever on coke, you'd start acting self-impressed and pretentious, then think, *Wow, I'm the self-impressed, pretentious cokehead guy,* then start drowning in a vortex of miserable self-awareness.

And there's another strike against you in the party scene, perhaps the biggest of all: you are the world's first and only Doogiesexual. Wherever you go in public you are reminded of this bizarre meta-reality. Almost every girl you meet at clubs thinks of you as Doogie. More often than not, they *call* you that. You do occasionally parlay your doppelgänger into some action: the loss of your hetero virginity dates to this time, a squalid, 4½-minute limp-dicked affair at a house party in New Mexico that was the direct result of one of the girl's friends daring her to sleep with Doogie. (Given the quality of your performance, the dare could not possibly have been worth it.) But for the most part your encounters with women are not so much flirtations as bemused interrogations of a fictional doctor. Your actual sexual identity at this time is a mystery, even to you. *Especially* to you. It's not that you're suppressing anything; you haven't even evolved to that point. You're not *aware* of anything. You know that Doogie is playing wingman for you, but you have no idea he is also your inner beard.

To delve more into the tenuous netherworld that is your adolescent sexuality, turn to page 27.

If you prefer to keep those kind of issues hovering in your subconscious for now, go on to the next page.

For all this you still enjoy hanging out with your friends and watching the night unfold from a distance, laughing at yourself for the way you spend night after night breaking the law, wasting hundreds of dollars, and exposing yourself to earsplitting levels of music for the dubious privilege of having the exact same conversation with the exact same forty people from the night before.

But not everyone is as immune to the lures of the early-nineties club scene as you.

Scott Caan, for instance.

(Cue dramatic music sting!)

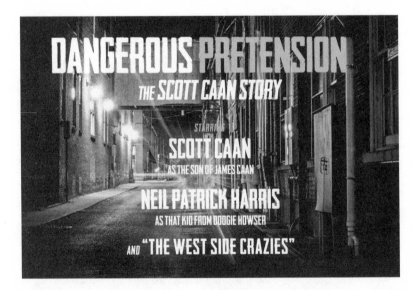

You are dating a very nice girl named Eden Sassoon, the daughter of Vidal. She was once Scott Caan's girlfriend but they've been broken up for a year. You and Eden are out at a club, sitting at a booth enjoying a vodka and cranberry, when someone runs up to you like he's in the cast of *Newsies*. "Hey, you gotta get out of here, see? Scott Caan's here, see? If you don't get outta here there's gonna be trouble, see?" And then he runs off and another guy comes up and says, "Scott's here, and he's looking for you, 'cause you're datin' his girl, see?"*

Not looking to cause trouble, see, you decide to leave. You are waiting for the valet to bring your car around when up walks the one and only Mr. Scott Caan, wearing a hipster porkpie hat with the brim up, like the one Ed Norton wore on *The Honeymooners*. Scott bumps his chest against yours. He turns his head sideways. Now his face is almost in your ear. And suddenly he begins repeating this mantra: "What's up with the West Side, yo? What's up with the West Side, yo? What's up with the West Side, yo?"

You are terrified and confused. Is this some sort of rap lyric? Children's book verse? Government code for an incursion into Gaza? None of the above: it turns out that Scott is in "The West Side Crazies." Is this a real gang? You're not sure. To you it seems like a self-styled group of hooligans comin' straight outta Brentwood, a cadre of young stars who've grown up deprived of deprivation trying to transform themselves into street toughs by forming ""gangs"" so devoid of street cred it's necessary to put the word in *two* sets of quotes. What kind of criminal activity are they engaged in? Script laundering? Agent smuggling? Film miscasting? Who knows. They think they have a posse when what they really have is a pose.

------

* You notice how strange it is that people in 1991 are ending sentences with the Edward G. Robinson–style "see?" that hasn't been used since 1938, but chalk it up to nostalgia.

Anyway, Scott Caan's dope-ass mob is named "The West Side Crazies," and if you can extrapolate from him, his fellow street-thugs are probably also the sons of famous actors. (Jake Busey? Kiefer Sutherland? Ed Begley Jr. Jr.?) And now, in defense of his honor and that of his gang, Scott Caan—whose father famously beat Carlo Rizzi to within an inch of his life in *The Godfather*—is repeatedly asking, "What's up with the West Side, yo?" and bumping his chest into yours, like some mighty ram bumping his horns against a small nerdy kid's chest.

Eventually your acerbic mind comes up with a simple, devastating response.

If your response to Scott Caan is "I'm going to do to your face what cancer did to your dad's body in Brian's Song," turn to page 66.

If your response to Scott Caan is "I don't know, Scott, what is up with the West Side?" continue reading.

In an alternate universe this is where Scott Caan takes a swing at you. In the actual universe, this is where Scott Caan begins acting like he desperately wants to take a swing at you if only his friends weren't holding him back. Only it takes them a few seconds to intervene, so he has to improvise looking like he's being restrained. None too convincing, you think. Then the whole thing ends as most things do, anticlimactically. The two of you are separated, and Scott, safely ensconced by fellow Crazies, flails his arms and screams, "You better get out of here, kid!" Which you promptly do.

Later in life you will remake the acquaintance of Scott Caan, and while you will like him much better you will still be kind of scared of him. He never brings up the incident. Perhaps he doesn't remember it. You don't feel the need to remind him. But you still hold out hope that one day he will offer you a little mea culpa. Like, "I'm sorry I acted like I wanted to kick your ass for dating a girl I'd broken up with a year prior." Or, even better, "I'm sorry I was un-self-aware enough to be a charter member of a gang called 'The West Side Crazies.' "

If you are ready to deal with another mercurial actor over a longer period of time, turn to page 115.

If you would like to put the Doogie period in general, and Scott Caan in particular, behind you, turn to page 67.

If you would like to learn a cocktail recipe far tastier than the vodka cranberries you'd been drinking just before meeting Scott Caan, turn to page 149.

If you would like to be verbally assaulted by Scott Caan, visit him on the set of Hawaii Five-0 *and tell him you dated one of his exes.*

Scott Caan does to your body what his father did to Carlo's body in *The Godfather.*

You spend the rest of your life in traction.*

THE END

---

* What, you thought this would be more specific? You really want to give Mr. Caan ideas of potential ways to harm you? Have you seen how he's built? And have you seen how *you're* built? Seriously, go look at yourself in *Doogie.* That *Brian's Song* joke was a bad idea, man.

D*oogie Howser, M.D.* ends in 1993, as do your teens. Together in life, together in death.

The series makes it to syndication, which bodes well for your ability to support yourself, at least in the short term. It also means that it won't be easy to escape the shadow of your fictional alter ego. You have managed to navigate the waters of child stardom without crashing into the rocks of egomania, the shores of self-entitlement, or the Cape of Cocaine.* You are eager—or so you think—to move on to the next stage of your career. But others seem less so, and when you focus your attention on returning to movies, you hit a brick wall. You are repeatedly rejected by producers and directors who see you as a TV actor forever linked in the public consciousness with one particular role, like Adam West as Batman or Snuffleupagus as Snuffleupagus.

You also find no luck when you audition for new recurring TV roles. But you do find work in the bastard stepchild of movies and TV known as made-for-TV movies. You appear in six in quick succession, four in 1995 alone, and will ultimately do over a dozen. The good news is the money's pretty good. The bad news is they are of varying quality and little to no artistic merit.

You begin to feel a little frustrated. You're in your early twenties, and sometimes you have daymares in which strangers yell "Yo, Doogie!" at you for the rest of your life. Then you're buried alive in a tomb engraved with the words "Here lies Doogie

---

* It's off the Santa Monica Pier.

Howser, R.I.P." You feel adrift, both professionally and personally. Nothing is grounding you and you don't know how to go about making that happen.

One day on a whim, you overcome your innate cynicism of infomercials and buy a set of Tony Robbins audio lectures. To your surprise you find them genuinely stirring. Inspired, you decide to attend one of Tony's weekend seminars in Hawaii. Although lacking the dramatic walking-on-hot-coals and/or climbing-onto-a-big-pole-and-jumping-onto-a-trapeze-style activities you were hoping for, the event is nonetheless profoundly transformative. It's terrifying but revelatory to spend twelve straight hours in a group of two hundred strangers sharing their stories. You realize that hearing teens yell a fictional name at you ten times a day is a far lesser ordeal than that of, say, a man who's been through four marriages, or a woman who was repeatedly molested by her father as a child. The weekend makes you realize you have no excuses for being the slave of your own story. As Tony might say, you have to move on from your past, live in the present, and create your own future by following your passion.*

The getting-out-of-LA thing feels nice. No doubt about it: a change would do you doogie. Rejuvenated, you pay a visit to your childhood friends Louis and Elizabeth Rutherford, a married couple living in the tiny New Mexico town of Placitas. Louis, Elizabeth, and their dogs spend their days hiking and mountain climbing and cooking and staring up at the magnificent night sky. Damn, you find their way of life appealing. You decide to move to Placitas, reasoning that since the TV-movie jobs you're getting offered don't require auditions, you're free to base yourself anywhere. You take up residence in a little adobe house, returning to California only for the occasional shoot. Ready to embrace liv-

---

* You are also befriended by Tony, who takes you on a helicopter ride to a friend's house in the middle of a Hawaiian rain forest to have lunch. This is less profoundly transformative and more just really frigging cool.

ing in the moment, you spend eighteen wonderful months doing little more than climbing, hiking, working out, writing, visiting your family, and watching the tube. It's a happy period of your life worthy of a cheery montage in one of the TV movies you're shooting, set to the tune of, oh, Howard Jones's "New Song." It's surprisingly easy to part with your LA life, and surprisingly comforting to learn the only suitcase you really need to travel with is the white bony one covering your brain.

You also briefly experiment with psychedelic drugs. You take mushrooms a few times, beginning each session hopeful the trip will expand your mind, ending each one staring in the bathroom mirror muttering, "Pull yourself together, man! You can do this! You can *do* this!" So you go the extra mile and drop acid with a group of friends. Afterward the only thing you remember is staring at a weeping willow tree in front of your house and watching its leaves turn into frogs hanging by their hind feet and one of the frogs turning his head and shrugging at you as if to say, "Yep, a tree filled with frogs. What are you gonna do?" You emerge from your one and only LSD experience as one of the few people to find the drug neither transcendent nor horrific, just kinda weird.

Above all you are preparing. You have no intention of giving up show business; it makes you feel too alive, awakens too many nerve endings in you. It's something you want to do for the rest of your life. But you need to reconnect with yourself, to spend some time a thousand miles away from Hollywood, far enough to hear the quieter stirrings of your own body and deepening soul.

The payoff of this period takes place in Albuquerque, at the Landmark Forum, another popular series of intensive weekend group self-help sessions. You are psychologically ready for the trek back to the West Coast but you'd like some tools to deal with the expectations other people will put on you. The Forum gives you these tools, teaching you to recognize the ways people project their own layers of subjective meaning onto reality, to distinguish personal agendas from objective truth. Through exercises you come to understand why it is that, for example, when you innocently tell someone "You look great today," they are less inclined to respond with "Thank you" than "Why, do I normally *not* look great?" or "Dude, are you hitting on me?" Such insights into human motivation and behavior are not only wonderful in navigating the world of other people, they mark a crucial step toward eliminating such distortions in yourself.

And in that spirit, after much reflection, and insight, and quite possibly a shot or two of whiskey, you boost up your courage and, when asked to say something about yourself in a small group discussion, stand up and haltingly but confidently say, "I am bisexual."

There's a long pause. Then one of your married friends who's attending the weekend with you says, "Really? Cool, so am I." You find that nice to hear, as opposed to, say, "Get out of my face."

In retrospect your admission of bisexuality will come to seem like a half-truth. But right now it *is* the truth, the whole truth, and nothing but the truth . . . insofar as you are prepared to acknowledge it at that moment. It's a very important step. It boosts up your courage. Not every veneer comes down at once, but once they do, they start dropping like lemmings.

In the meantime, life doesn't stop. The show must go on . . . or the movie. But which?

To re-experience the wonder that is the made-for-television movie, turn to page 89.

To attempt to embark on a stage career, turn to page 98.

To return to LA and make another push to star on the big screen, turn to page 124.

Over the decades you guest-star on episodes of more than a dozen different TV sitcoms and dramas. Without exception, each one is very special.

For instance, you do a very special episode of *B. L. Stryker* starring Burt Reynolds in 1989. (You're asked to do it because the previous year Burt's wife Loni Anderson had drowned you in a lake in the TV movie *Too Good to Be True,* and evidently she was impressed by your drowning technique.) You play a precocious young evangelist whose life is being threatened until B. L. comes on the case. At one point you are hanging out with Burt, who's a lovely guy, sitting in the passenger seat of a convertible filming a scene. As a joke at the end of one take, Burt leans over and kisses you square on the mouth. The crew thinks this is very funny, but it makes you uncomfortable. Uncomfortable and, it will ultimately turn out, gay. Burt Reynolds's kiss makes you gay.

You are on a very special episode of *Blossom* starring your lifelong friend Mayim Bialik. They're doing a parody version of the Madonna documentary *Truth or Dare* and you play Warren Beatty's part. You make out with Blossom and persuade her to fire her father-manager. Then you make out with her some more. It's far more action than you ever get on *Doogie Howser, M.D.**

You do a very special episode of *The Simpsons* called "Bart the Murderer." It's so cool! You're not a die-hard *Simpsons* fan, but just

---

* Granted, several times you get to third base, but that's because you're assisting in a birth.

being part of that world for an afternoon is unforgettable. In the episode Bart becomes involved with organized crime, and at the end he sits down to watch a fictionalized TV-movie version of his own story, and you are "cast" as him. This might make you the only voice actor other than Nancy Cartwright to play Bart.

You are on a very special episode of *Roseanne*. It's a quasi-Doogie cameo: after deciding to get a breast reduction, Roseanne has a nightmare in which she wakes up to find her breasts have actually *grown* in size. The operating room door opens, you appear, the crowd gives its standard-issue recognition applause, and you say, "What's wrong? Not big enough?" All the backstage stories you've heard about the show appear to be true. As you wait to rehearse, you watch Roseanne and her then husband Tom Arnold whisper to each other. Roseanne screams, "You gotta be fucking kidding me!" and storms off, and then everyone waits a half hour until the first assistant director sheepishly says, "Okay, everyone, that's our day, thank you!" Not the most emotionally stable set, *Roseanne*.

You are on a very special episode of *Murder, She Wrote*, your mom's favorite show. You play a grocery boy wrongly accused of the eponymous offense.* You harbor directorial ambitions, and Angela Lansbury is kind enough to let you be an "observing director," meaning you get to spend the week shadowing the director and asking him annoying questions like "Is this a camera?" and "Where's the bathroom?" Angela is the consummate pro. And she is a longtime outstanding Tony host. And the two of you make sweet, sweet love in her dressing room. What a week.

You are on a very special episode of *Quantum Leap*, which is awesome because it's one of your favorite shows ever. You love the time-travel premise, you love Dean Stockwell, and you *love* Scott Bakula. He's a sexy, great actor whose work you've already

---

* Murder, not writing.

admired in the criminally underrated Broadway musical *Romance/Romance*. It's odd casting, though, because you're playing a bad-guy hoodlum in the fifties, and you look nothing like a bad guy. Your neck is long and your ears stick out of the side of your head and you look like Beaker from the Muppets. Your dialogue may as well be "Mi mi mi mi mi!"

Shortly thereafter *Doogie* ends, and you don't land another guest spot for a few years, and not another *very special* guest spot until 2000. That's when you appear on *Will and Grace* as the leader of an ex-gay conversion therapy group whom Sean Hayes tries to out. Your public sexual status at the time is closeted-but-suspicious, so it makes for an interesting week. You love the cast and admire how well they work together, but given where you are in your personal life you're a little freaked out to be playing a character like that on what's widely seen as the gay-friendliest program on TV. It seems like a big bold move, but when it comes out no one bats an eye. You are happy to maintain your low eye-batting average.

Then you do a very special episode of the Howard Stern–produced *Son of the Beach*. Here's how special: the episode is called "Queefer Madness." You kid you not. You play a member of David Arquette's biker gang. You get to make out with the super-hot-but-very-cool Jaime Bergman. You are confused why you're offered a role like that. It turns out that the part was written for your once good friend Stephen Dorff *expressly because he wanted to make out with Jaime Bergman*. Then at the last minute for some reason he couldn't do it, so he suggested you. And that's how you get to suck face with David Boreanaz's future wife.

The next year you shoot a very special episode of *Touched by an Angel* in Salt Lake City. You have a sweet, wholesome part in a sweet, wholesome show. That night you receive an "in-room massage" from an anonymous gentleman you meet on AOL. Ah, the irony.

You do a very special episode of *Law & Order: Criminal Intent*.

You play a guy who captures a woman and then bores a hole in her brain with a drill bit. It's one of the first times in your life you get to do that.

Two years later you appear on a very special episode of *Big Brother,* which is particularly gratifying for you because you're obsessed with that show. You love the whole idea of filling a house with strangers and cameras, of people *knowing* they're being filmed all the time and yet inevitably losing sight of that along the way amid all the playing around and hooking up and voting off. One night you're at home when a friend calls and says, "Did you see what just happened? Go on *Big Brother,* watch the live feed!" One of the greatest players of all time, Will Kirby, a/k/a Dr. Will, who is awesome and hot and sort of a villain, is bored and talking to one of the outside cameras and saying that his favorite actor in the world is Neil Patrick Harris. Which is *so* meta, because *your* favorite show is *Big Brother,* and your favorite player is Dr. Will. It's one of the coolest moments of your life up to that point. And then next week the producers call asking if you want to be on it. Well, duh. You do a Secret-Santa-in-July thing, sneaking into the house in the middle of the game, waking people up and giving them presents. When you sneak into Dr. Will's room and rouse him he admits, upon questioning, to having morning wood. Man, is it fun to see your *Big Brother* man-crush's little brother full-throttle.

And finally you do a very, very, *very* special episode of *Sesame Street* in 2008. Seriously, this is very special—the bucket-list check-off of all bucket-list check-offs. Your life partner (you'll meet him later) is friendly with an amazing actress named Kerry Butler, whose husband is one of the executive producers of *Sesame Street,* Joey Mazzarino. You all become friends, and one day you get a call: "Hey, would you ever want to be on *Sesame Street*?" Well, *doy!* They say, "We want you to be a character called the Shoe Fairy, who grants wishes in shoes. Abby Cadabby and Sully would sing, and you would appear and sing a song called 'Shoes!'" You say, "I'm in, but may I make one suggestion? Can we change the name Shoe Fairy, so it doesn't emphasize the 'fairy' so much? Because it's me, I wouldn't want any confusion or distraction about the gay association with the word 'fairy.'" So they turn the noun into an adjective and you become the Fairy Shoeperson, and record this great song and wear a crazy costume made of shoelaces all down the front and part your hair in the middle and speak with a borscht belt accent for no good reason. Acting with puppets is the best. It's another type of magic show. As you perform you peer down and see the puppeteers smooshed below at odd angles, wearing headbands with microphones, staring at little tiny monitors with scripts taped to them. As always, you love being made privy to the secret machinery behind the process. And as (almost) always, you love seeing how absolutely flawless and magical it winds up looking on TV.

It's one of the best days of your life. The kids you will soon have will enjoy watching the tape of that.

To work with Sesame Street *again, turn to page 242.*

If you are really enjoying making short appearances on a variety of different TV shows, turn to page 215.

If you yearn for the legitimacy of stage work, or are just jonesin' for some hot manlove, go on to the next page.

Despite your love for the stage you are far too busy rescuing patients from a variety of camera-ready ailments to appear on it. But when Doc Howser hangs up his stethoscope you are eager to once again tread the boards, for the first time since high school. In rapid succession you star in James Lapine's *Luck, Pluck and Virtue* at the La Jolla Playhouse in San Diego and Jon Robin Baitz's *The End of the Day* in Los Angeles.

They're both great roles, but they prove mere preludes to the first great event of your stage career, and one of the most pivotal events of your life. In 1997, while shooting a movie in Boston, you attend the opening night of the first national tour of *Rent*. As is your wont, you seek out and befriend members of the cast. They are every bit as diverse and bohemian as the characters they play. They are black and white and brown and skinny and fat and butch and gothy and gay and supergay and wonderful and creative and welcoming and you love them, and you love the world they inhabit, and dammit, you want in.

So a few months later, when the producers announce the formation of a *second* national tour, you audition for it. No half-hearted, half-assed audition here—you go full heart and total ass. Your audition song is Billy Joel's "Captain Jack," 'cuz it's edgy and mentions "junkies and closet queens." And you get the role of the narrator, Mark Cohen. Overjoyed, you go down to La Jolla and begin an unforgettable, life-changing experience.

There's a reason actors who've done *Rent* speak of it in such personal, reverent tones. When you act in *Rent* you have to own its ideals: no day but today; forget regret or life is yours to miss; there's only us, there's only this. You instantly embrace the beautiful worldview of the show, a view only deepened by the poignancy of the tragic death of its author, Jonathan Larson. Your director, Michael Greif, has been with the show since its inception. He understands it better than anyone, and with a few exceptions the people he has cast are not just amazing actors but amazing *souls*. No one judges; no one condemns; no one feels hampered by other people's notions of what you're supposed to be. And of course it's very free sexually. You're very flirty with lots of people who are very flirty with you. You make out with one of the understudies; you have an affair with the girl playing one of the leads. And both on- and offstage, there's lots of representations of gay: proud gay, happy gay, defiant gay.

So you hook up with a dude.

If you want to hook up with a dude, go on to the next page.

If you want to rock out onstage even harder and more transgressively, turn to page 267.

If you're not ready for that yet, but are still interested in pursuing a life in theater and/or learning titillating gossip about Kelsey Grammer, turn to page 98.

If this whole thing is getting too gay for you, snort a line of coke off a stripper's ass and turn to page 102.

Here's a peculiar and rather disappointing fact about you: you're not much good at remembering the intimate details of your sexual history. To be honest, you're not much good at remembering the broad generalities either. You are not by nature a hedonist, sensualist, or Casanova, and so when one day you look back on your life you will find you don't have particularly vivid memories of where you've stuck your stuff. And you will realize that part of the reason for that quasi-amnesia—perhaps most of it—is that you spent much of your life trying to engage in entirely the wrong type of stuff-sticking.

But your first gay hookup, *that* you will remember vividly. His name is Andy, he's in *Rent* with you, and from the moment you see him you kinda sorta know it might go that way. One night during previews he lures you back to his place with the "I'll happily give you a back massage if you want one" line. (Even then you knew that was a line.) In fairness, you *do* really need a massage because you *do* feel genuinely, physically beat the eff up from the kind of hard dancing you have to do in *Rent*—the kind with lots of explosive movements and writhing gestures and . . . well, you can see how the show can't help but get you feeling sexperimental.

So you go to his place, and he starts rubbing you, and whoops, his hand wanders, and whoops, your hips rotate, and hey, look what the two of you find yourselves doing just because it happened to happen this way, and you have your fun, and you're lying there post-boytally, and in the wake of your "bisexual" breakthrough at the Landmark Forum a year earlier you know

you're *supposed* to be thinking *Of course, now it all makes sense!*
Finally, this feels so right! But that's not what you're actually feeling.
It's less an escape from self than a brutal collision with it. The
excitement and anxiety of what's happening drives you into an
even more analytic, introspective, meta-angsty place than usual.
Any chance of surrendering to and thus enjoying the moment is
cut off by the constant internal monologue now set to hyperdrive:
*No one can know, you can't tell anyone, this can't happen again but
what if it does . . .*

On the plus side, you did have an orgasm, which, like Andy
himself, is nice to come by.

Andy accompanies you on several more tentative dips into the
Great Sea of Gay. When *Rent* is over you stay with him in New
York on your frequent trips to see Broadway shows. He continues to offer you "massages," and you continue to allow him to
give them, and sometimes it doesn't lead to something else, but
sometimes it does. It's like a friends-with-benefits situation, with
the benefits somewhat limited. The two of you walk around the
West Village like bros and then at night sometimes you cuddle
up. It's hardly a relationship, but it's a necessary tentative first
step toward a new life, and it's great to be doing it in New York.
The physical reality of a new and vibrant city makes it feel like
a safer place to engage in authentic self-exploration, and not just
sexual either. Are you closeted? Maybe. A better word would be
"un-self-actualized."*

You soon find the sporadic hookups with Andy aren't enough.
You want more. Fortunately for you, it's the late nineties, the
golden age of AOL, and soon the shrill screeches of dial-up internet become your Pavlovian cue to start feeling horny. You enter a
chat room, say "M4MShermanOaks5," with a bunch of other glo-
riously unknown people, type "Hey, everyone!" and then wait to

---

* Better but much more pretentious.

get an IM. When you have a private conversation the other person usually requests a picture, and you send him an image of either someone else or a body part, and by "body part" you seldom mean "pancreas." And a few times you actually go and hook up with someone in full clandestine mode, spending the whole time with a baseball cap low over your head, wondering if you're going to be exposed, if it's all a big setup, if there are hidden cameras in corners. The whole covert-ops-ness vibe is nerve-racking and heart-pounding and, both despite and because of this, intensely hot.

But random hookups on the down-low are not your thing. You've sown a few wild gay oats in the shadows, but now you're ready to spread some in the sunlight. Which is why on some sub-conscious level you jump at the chance to visit your old friend Ed Alonzo, who is performing his magic show in Berlin. It's a perfect opportunity. Ed, who is straight, happily married, and the father of a little girl, is a familiar and comforting presence. But if you go visit him in Germany you will be among people who don't even speak English, much less Doogish. You will be alone. You will be unknown. And you will be ready.

On your second day in Deutschland you decide to wander. You walk outside Ed's theater and, in an astonishing *Zufall*, dis-cover a massive procession going on. It's the annual Love Parade, a glorious Teutonic rainbow freak show with lots of barely clad dancers shimmying down the street on supergay floats. Every-body's smiling and having fun, and, having nothing better to do, you follow it.

For the first time in over a decade, you feel truly anonymous in public. It's gleefully liberating to be wandering among the throngs without having to disguise yourself. You feel empowered to walk tall—not just physically, but emotionally. Because you've been in the public eye since puberty, you have never felt free to privately experiment with your identity, to say "I'm going to be goth for a month," or "I'm going to try wearing glasses and be a scholar and talk about Kierkegaard." Or "Today, I'm going to be actively bi-curious," to be more . . . germane.*

But here are teeming throngs of ordinary people who are happy, authentically celebrating who they are, giving not the slightest fraction of a shit about your history. It's a similar vibe to *Rent,* but that was just a show, and even in that context the characters were countercultural outcasts. These are regular, everyday people just marching around having a blast.

The next night you're psychologically ready to go out and cut loose, but you're still a little hesitant. You chat online with Andy, your friend-with-benefits. And he says, "Why don't you just go out?"

"Right now?"

"Yeah, why not?"

"Well . . ."

"Do it, no one knows you there, just go out."

And so you go out, and God bless Andy.

You go by yourself to a loud punk-industrial gay dance club, mostly empty. You sit in the corner, nervous, beer in hand, passively waiting for adventure. A good-looking guy from Austin sits next to you and recognizes you. *Oh no,* you think, *this was a bad idea.* But then Ed's friend Ully, whom you've arranged to meet, shows up with his friends, the Europeanly named Christophe and Rodrigue. They're variety performers. They do a single trapeze act where they flip and catch each other. They are young. They are ripped. They are hot. This is good. This is *very* good.

And now, blissfully, your self-monitoring switch turns itself off, and you're actually dancing in a gay bar with two superhot circus performers. It's incredible. Before this you have *never* danced for purposes of seduction, ever. Sure, you've danced at weddings and proms and such, but never as a means of flirting. So to find your-

---

* See what you did there?

self doing it for the first time, and being okay at it, and enjoying it, is almost otherworldly. And a few beers later, amid the cacophony of earth-shattering techno, you lean over and start making out with Christophe. *In the club.* Big step. So, so great.

They invite you back to their place. Your internal alarms go off and you think, *Oh jeez, now it's getting XXX-rated.* But it's not that way at all. Rodrigue goes to his room to practice circus acts. (Ninety-nine times out of a hundred that's a euphemism for sex, but in this case that's literally what he was doing.) You and Christophe end up in his bedroom, in his bed, and you spend the night, and it's *fantastic.* He barely speaks English and you speak no German, so you smoke cigarettes laced with hashish, have very rudimentary, comical conversations interspersed with very nonrudimentary, noncomical sex, and it goes on all night, and you don't want it to end.

You spend the next day together. Randomly, you visit the very first Bodies Exhibit—the one where they have actual skinless cadavers posed like they're having a knife fight or riding a horse. (Romantic, right?) That night you go out again. This time you bring Ed with you, which is another big step: here's this guy I'm fooling around with, is that okay, Ed? Answer: of course it's okay, Neil, calm down. And you all go out and dance and have a blast.

Then it's time to go back to the States. Saying good-bye to Christophe is hard. Never before have you been intimate with a guy and not woken up the next day in quasi-denial mode, saying, "Hey, bud! Good to see you, bro!" You've had a little fling, and it is sweet to give a hug and know that you probably won't see each other again. Sweet and sad. It's the first time you feel that kind of waving-good-bye-on-the-bus-home-from-summer-camp sadness, but even that, in its melancholy way, has its charms.

It is, in every sense, a seminal week.* All the things you've

---

* You *know* you saw what you did there.

done—walk next to gay people in a parade, dance with other men in a club, make out in public—had only last week seemed so taboo in your mind, unachievable, horrifying, potentially life-destroying. And yet when you do them, they are fun, and—get this—not that big a deal. In hindsight, the fears you've faced are revealed as eminently overcomeable. There's a parallel with magic. The secrets seem so awesome and huge, but once you know them you see they're manageable and very much of this universe, and you're left with the pure joy of an authentic experience.

You're not much for life lessons, but you will happily quote the brilliant Dan Savage: "It gets better."

Better, and easier.

If you're ready for it to be better, turn to page 107.

If you're ready for it to be easier, turn to page 168.

If you're ready for neither and this whole thing is giving you gay anxiety, turn to page 94.

D*r. Horrible* is one of the greatest and most satisfying experiences of your professional life. So when Joss Whedon calls you out of the blue to say he wants to discuss another possible project for you, you jump at the chance.

It's a beautiful day, so you decide to take a nice leisurely stroll to Joss's house in the desert. You start wondering what he has in mind. You lose yourself in happy speculation.

Suddenly you notice the world slowly rising all around you. Looking down, you realize you have stumbled into a silty Saharan pit. You are sinking in quicksand!

You desperately struggle to escape, but your efforts only cause you to sink deeper. You look around for something to pull yourself out of the quicksand with. A rope attached to a palm tree dangles tantalizingly a few feet in front of you, but you can't quite reach it.

With your last breath you scream, "Help me, Joss!" but your cry is quickly throttled by the sandy grit filling your throat. The last thing you see is Joss Whedon running to you wailing, "No, Neil! Not before we shoot *Dr. Horrible 2: The Desolation of Moist!*"

Your body is never found.

THE END

Once again, the real *Neil Patrick Harris.*

Thank you, thank you. Please. Sit down.

Now that you've begun to appreciate my miraculous pow-ers, I'd like to answer the oft-asked question "Why would anyone want to learn magic?" Simple: because if you can read someone's mind, you can figure out exactly what they're thinking. You can even hack someone's password. I'll show you how.

Begin by taking an ordinary deck of cards and removing nine of them. Any nine you like. I'll point out to you that I don't have any idea which nine cards you removed from the deck. Put your nine cards in a pile, and look at the bottom card, the one facing out. Since I'm not there with you, I can't ask you to pick a card, so we're going to say that's the card you just picked.

Of course, as long as it's on the bottom of the packet, it's easy to find. So I'm going to have you mix the cards, but in a specific way. I want you to think of a password, any word with just letters, and fewer than nine letters. It can be any password you'd like. A friend's name, a pet's name, a friend's pet's name. Don't say it out loud; otherwise I might hear it. Just remember it.

Now hold the cards face down and spell the password in your head, dealing one card on the table for each letter. In other words, if your password is "dog," you'd deal three cards, one at a time on top of each other, spelling "d . . . o . . . g."

When you're done, you will have some cards left in your hand. Drop them on top of the cards on the table and pick up the whole packet again.

I want to show you what's just happened. Keep the packet in order, but turn it face up and spread it like a hand of cards. You'll see that the bottom card is now moved, based on your own personal password. Don't change the order. Just put them in a deck again and put them back face down.

We're going to keep mixing them, and this time I don't want you to look at how they're getting mixed so you don't know where your card ends up. This time, I want you to spell the word "my." Just deal cards on the table, for "m . . . y." And drop the rest of the cards on top, just as you did before.

Now pick up the packet. You're going to do the same thing, but this time with the word "password." Deal the cards down in a pile, spelling with me: "p . . . a . . . s . . . s . . . w . . . o . . . r . . . d." Drop the extra card on top, then pick them all up.

And now one more time, the same thing, but now with the word "is." Deal two cards down. "I . . . s." Drop the rest of the cards on top and pick them all up. You just spelled "My password is. . . ."

Of course, those were words I told you to use, but now I want you to use your own personal password again. Spell your password one more time, dealing cards on the table. When you're finished, drop all the rest of the cards on top.

If you were doing that on a computer, making up a password and confirming it, you'd think that your information would be safe, and that right now, because you don't know where your card is, it's lost in the packet.

But using my best intuition, as well as a little special ability at hacking your password, I'm going to tell you exactly where you card is. Slide the top card off the packet, the first face-down card. And turn it over. That's exactly the card that you selected!

Thank you. I'll be appearing in this book through Saturday.

*If you'd like to take part in another magic trick,
turn to page 162.*

If you'd like to feel enchanted in a more romantic way, turn to page 107.

Or, check out the chapter starting on page 244. It doesn't really flow from this chapter but it's really cool. There's, like, a yacht and everything.

Between 1988 and 2001 you star in thirteen made-for-TV movies. You appear in so many that after a while you begin making up new ones in your mind for your own amusement. Thirteen years later, when the editor of your autobiography presses you for information about this period of your life, you can barely remember any details about the movies. In fact, you can no longer distinguish the real ones from the fake.

Title:	*A Family Torn Apart*
Character Name:	Brian Hannigan
Costars:	Johnny Galecki, Gregory Harrison
Synopsis (from IMDb):	A teenage boy finds his mother and father murdered in their home, but as the story goes on he reveals he knows more than he is letting on.
Memories:	You're pretty sure it turned out you were the killer. You remember filming for two days covered head to toe in fake blood, so yeah, it was probably you.

Title:	*Snowbound: The Jim and Jennifer Stolpa Story*
Character Name:	Jim Stolpa
Costars:	Kelli Williams, Michael Gross

Synopsis: Two thousand miles from home, Jim and
                         Jennifer Stolpa (with baby Clayton) lose
                         their way and are stranded in an endless
                         wilderness of deep snow, battling for sur-
                         vival against the elements.

Memories: You survived. The shoot was very cold.
                         The "haunted" hotel the cast stayed in
                         wasn't, but left mints on your pillow. The
                         real-life Stolpas ended up getting divorced.

Title: *Modern Family*

Character Name: Luke Dunphy

Costars: Ed O'Neill, Sofia Vergara

Synopsis: Three different but related families
                         face trials and tribulations in their own
                         uniquely comical ways . . . until a series
                         of murders forces one young man to con-
                         front his own demons.

Memories: This was later adapted into a popular
                         sitcom.

Title: *Stranger in the Family*

Character Name: Steve Thompson

Costars: Teri Garr, Randle Mell

Synopsis: When a car wreck leaves a teen with per-
                         manent memory loss, his resilient fam-
                         ily must help him relearn to read, write,
                         walk, talk . . . and, hardest of all, remem-
                         ber who he is.

Memories: None, ironically.

Title: *This Is One of the Fake Ones*

Character Name: Coltrane Q. Fraudington

Costars:	Traci Lords, Raymond Burr
Synopsis:	When a mysterious bacteria renders all of Connecticut's children lactose-intolerant, a down-on-his-luck rodeo clown teams up with a beautiful endocrinologist in one last desperate attempt to keep the Nutmeg State's most vulnerable citizens milk-safe.
Memories:	This was Alfred Hitchcock's last film.
Title:	*The Christmas Wish*
Character Name:	Will Martin
Costars:	Debbie Reynolds, Naomi Watts
Synopsis:	A cynical Wall Street trader returns to his hometown for the holidays and becomes tangled in a family mystery that teaches him about love, forgiveness, and the usual Christmas shit.
Memories:	You could tell even then that Naomi Watts was waaaay too good for this.
Title:	*The Man in the Attic*
Character Name:	Edward Broder
Costars:	Anne Archer, Len Cariou
Synopsis:	Based on a true story. An older woman hides her younger lover in the attic of her house for years without her husband suspecting.
Memories:	You spent half a day naked with your head six inches from Anne Archer's crotch while shooting a sex scene. One of those great "if my parents could see me now" moments.

Title:	*The Man in the Basement*
Character Name:	Edward Broder Jr.
Costars:	Anne Archer, Len Cariou
Synopsis:	Sequel to *The Man in the Attic*. An even older woman hides her even younger lover in the basement of her house for decades without her three husbands suspecting.
Memories:	Felt a bit forced.

Title:	*Joan of Arc*
Character Name:	Charles VII of France
Costars:	Leelee Sobieski, Jacqueline Bisset, Peter O'Toole
Synopsis:	Duh.
Memories:	Working with Peter O'Toole was a true career highlight. Hearing his fantastic stories, in which he often employed the word "cunt" as a term of affection, was even more so.

Title:	*The Christmas Pie*
Character Name:	Nehemiah Featherbones
Costars:	Dame Maggie Smith, Dylan McDermott
Synopsis:	The hearts of a rural Welsh coal-mining village are gladdened on Christmas Eve by the sudden appearance of a magical mince pie that brings love and peace to all who nibble it.
Memories:	A musical. Songs included "Coal!" "Quit Mincin' Around," and an ode to the town in which it was set, "Llybrugghyrhurgyrm."

Title:	*Decisions: The Neil Patrick Harris Story*
Character Name:	Neil Patrick Harris
Costars:	N.A.
Synopsis:	In an interactive format, viewers themselves get to choose whether they now wish to get cast in *How I Met Your Mother* (page 133), hang out with Sir Elton John (page 244), or meet Harold and Kumar (page 102).

WHEN WE HERE AT *TOTALLY STRAIGHT GUY* MAGAZINE WERE TOLD NEIL PATRICK HARRIS WAS INTERESTED IN SITTING DOWN FOR AN INTERVIEW, WE WERE SO EXCITED WE ALMOST SPILLED THE BEER WE WERE DRINKING WHILE WATCHING UFC AND TALKING ABOUT CHICKS. SEE, WE'VE BEEN CURIOUS ABOUT NPH FOR A LONG TIME. THERE'S SOMETHING ABOUT HIM THAT DOESN'T . . . IN MANY WAYS HE SEEMS LIKE HE SHOULD BE . . . WELL, LET'S GET TO THE INTERVIEW.

TSG: Neil, thanks for sitting down to talk to *Totally Straight Guy* magazine.

NPH: My pleasure.

TSG: So, let's get right to it: are you gay?

NPH: Yes.

TSG: Really?

NPH: Yes.

TSG: *Really?*

NPH: Yes. I am a gay man. *[Pause.]*

TSG: So like, *homosexual* gay?

NPH: Right. I am a gay homosexual man.

TSG: Okay. *[Pause.]* 'Cause here's the thing: you *seem* totally straight.

NPH: What do you mean?

TSG: Hey, don't be offended. I mean that as a compliment.

That's the definition of gay.

NPH: Don't be offended as a gay man when you say that seeming straight is a compliment?

TSG: No no no, you're misconstruing me, Neil. Look, I'm not homophobic. I have absolutely no problem with the gays.

NPH: "The gays"? Is that a band?

TSG: Hahaha, no, but you know what I mean. Like, with most gay guys, they act, you know, what's the word . . . "gay."

NPH: Uh-huh.

TSG: Like, they gay it up. They gay things. They go around gaying.

NPH: Mmm-hmmm.

TSG: And so, when you see them,

you know ... you *know* ... you know?

NPH: Uh-huh.

TSG: Whereas with *you,* if I were hanging out with you, even for a *while,* I'm not sure I would necessarily know that, that you—

NPH: That I'm sexually attracted to men?

TSG: Umm, well, that's one way of putting it.

NPH: That's *the* way of putting it. That's the definition of gay.

TSG: Right.

NPH: My partner David, for example. I'm sexually attracted to him.

TSG: Okay, but—

NPH: So we have man-on-man sex.

TSG: Okay, but let's—

NPH: Shall I describe it to you?

TSG: *No,* let's move on, because you, I mean ... Okay, I guess here's what I'm having trouble with: Barney Stinson.

NPH: Right.

TSG: Horndog. Lothario. Total womanizer.

NPH: Absolutely.

TSG: You were amazing as Barney.

NPH: Thank you.

TSG: So ... was that just acting?

NPH: Well, traditionally, when you are paid money to play a fictional role in a comedic or dramatic performance, that is considered acting, yes.

A big erection.

TSG: I have to say, even talking to you right now *about being gay,* you don't seem gay.

NPH: Well, looks can be deceiving. I mean, you don't seem gay either, and yet it's quite obvious to me that you have an erection.

TSG: *[Looking down]* Oops.

NPH: A *big* erection. I mean that as a compliment.

If you've had enough of this interview and want to go meet the aforementioned man-on-man sex partner of your dreams, turn to page 107.

If you want to hear from Barney Stinson himself, turn to page 145.

To read the rest of the interview, buy a copy of this month's *Totally Straight Guy* magazine, now on sale at newsstands, bookstores, and airports around the country.

Congratulations! You have found the hidden page. No other section leads to this one, and it's impossible to imagine anyone violating this book's explicit instructions by casually flipping through it out of sequence.

So how were you able to find it? Because you, sir or madam, are a rare breed of individual. You are diligent and intrepid. You are also confident, suave, and alluring, with a keen sense of self, a gift for problem solving, and a unique sartorial style. In fact, you, Neil Patrick Harris, remind me very much of *me*, Neil Patrick Harris. I have a feeling that if we ever met, we would be besties. Or at the very least, pretty goodies. We would share confidences, or a secret handshake, or a time-share in Sun Valley.

In short, we are *simpático*, as a Frenchman might say, if he also spoke Spanish. So let us do something special to commemorate our newfound kinship. Since no one else knows of this page, let's you and I come up with a code word, so that when we finally meet in person we can whisper it to each other and seal our bond. I propose the word "Kungaloosh." Do you object to this word? If so, speak up now.

I can tell by your silence that you approve.

We are truly, in every sense, on the same page.

For now, feel free to come here whenever you need a rest from the day-to-day travails of the busy life you lead as Neil Patrick Harris. Relax in the cozy chair below with a drink from page 45 or 149 and kick back with a good book. This one, for example.

Once again, congratulations, my new boon companion.

Until we meet again, I bid you a hearty Kungaloosh.

R*ent* gets you a lot of action, and not just offstage. It raises your standing in the theater community, and shortly thereafter Dan Sullivan, one of America's great stage directors, asks you to play Romeo opposite Emily Bergl's Juliet at San Diego's Old Globe Theatre. It's another liberating moment for you, though in a more purely professional way. Eight years of working almost exclusively on television has left your acting persona feeling trapped in perpetual close-up. Even your character in *Rent* wasn't the most physical guy in the world. But Dan wants Romeo to be a freewheeling, heroic lover, so you find yourself onstage every night fighting with broadswords and daggers, climbing balconies, braining Tybalt with a rock, and doing all kinds of cool bodily shit. (One reviewer describes your "nimble shimmying," which sounds almost pornographic.) To get so overwrought with emotion by the death of your lover that you cry, weep, bang your head on the floor, and flamboyantly kill yourself even *once* is cathartic. To get to do that eight times a week for two months is positively therapeutic.

Shakespeare is dead, but the modern-day Shakespeare is alive and well. His name is Stephen Sondheim, and your next role is in a staged reading of one of his masterpieces, *Sweeney Todd.* You play Toby; the sublime Christine Baranski is Mrs. Lovett; and Kelsey Grammer is Sweeney. At least he is allegedly. You and your cast-mates are surprised to learn as you begin rehearsals that Kelsey and his wife, Camille (and what a great couple they are; no doubt they will last forever), have gone to Hawaii for a vacation.

A week later everyone's on a soundstage working on the big production number when Kelsey shows up and marvels at how good you all are. Which would be a nice thing to hear from an audience member. Only he's not an audience member, he's the star of the show, and shouldn't he, you know, maybe be onstage doing this with you right now?

You're well aware of the different levels of focus and preparation needed for TV work and stage work. But Kelsey . . . well, Kelsey is becoming aware of it *now*. His voice grows more and more strained as he rapidly realizes how much work he should have been doing and how much he should have already gotten down. On a weekly series you can learn a lot of material quickly, and no doubt he had often done so, and brilliantly, but it doesn't work that way with theater—much less within the limited rehearsal period of a staged reading, and much much less when it's Sondheim, and much much *much* less with a show as elaborate and musically challenging as *Sweeney Todd*.

So come the night of the performance the director makes the ultimate TV-star concession: he puts *five* teleprompters onstage. Five. Two in the front, two in the wings, and one in Mrs. Lovett's pie shop. For the rest of the cast it's kind of like doing *Sweeney Todd: The Infomercial*, because when you're talking or singing to Kelsey he's staring away from you, reading his next lines on the screen behind you or beside you, or the one stuck smack-dab in the middle of a goddamn Victorian-era bakery/barbershop.

It's a little awkward. But it's totally worth it for this: Sondheim singles you out for praise! There's a section of the show where Toby rhythmically chants an improvisation on a children's rhyme:

Pat-a-cake, pat-a-cake, baker man.
Bake me a cake—
No, no,
Bake me a pie—

To delight my eye,
And I will sigh
If the crust be high . . .

Sondheim had only put *x*'s in the score, to indicate that the words had a rhythm but not necessarily a melody. But you make up some weird singsongy tune to do it to. Sondheim comes to see the performance, and afterward, in an elevator full of people, he tells you he likes your tune so much *he's going to change the notes in the score to match your melody.* When he leaves, the rest of the elevator turns to you and squeals like schoolgirls, which is exactly what you would do. Oh wait, you're squealing too, actually.

You have no idea if he ever followed through on his pledge. It's possible he did. It's possible he didn't. A quick glance through the most recently revised score of *Sweeney Todd* would reveal the answer. Which is why you never glance through it. Because as long as you don't, *last you heard,* Stephen Sondheim changed his score because of you.*

To work with Stephen Sondheim again, turn to page 154.

To continue your theater career in a less illustrious way, turn to page 115.

To go to Ireland, 'cause why the hell not, turn to page 156.

---

* Years later, Stephen Sondheim will be gracious enough to contribute this verse to your memoir:

Neil Patrick Harris,
Who's hard to embarrass,
Can be found in your browser
Under "See Doogie Howser."

Along with this explanatory note:

It's a cleribew, a form of personalized quatrain invented by E. C. Bentley, in which you use the subject's name as the first line.

Double squeal!

Have courage, Neil. Don't be scared. Life is an adventure. An opportunity like the one you have now may never come again, at least not in this book.

Sure, you're a little afraid right now. The thing/activity/career path you're considering doing may seem a little frightening. But it's also the path to growth and self-discovery.

So pluck up your courage and take that risk! Add another story to the book of your life. Even if it doesn't go the way you planned or wanted, you'll still learn from it. Adventure elicits action, and through action comes change.

And change forces new experience.

And experience yields knowledge.

Now turn back to the page you were just on and say yes to adventure!

Two of the most important people you meet in your post-Doogie life turn out to be a couple of stoner dudes from Jersey. Not that you set out to meet them. Or any dudes, for that matter. Because in the wake of your star-making four-season TV run, when you ask yourself, *What's the best way to capitalize on your medico-televisual fame?* the answer is obvious to you and to anyone who knows Neil Patrick Harris: fuck as many women as humanly possible.

So you spend the next few years hitting and quitting almost every cooch you come in contact with. Eventually, you pork your way through the entire LA snizz scene and start traveling the country in search of new vaginal adventures. One day you find yourself at a party on a movie set in New Jersey. You're disappointed by the level of talent until your friend Charlie arrives with his new girlfriend. She's a 9, easy, with the face of Ava Gardner and the tits of a *Square Pegs*–era Sarah Jessica Parker. Her intoxicating fragrance is redolent of lilacs, juniper berries, and cooze sweat. Your hard-on instantly becomes a harder-on. You desperately want to do her, but what about Charlie? How are you gonna bang his girlfriend when he's standing right there?

As you deliberate, Charlie asks if you want to bounce with him and the skirt to another party. Then he offers you ecstasy. You tend to be more of a Quaaludes/barbiturates kind of guy, but when it comes to drugs you're willing to try anything because you, Neil Patrick Harris, love doing drugs.

At first nothing seems to be happening, but then, just as you get in the limo and take off, the ecstasy starts kicking in. Your lust overpowers you. Your balls are about to explode. You wait until Charlie isn't looking, then stick your hand under his girlfriend's skirt and commence fingerbanging. Much to your delight, she is into it. But then, just as you take your fingers out so she can taste her own cooch cream, Charlie catches you, punches you in the face, opens the door, and pushes you out.

You tumble onto the pavement and get up relatively unscathed, but now you're stuck in the middle of fucking nowhere without a car. Luckily, you flag down a car and hop inside, and that's when you meet them: the driver, an Asian dude in his twenties, and his passenger, another dude in his twenties who looks Indian or Pakistani or something. They say their names are Harold and Kumar, but you don't care; all you want is for them to take you to the nearest strip club. But they insist on going to White Castle instead.

This is the moment you realize they're probably gay.

You wait until they pull over at a convenience store, then hop into the driver's seat and jack their car. Next stop: your favorite NJ strip club, Flaps, in Piscataway. Strippers always love it when cute, innocent Doogie walks in—and that's how you lure them into leaving the club with you. You pack 'em into the H&Kmobile, pull out an eight ball, and keep the party going down the open road. Once you're done giving them the business, you drop them off like the gentleman you are. You're starving and White Castle is still fresh in your mind because of those gay dudes who kept talking about it so you go to one . . . and turns out they have a happy ending (but not the fun kind), 'cause there they are holding a whole bunch of meat (which they must love since they're gay). You buy their meal, give them back their car, and walk off into the sunset, expecting your encounter never to have a sequel.

But you're wrong. Cut to a few days later. You get a call from another buddy throwing a wild rager down in New Orleans. Faster than a speeding penis you're in a hotel room overlooking Bourbon Street. Within five minutes you're banging some broad on the balcony, hard against the railing, NPH-style. Then you hear police sirens. Turns out all the ladies there are professionals and you're getting raided. Your buddy tosses you the keys to his car and tells you to get the hell out of Dodge. You do exactly as told.

But you didn't finish your business, and your balls are bluer than a Smurf in a cloudless sky, so you decide to head to Madam Sally's, the Texas whorehouse you used to frequent during the *Doogie* hiatuses of yesteryear. On the way you spot a couple of dudes hitchhiking on the side of the road. You remember that nice gay couple that picked you up in Jersey a few days earlier and decide to pay it forward. So you pull over and let them in. But wouldn't you know it—the hitchhikers turn out to be *those same* gay dudes, Harold and Kumar! Them again! If this were a movie it would be *Harold and Kumar 2*!

You all make your way to Madam Sally, who presents you with a glittering array of prostitutes. Naturally you pick the biggest-titted whore of the bunch (her name is literally Tits), then tell Sally to hook up Harold and Kumar with a couple of girls. Knowing them, you assume they'll end up rubbing their dicks together or something, but that's *their* problem. You and Tits get undressed in one of the private rooms, and dive into a typical Neil Patrick Harris fuck session, which consists of:

1. Kissing.
2. Super sloppy wet blowjobs (the more spitting the better).
3. Tit slapping . . . first with your hand, then your dick.
4. Golden showers.
5. Chocolate hailstorms.
6. A few minutes of cuddling (after she wipes off the remnants of your hailstorm).

7. Branding her with your initials, officially making her your bitch.

But alas—as Fredrick Douglass once said—"bitches always act like bitches." The moment you brand Tits she runs out of the room and starts crying to Sally. Next thing you know, Sally's pulling out a shotgun. You make a break for the car with H&K, but before you can get to them, she cocks her shotgun and blows a load right through your chest. You fall to the ground as everything around you fades away. . . .

You've heard of people talk about near-death experiences before, but yours is the real deal. You actually go to heaven and meet Jesus. He's a little Jewy for your taste, but he's got a couple of hot medium-meloned angels around his arms. Naturally you make a move on them when Jesus isn't looking. But before you can dip your wick, Jesus catches you and gets his dad to send you back down to Earth. Whatevs.

With a new lease on life, you realize you need to change your ways. For the next eight months, you give up booze and broads. You score an audition for a CBS show entitled *How I Met Your Mother,* and soon you're once again on every TV set across the country. Before long, you're catching a whiff of that sweet smell that can only come from a certain female orifice, and you're sticking it to every chick on the show . . . even the unknown mother herself. But when your agent catches wind he reminds you you're on a family network and shouldn't do anything in the public eye that could hurt your chances of getting this show into syndication. That's when you remember those two gay guys, Harold and Kumar. They were friendly. They were harmless. They were sweet. So you come up with a brilliant idea—convince the world you're gay!

You make the big announcement to the press and they buy

it. It works like a charm. Now you can grab whatever snatch you want and no one will see it coming. True, now you have to pretend to be an advocate for gay rights, but you quickly learn that hot chicks show up to gay rights rallies. Still, when you bump into the boys for a third time—backstage at Radio City Music Hall—they start giving you slack for pretending to be gay. You assume they're offended at how you have been portraying their lifestyle, so you appease them the only way you know how—by giving them a Christmas tree and a robot. They leave on good terms, and that's the last you ever see of them.

But in the years to come you will occasionally pause to reflect about them. *Those two dudes,* you will think, *were there during some of your lowest lows and highest highs.* In many ways, Harold and Kumar change your life. You wonder if you'll ever meet up with them again. The odds are unlikely—but "randomly" bumping into them through the years has made you a believer in fate. Maybe the next time you're on one of your awesome adventures, your paths will cross for a fourth time. Until then, here's hoping they're doing well.

Woohoo! To be the subject of a profile in Totally Straight Guy *magazine 'cuz you're so totally straight, turn to page 94.*

To go out on a date with the kind of hot chick a raging heterosexual man like you can get anytime he wants, turn to page 264.

If all this adrenaline has you ready for a climactic car chase, turn to page 207. (It's a gay car chase, though.)

A nd then comes David.* *(uh-oh)*

A revival of Sondheim's *Into the Woods* is playing at the
Ahmanson Theater. You go to the opening night and, as has been *(like you always do!)*
your theatergoing pattern for most of your life now, you finagle
your way backstage afterward to find out how the set works, who *(Too friendly)*
(Theatre Geek) has what dressing room, and all that stage-door-Johnny stuff. You *(if you ask me.)*
mingle and become friendly with a lot of the cast. They come
over to your house, you party, you bond. They are theater people, → *(The best kind.)*
and they're wonderful, and you don't get to hang out with a lot of
them in LA. *(—which is where I 1st fell for you!)*

A year later you return to New York to do *Cabaret*. You're walk-
ing down Eighth Avenue around Forty-seventh Street when you *(The Fabulous)* *(The better one)*
run into your *Into the Woods* buddy Kate Reinders, freshly cast in
the Sam Mendes–directed Broadway revival of *Gypsy*. Accompanying her is this rakishly handsome James Dean–like hot dude in *(I wish!)*
a leather jacket and T-shirt—with a little gray hair, which is always *(Mötley Crüe)* *(Premature)*
a plus. So you say, "Hey, I'm Neil," and he puts his hand out with
great indifference and says, "Hey, I'm David." And that's it. You *(I didn't want him to know I knew he was a celebrity.)*
keep talking to Kate about this and that, but in a private moment
when David turns away for a minute you whisper, "Well done,
you!" And she replies, "David? Oh, no, he's totally gay." *(To pretend to text.)*
(I'm a good actor) Contrary to popular belief, gaydar technology is still imper- *(you know it guuurl!)*
fect, even among gays. You find that when you spend an hour

---

* You have asked David to annotate this chapter with his own handwritten notes. He
has graciously agreed. He better not have messed with this footnote, though. That
would be way too meta.

with someone you tend to figure it out based on voice inflec-
tions and general impression, but on first blush it's not always
easy to know. You've met guys you found extremely effeminate
who turned out to be married with kids and straight, and you've
met guys you never would have thought were gay turn out to be
flaming man-whores. So you don't know. And David isn't swishy.
So when you see him with Kate, who's hot and blonde, you just
assume they're together. *If I WAS STRAIGHT I WOULD HAVE hit that!*

*WHAT DID YOU
CALL ME?!?*

*You
OBVIOUSLY
DIDN'T
KNOW
ME.*

They're not, of course. *(Yes!)* But he's in a relationship, and
even worse, that relationship is with a ^Hot Hollywood publicist. Well
then, that's not going to work. Try to steal him away from his jealous partner has the power to sabotage your career with one swift
broad-stroke e-mail. *BUT HE WOULD NEVER DO THAT, CAUSE HE IS A STAND UP GUY
♦ KARMA SUCKS!*
But you hear through the gayvine they weren't doing great, *IT WAS A LONG DISTANCE RELATIONSHIP. WHAT
DO YOU EXPEC*
and Kate kindly keeps you informed as to where she and her BFF
David will be on any particular night. So over the course of a couple of months you "happen" to be at the bar they're going to that *STALKER*
night, or just happen to go to Kate's to watch *American Idol* along
with David and ~~ten~~ 4 or so other members of the cast. Again, you're
not trying to steal ~~him~~. That would be uncool and stupid. But *YEAH RIGHT.*
you just want to make sure he sees you're interested and around.
You're like an unusually considerate hawk, *OR VAMPIRE,* politely waiting for the
opportunity to swoop down and attack. So you become friendly,
and eventually David and the publicist do break up *(double yes!),* *THANK GO
it WORKED
THE WAY
it DID.*
and shortly thereafter you go out on an actual proper date. *WHICH HE
DID VERY
WELL. HE*
It's natural. It's familiar. It's as cozy as an old shoe. You've *YOU CALLING ME OLD?!*
met the right man, and luckily you've done so at the right time. *PASSED
THE TEST*
Your experiences of the past few years have prepared you. You are *MAYBE CAUSE
HE COULD KEEP
UP WITH MY*
no longer scared of being someone's significant other, of meet-
ing someone's parents, of emotional intimacy. You are ready, and *FAMILIES,
EATING ♦
DRINKING.* *THEY ARE
POLISH BTW,*
David is ready. He has already lived such a full life. He's gone to
acting school, just won the Fred Astaire Award for Broadway's
best dancer for his work in *Gypsy,* been involved in long-term rela-

tionships, and, most amazingly, already raised twin two-year-olds (more on that later). He isn't ~~the stereotypical~~ SOME flighty dancer guy, unsure of what he wants out of life. He is well rounded in a way *you calling me fat?* that makes you confident he's not just looking to date another *if you play your cards right!* guy after you. It seems like if he's interested in you it's because he's decided you're the kind of guy he wants to be with long-term. Longer-term. Longest-term. *(for forever term)*

And so your adventure together begins. Within a few months *we were practically lesbians.* you begin talking about getting a place together in New York. You're both theater gypsies living in furnished sublets, so when it comes time to move in together you don't have to make the "whose house do we live in" decision: you'll find a new place. At first you look on the Upper West Side, and everything you see is *and stuffy.* tiny and sad. For $1,800 a month you get one tiny square living room with a tiny square adjoining bedroom with a half closet and half bath. So you decide to try Harlem, where you hear you can get a lot more. And while David is away you find a great place *performing in meet me in St. Louis.* that's just been vacated after forty years. It's in a tenement build-*in St. Louis.* ing but it's a really great space. You like it despite its utter disar-ray. The ceilings have caved in and the bedrooms are filled with trash bags (evidently the last tenant was a hoarder). But the three landlords who own it are trying to gentrify the building and are more than happy to have a well-known white gay couple move in. They're Hasidic Jews, but if they're homophobic they don't show it. They upgrade the electric, redo the floors and ceilings, and generally make you feel wanted. *(cause gays are a-gay-zing!)*

And as they do the upgrades, you set out on our first trip to-*Yo Penske!* gether. You rent a big Penske truck ~~tip: if you ever need to relax, try saying the word "Penske" a few times; it never fails~~ in LA and *so much fun! we love road trips!* pick up some of your stuff. Then you take a weeklong transconti-nental road trip, stopping at various places and filling up the truck with more stuff. You stop at Albuquerque to visit your parents and get more stuff. You go through Memphis, buying additional stuff,

We saw the actual Elvis!

110

IN All 1960's VIBE. RETRO ₹ AWESOME.   _THAT WAS FUN GETTING IN THE TRUCK_

like end tables and bric-a-brac, at a series of thrift stores. You drive up to Detroit, where David's parents are, and the pattern of stuff-picking-up continues, this time including a (piano) By the time you get back to Harlem the truck is loaded with the cornucopia of stuff the two of you will use to start your lives together.

You're not yet sure if that means "the rest of our lives." It's still _— IT BETTER BE !!_ a little tentative. Hypothetically it could wind up being another semitransient chapter of your romantic life. You could break up and move back to LA, and he would keep the apartment, and it would be fine. _EWWWW — I hope I don't have To GO BACK._   _— YELLOW ₹ ORANGE_

But that's not what happens. You unpack, paint the walls, put up fixtures, and move in together for the rest of your lives.

HAVE BABIES, MOVE A COUPLE MORE TIMES AND IVE HAPPILY EVER AFTER.

To take a vacation with David, turn to page 121.

To tell the world you love David, turn to page 168.

To start a family with David, turn to page 194.

To sing a song with lyrics by a different guy named David, turn to page 227.

FRESH PASTA WITH BOLOGNESE SAUCE

For most of his life, whenever David was feeling down in the dumps, sad, or bored, he cooked. He made homemade chicken soup when he didn't get a job; he made chocolate cake after a fight with a friend. This love of food led him to go to cooking school and become a professional chef. At the start of his career he had a chance to work at the legendary restaurant Babbo in New York under the tutelage of the great Mario Batali, where he learned how to make Mario's famous Bolognese. The recipe below is David's personal take on the recipe. You're addicted to this dish and it's quite possibly your favorite thing David makes. Whenever he goes out of town he makes sure there's plenty of this ragù stocked up in the freezer. David says this sauce is best with homemade pasta but in a pinch dry pasta will do just fine. You say, oh sweet Babbo, is this good.

FRESH PASTA

Although the sauce will work on any type of dried or fresh pasta, David likes to make his own. Yes, it can be time-consuming, but it's totally worth it.

Serves 4

2 cups all-purpose flour, plus additional as needed

2 eggs

I teaspoon olive oil

Salt

Water as needed

Note: The ratio for pasta dough is always I cup of flour to I egg. You can increase the amount if desired.

1. Place 2 cups of flour in a pile on counter. Use your fingers to make a hole in the center of the flour (a "well").

2. Break the eggs into the well; add olive oil and a pinch of salt.

3. Break the yolks with a fork, and in a swirling motion beat them slowly to incorporate into the flour. You can swirl to your favorite late-'80s dance song—David prefers Technotronic's "Pump Up the Jam." Be careful not to break the walls of the well until the eggs are fully incorporated.

4. Add a tiny amount of water and knead with your hands until a dough forms. *(Note: Add only enough water to make the flour sticky, but not wet. If you add too much water and your hands get sticky, use a little more flour.)*

5. Continue kneading 5 to 10 minutes, until the dough is smooth and bounces back. *(To test the dough: Press your finger into it to make an indent. If it bounces back, the dough is ready. If it screams in pain, something's gone horribly awry.)*

6. Form a flat disk with the dough, cover in plastic wrap, and let rest for 30 minutes on the counter.

7. Set up a pasta roller; place die setting to 1 (the widest setting).

8. Take *one-quarter* of the dough (leave the rest covered) and flatten it out with the palm of your hand or a rolling pin to about ¼ to ½ inch thick. Place the dough on the pasta roller and crank through each setting twice, starting on the lowest setting. When you get to setting 6, pull through only once.

9. Using a pastry wheel, cut 1 x 9-inch strips for pappardelle. Put the cut pasta in layers on a baking sheet with parchment between layers to keep them from sticking. Keep the pasta covered so it won't dry out as you repeat step 8 with the remainder of the dough. Remember to turn the setting back to 1 with each new batch of dough.

10. Store fresh pasta, covered, in the refrigerator until ready to use. Do not allow loved ones to snack on it. Use force if necessary.

BOLOGNESE

Serves 4 to 6

2 ounces extra virgin olive oil

1 cup onions, cut into very small dice

½ cup celery, cut into very small dice

½ cup carrot, cut into very small dice

Salt

3 cloves garlic, very thinly sliced

½ pound ground veal

½ pound ground pork

4 ounces ground or finely diced pancetta

4 ounces (⅔ can) tomato paste

½ cup dry white wine

½ cup whole milk

¼ cup chicken stock or broth

½ teaspoon fresh thyme leaves, minced

½ teaspoon fresh oregano, minced

Red pepper flakes

Pepper

1 tablespoon butter

Parmesan, for serving

1. Heat a large, shallow saucepan over medium-low heat. Add the olive oil, onions, celery, carrots, and a pinch of salt. Sweat until translucent (approximately 10 minutes), stirring occasionally (do not brown).

2. Add the garlic and continue to sweat for 2 minutes. (The garlic, not you.)

3. Increase heat to high and add the veal, pork, and pancetta. Brown the meat, stirring frequently to break it up while combining with the vegetables.

4. Once the meat is browned, add the tomato paste, wine, and milk. Bring to a boil.

5. Add the chicken stock, thyme, oregano, and a pinch of red pepper flakes (or more if desired). Return to the boil, then reduce heat to medium-low and simmer for 1 to 1½ hours, uncovered, stirring occasionally.

6. Season with salt and pepper to taste.

7. Add the butter and stir until it is incorporated. Place in a large serving bowl.

Serving Suggestion

1. In a large pot bring at least 6 quarts of salted water to a boil.

2. Put fresh pasta in the pot and boil for 2 minutes, or until it floats *(do not drain)*.

3. Transfer the pasta and a few tablespoons of pasta water from the pot to the serving bowl with the Bolognese.

4. Delicately combine the pasta and sauce.

5. Serve with shaved Parmesan to your loved ones.

6. Enjoy their moaning.

7. Make them do the dishes.

To tweet food porn about this delicious meal, turn to page 252.

To share a meal with one of your best friends, Kelly Ripa, turn to page 219.

To bask even more deliciously in David's love, turn to page 280.

In 2002 you are hungry for a starring role on Broadway, and you think you may have found one in *Proof,* David Auburn's beautifully written Pulitzer Prize–winning play. Although the play centers on the brilliant but troubled young female mathematician Catherine, the role of her boyfriend Hal is enormous, meaty, and fun.*

Catherine is played originally by Mary-Louise Parker, then by Jennifer Jason Leigh. When Jennifer leaves, the producers decide to break with tradition and cast someone with only two names, Anne Heche. At the same time, the role of Hal becomes available. You're very interested, and so are the producers, but they're concerned you might look too young opposite Anne. So your agent—who's Anne's agent also, and isn't that nice—finds a recent video of her auditioning for a film in which she looks young and glowing and radiant, which gives the producers confidence it won't look too oedipal when you kiss her.

You begin a month of rehearsal with Anne and the other new members of the ensemble, including the glorious Kate Jennings Grant and Len Cariou, the original Sweeney Todd. The cast is great. The material is exquisite. The stars seemed to be aligned. But from the very first rehearsal one unexpected obstacle emerges: Anne Heche. After her very public breakup

---

* You can imagine the kind of joke that goes here.

with Ellen DeGeneres, she has by her own admission done a lot of prescription drugs. She was recently found on a highway in Napa Valley speaking to aliens. She has just come out with a book called *Call Me Crazy*. And now, as you sit in a circle discussing the play, she looks at you, pulls her sunglasses down (note: you are indoors), and, in a loud, helium-pitched voice, says, "Wow, how do you theater people do it? How do you theater people do the same thing every night? I just don't get it, I don't work that way."

At which point you think, *Heeeere we go.*

From night to night Anne refuses to do the show the same way twice. You've worked with several great actors, like Denis O'Hare, who choose to perform their roles slightly differently each time. But they always do so within the constraints of their character, and with a clear understanding of what the pace and rhythm of any given scene should be.

That is not Anne Heche. Anne Heche is the kind of actress who asks the wardrobe department to make her a whole bunch of different outfits so she can choose which one to wear during any particular performance. She is also the kind of actress who, when the wardrobe department refuses her request, starts doodling in permanent marker on her outfits, forcing them to get her different ones. Anne Heche is the kind of costar who decides one night, for no reason whatsoever, to shout all her lines. And on another night not to pause for the *entire* performance. One night you watch as she delivers all her lines as single rapid-fire eruptions as if every monologue is a single unimaginably long German compound word. But of course, unlike the audience, you can't just *watch* her doing this; you have to act alongside her. Fall in love with her, in fact. What is she doing? Is she mad at you? Is this some kind of passive-aggressive attack? "No," she tells you afterward, "it wasn't about you at all. I just wanted to see what that would feel like."

To be clear: She isn't mean. She's . . . volatile. And given the mental and emotional volatility of her character Catherine, she is in many ways perfectly cast. No doubt much of the audience considers her performance galvanizing and spontaneous. And it is spontaneous, insofar as she is *genuinely* doing things she's never done before. But in your mind it's a little unfair to the author. And the director. And the rest of the cast. And the crew. And the wardrobe.

There's a scene in the play where your character runs down the stairs, opens the screen door and finds Catherine fighting with her older sister, played by the luminous Kate Jennings Grant. You interrupt them, at which point Kate angrily goes upstairs and you continue the scene with Catherine. One night you come running down the stairs, open the screen door and see only Kate. Anne's not there. Where is she? Then you hear her voice and turn your eyes to the wing, past the corner of the stage, almost in the front row, where Anne, hands over her head, spins in a circle singing her lines. *In complete darkness.* 'Cause there's no lights on her. 'Cause that's not where's she's supposed to be.

And at that moment, Kate leaves, and with a shudder you think to yourself, *Oh, good, she's all mine now.*

After a while, sustaining the illusion of being in love with her becomes difficult, and making out with her (which you must do several times a show) feels kind of icky . . . and not because you're kissing a chick. It feels kind of icky because, during one show early on, she makes the conscious decision to act as if kissing *you* is disgusting. Not because of anything you did offstage, mind you. Just because Anne Heche feels her character would consider kissing you disgusting *on that particular night*. Which, in the world of the play, is the same night it always is.

On the plus side, the two of you share several pleasant dinners.

If you need a drink to calm down, turn to page 45.

If you need to wake your brain back up, turn to page 150.

To continue your stage career, willkommen/bienvenue/welcome im/au/to page 130.

To attempt to relaunch your movie career, turn to page 124.

You, age 1½. Unlike all other children that age, you were adorable.

You, age 6. Note the orange stripes in the shirt. That color would be declared illegal in 1982.

You, age 8, going through not only your "awkward stage," but that of six other classmates.

You, age 26. You were a very late bloomer.

Your family. Pictured: Brian, Mom, Dad, you. Not pictured (but strongly implied): President Gerald Ford.

You and your brother, Brian, whom you admired for his coolness, creativity, and reluctance to be photographed holding wash basins.

Your beloved cat Cosette, staring at you with her beautiful loving eyes as if to ask, "Why did you not mention me anywhere else in the book?"

This is an actual picture of you getting the news you'd been cast in *Clara's Heart*, meaning your family would finally be able to afford its own phone.

A scene from *Clara's Heart*. Note the milk carton with the missing girl. She eventually turned up safe and sound and went on to become Alyssa Milano.

Signing autographs at the premiere of *Clara's Heart*. All those writing lessons finally paid off!

A publicity still for *Doogie Howser, M.D.* The creation of this pompadour required the day-long application of a rare imported mousse distilled from the secretions of an opossum's thyroid gland.

Your appearance on *The Tonight Show with Johnny Carson* remains one of the highlights of your career, even if it did drive him into retirement.

You and fellow actor Stephen Dorff in 1990. You used to go out and try to get laid looking like this. With women. And you weren't even straight.

The Music Man, 1985

Rent, 1997

Proof, 2002

Cabaret, 2003

Assassins, 2004

Hedwig and the Angry Inch, 2014

Your theater career spans more than 30 years and a variety of genres, from your early role in the gender-bending, taboo-busting *The Music Man* to your most recent work in the old-fashioned, family-friendly *Hedwig and the Angry Inch*.

The *HIMYM* crew: Carter Bays, Pam Fryman, Josh Radnor, Jason Segel, Cobie Smulders, Rob Greenberg, Alyson Hannigan, Craig Thomas, and you. Staring at this photo gives you the feels.

You and David on one of your first dates. Is he good-looking or what? Seriously, dude, you scored big-time.

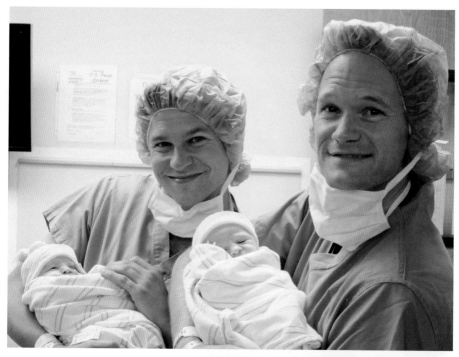

Gideon and Harper,
Day 1, 10/12/10

Gideon and Harper,
Day 1,338, 6/12/14

Gideon and Harper on the set of the 2014
all-preschool production of *Rent*, hailed
by the *New York Times* as "breathtakingly
inappropriate."

The finale of "Bigger," the opening number you performed at the 2013 Tonys. Unique among the major entertainment awards, the Tony Award is actually 20 feet tall. When you win one yourself the following year for *Hedwig and the Angry Inch*, you end up converting the base into a toolshed.

And now a word from your friend . . .

AMY SEDARIS

Neil, you and I met—as of course you know, so why am I saying it, it's as if I need to create context for some imaginary third party who might be reading this, which, why would I do that?—on the set of that small little movie we did, *The Best and the Brightest.* We were introduced the same day Michael Jackson died. I'll never forget the day I first shook your hand, because I'll always associate it with tragedy.

You're a great performer whom I have long admired, plus a genuinely nice person whose friendship I treasure, but probably everybody is writing sappy stuff like that. So here are some more specific things I associate with you:

1. You consume an astonishing amount of Red Bull. It's . . . amazing. I once saw you do a back flip in a hotel room. (Or was that David?) I don't remember the context, but I do remember being impressed, and I remember thinking such a display of reckless acrobatics could only be driven by a large amount of a certain color combined with a certain male farm animal.

2. You *love* performing magic, and you also love propagating it. I recall that time you gave me a generous supply of magician's flash paper and a device that secretly ignites it. You carefully instructed me *never* to ignite more paper at a time than the amount you used to

show me how to do the trick. Of course that only encouraged me to use more paper, and I ended up severely burning my hand and very nearly lighting my rabbit ablaze. As it turns out, you are not only a talented magician, but also a responsible one.

3. You are a great friend. And a unique one. I still have that taxidermy beaver you and David got me. I mean, of course I still have it. As far as dead animals go, it's beautiful. Did you get it from a museum of natural history or something? I don't know, but I know it came in a box the size of a chest freezer, and that as I struggled to open it the first thing to emerge was a root-beer-brown-colored beaver-flap, not unlike a canoe paddle. It's not every day you open a gift and an animal tail flops out. And until the day I received it, I never would have guessed that the one item needed to tie my apartment décor together was a large taxidermy beaver.

So to sum up: You are a multitalented performer continually hopped up on questionable beverages meant to improve stamina, a sensible magician who has a childlike wonderment for sleight of hand, and a good friend who sends me odd yet thoughtful gifts.

By the way, Neil, my bathroom's looking a little sparse, and I really love otters . . .

Amy is so awesome. It's too bad you won't get to work with her on any of the very special TV guest spots you are now going to do on page 71.

Or in any of the kids' movies on page 233.

You and your boyfriend, David, are in the middle of a Costa Rican vacation. You spend the first few days in an honest-to-God tree house—a fifty-foot-high hotel room in a tree, with its own plumbing and everything. To order room service you have to call the front desk and lower a Swiss Family Robinson–style basket, which they fill with either beer or rum, depending on . . . you're not sure, exactly. Then they ring the bell and you pull it up and slide off the retractable roof and sleep under the stars and man, is it nice.

One day you decide to leave your little jungle paradise and head off on a two-day white-water rafting adventure. You spend the day navigating some surprisingly hard rapids in an incredible tropical setting. Then you and the rest of the group prepare to spend the night in little jungle cabins, under a billion stars, with no streets or cars or lights or any other sign of civilization except *guaro*, a drink made from fermented sugarcane that is approximately 175 percent alcohol.

You and David are both good and *guaro*ed when two of the guides, both darkly attractive, offer to take you to some nearby zip lines that are scheduled to be part of tomorrow's platforms.

If you decide not to go, turn to page 101.

If you decide to go, keep reading.

You and David are very excited to climb up to the platforms. One or both of you may or may not also be excited about the possibility that one or both of the darkly handsome guides could take things all crazy junglesexual.

The four of you head off into the moonlit night and, after half an hour, find yourself standing on a small but sturdy zip-line platform about twenty feet off the ground. A two-hundred-foot-high cliff juts out just below you.

The guides have brought blankets, pillows, and candles. They proceed to get the platform very cozy. You're drinking *guaro* when the guides *both* pull out joints, *both* light them up, *both* inhale, and *both* pass them to you and David. After ten minutes, you are both as messed up as you've ever been in your life.

You're all mellowly hanging out, telling stories, having a grand old time, when David stands up and says, "I'm going to go take a leak." He turns, takes a casual step off the twenty-foot platform, drops into the Costa Rican darkness, and vanishes.

Disappears. Like a cartoon. Step; vanish.

If squiggle lines indicating rapid downward motion appeared where he had just been standing, it would not surprise you.

David is gone. Judge Crater gone, Amelia Earhart gone. Neither the guides nor you hear any sound of landing, soft or hard. It seems as though he must have plummeted not only the twenty feet to the ground, but the two hundred feet off the cliff. You are sure he is dead. The guides are sure he is dead. You are also pretty sure that the guides are pretty sure they're both in deep shit.

You run down the steps calling for him. And miraculously, against all laws of motion and thermodynamics, you find him on the railroad ties that guard the edge of the cliff. He lies there and goes through a bodily checklist and is delighted to learn he still has exactly as many of everything as he is supposed to. It seems physically impossible given the (literal) gravity of the situation, but the worst thing that's happened to him is he's lost a flip-flop, the lucky son of a bitch.

In later years the two of you will recollect this moment often, and the primal fear (in your case) and the horrible vertiginous feeling of falling through the air in the darkness from the canopy of a Central American jungle (in David's) will return. You both agree it belongs solidly in the moments-that-brought-you-closer-as-a-couple file.

You also both agree the human body is better able to withstand twenty-foot plummets onto railroad ties when that body is drunk and stoned out of its mind.

To go on another vacation with David, turn to page 156.

To experience the coolest vacation/birthday present in the history of mankind, courtesy of David, turn to page 280.

It's been nearly ten years since you appeared on the big screen in *Purple People Eater*, the movie that was incredibly successful and made you a mega-superstar in an alternate universe. In the interim you've become a very successful TV actor, but in the eyes of Hollywood directors there's an enormous gap between "TV actor" and "movie star," and crossing that gap proves difficult. You audition for dozens of film roles and come up pretty much empty. You keep hearing the same feedback through your agent: you're (a) too Doogie, (b) too white and all-American, and (c) still too Doogie. But you keep at it, and your persistence pays off when Paul Verhoeven casts you in the sci-fi adventure *Starship Troopers*. He's looking for a master-race vibe, so the eerie Aryanness of your appearance plays to your advantage.

The filming will be at a beautiful place in Wyoming called Hell's Half Acre, which looks like a cross between *Lawrence of Arabia* and Carlsbad Caverns. As someone who's come to love the process of bonding with your theater cast-mates you look forward to the same thing happening here. But it's not to be. Your character, Carl Jenkins, is the smart one who *doesn't* get involved in the exciting man-on-alien fight action, so the director deliberately excludes you from the three-week paramilitary training session the rest of the cast has to go through. While they train for their roles by wearing armor and fighting till they pass out in 100-degree heat, you are forbidden from taking part, because your role in the movie is essentially to show up, look at all the dead bodies, cry,

"This is an outrage! Carry on," and walk out. Oh, and to talk to your pet ferret.*

Starship Troopers turns out to be a really good movie, but its massive $105 million budget makes it a bit of a financial flop in theaters. It is Exhibit A in a pattern from which your film career will only occasionally deviate: every time you're cast in a movie that's *sure* to be a hit, it isn't. Exhibit B is your next major screen role, alongside Rupert Everett and Madonna in *The Next Best Thing*. Rupert Everett has just scored a giant success in *My Best Friend's Wedding*. Madonna is Madonna. What can go wrong?

A lot. The movie gets killed both critically and commercially. For starters it's rewritten to death. Rewritten *from* death, more accurately. In the original script your character (Rupert's best friend) ends up dying of AIDS in a hospital, but not before setting Rupert straight about life from his deathbed. But a few days before shooting the producers tell you, "We're going to have you come film in the final courtroom scene. We'll see you briefly in it and you'll give a thumbs-up."

"But I thought I was dead from that dying scene. You know, the one where I died," you note astutely.

"Yeah, but we're considering an option where we don't really do that scene and you're fine."

"But the entire arc of my character is that he starts out healthy and his sickness is what jars Rupert's character into making the decision he makes."

"Yeah, but the whole AIDS thing, we're not sure that's going

---

* Acting with ferrets is far more tedious than you imagined. You have to take your place in the shot, then literally stand still and wait for the ferret handler standing behind you to yell "Skipper! Up Skipper!" You have to wait until it stands up to say your line. And you have to film each scene countless times. It is hilariously frustrating. By the end of the movie you and Skipper are no longer on speaking terms.

to test super well, so we'll maybe have a version where you're in the courtroom."

And sure enough, in the final cut there's you in the climactic courtroom scene giving Rupert Everett a thumbs-up, very much alive, and for very much no reason whatsoever. Committee filmmaking at its finest.

Madonna is . . . Madonna. She's perfectly nice to you, but she's always so surrounded by her retinue it's hard to get to know her. Her team worries *way* too much about how she looks on camera. After lots of screen tests they conclude she looks best when she has shadows over her forehead and her chin is lit diagonally across a certain part of her face. So in every scene in the movie she is lit *exactly* like that, and she's either sitting or standing perfectly still. Does it make for the most dynamic performance? Only true *cinéastes* know for sure.

As for Rupert Everett, you are surprised at how blatantly disrespectful he is to your director, John Schlesinger, a perfectly lovely guy and prolific filmmaker responsible for classics like *Midnight Cowboy* and *Marathon Man*. You're not sure why he's so contemptuous, but as years go by you will see Rupert Everett be equally contemptuous to a variety of different people, the LGBT community included. A shame, that. But he was friendly to you, so here's hoping he cheers up soon.

Next up, Exhibit C in your catalog of surefire-hits-that-aren't: *Undercover Brother*, based on an animated web series. It's sort of an urban James Bond meets Austin Powers. Playing to type, you're cast as the white guy. Your costars are Dave Chappelle, who is as hilarious as he is nice to work with, and Denise Richards, with whom you're already friendly from *Doogie Howser* and *Starship Troopers*. But Eddie Griffin plays the Undercover Brother himself. Eddie, as they say in Hollywood, is "having a moment," and he seems to be . . . enjoying it. A lot of time is spent waiting for him to come out from his trailer. On one occasion he refuses to emerge until the studio gives him a motorcycle. On another occasion he demands a giant-screen TV for his trailer. In his defense, he gets 'em both.

On a side note, you learn a valuable lesson about the limitations of verisimilitude in performance. There's a scene where you get out of a van filled with pot smoke. Your character is supposed to be really high in the next scene. So you have the brilliant idea, "Hey, I've never done this before, but since I'm supposed to be stoned, why don't I just actually *get* stoned?" Worst acting idea *ever*. Part of filming a comedy is being sharp and spontaneous and quick on your feet, especially when you're working opposite a master of improv like Dave Chappelle. But you spend the next ninety minutes unfunny and hyperparanoid. Your only thought is that everyone knows you're high and is laughing at you.

You learn your lesson: you, movies, and drug use should never mix.

Then you forget that lesson and salvage your film career.

To learn how your hard-core drug use affected two cheeseburger-seeking New Jerseyites, turn to page 102.

To go back to a simpler, happier, drug-freer time, turn to page 8.

To be the biggest movie star in the world, go on to the next page.

In 1997 your life changes forever when you, Neil Patrick Harris, are cast as Jack Dawson in *Titanic*.

Looking back it's hard to believe, but at the time some people in show biz are actually skeptical. "Neil Patrick Harris?!?" they say. "*He's* going to star in *Titanic*?!?" An Academy Award for Best Actor and $1.8 billion later, those critics are silenced. You are, truly, the king of the world.

You follow up *Titanic* with a riveting star turn as Captain John Miller in Steven Spielberg's WWII drama *Saving Private Ryan*. The role earns you your second consecutive Best Actor Oscar, along with the first-ever Nobel Prize for Acting—a category specially created to honor your brilliance. It also raises your asking price to $50 million a picture, and cements your status as the number-one leading man in Hollywood.

From there the roles just keep on coming. You, Neil Patrick Harris, earn fame, fortune, and seven more Best Actor Oscars for your work as Neo in *The Matrix*, Frodo Baggins in *The Lord of the Rings*, Anton Chigurh in *No Country for Old Men*, and the title characters in *Spider-Man, Lincoln, Django Unchained*, and, in an extraordinary display of acting range, *The Queen*.

Your films are *always* top quality and *always* overperform at the box office. You are *never* saddled by unprofessional costars and *never* have to play supporting roles. No one *ever* scrolls through your IMDb page and says, "Wow, I've never heard of a lot of these movies" or "Wait, Neil Patrick Harris was in that?"

How could they? You are Neil Patrick Harris, the biggest movie star in the world.

Then, one day, out of nowhere, during a daydream, you hear an unfamiliar voice . . .

Turn to page 19.

It's 2003 and you're stepping into the boots Alan Cumming once wore as the emcee in the Sam Mendes/Rob Marshall–directed Broadway production of *Cabaret* at Studio 54. You love everything about it, starting with your costume and makeup, both full-body Weimar bizarro: a custom-fitted harnessed outfit made of a ripped tuxedo, white suspenders wrapped around your junk, and an SS trench coat, all lovingly topped off with track marks, blue-black body hair, gold glitter on your nipples, and a swastika tattooed on your ass.

With the exception of the swastika, it's a completely new look for you.

One of the rules in this version of the show is that the emcee has carte blanche to do whatever he wants to whomever he wants at any time. He's an eerie metaphor for fascism, and the great thing about being an eerie metaphor for fascism is you get to mess with people. You can make out with or grope or fondle or bite or spit on anyone in the cast at any time, bound only by the laws of the State of New York and Actors' Equity, which you discover draws the line somewhere between grabbing a girl's cans and an over-the-pants handjob. Nor is your reign of terror limited only to your cast-mates. Studio 54 has (appropriately) cabaret-style seating, with the audience sitting at tables, and you are free to roam among the crowd, sit on laps, flirt, dance, maybe lick a neck or two. You know the point of the show is that power corrupts, but gosh, the corruption is fun.

It's a joy, but a grueling one. Before every show there's an intense vocal warm-up, then forty-five minutes of makeup, then a half hour of costume, then stretching, then five minutes of weight lifting right before curtain to get your muscles rippling. You are actually unable to complete your scheduled run in the show because you stomp around so hard in your combat boots that you develop stress fractures in all the bones in your feet, of which, you painfully discover, there are a lot.

Emboldened by *Cabaret*, you go back to LA and act in *The Paris Letter*, your second appearance in a work by the master playwright Jon Robin Baitz. The unique thing about this role is that you have to do full-frontal nudity. Not just that: You are required to be naked onstage with another naked man, to make out with him, and seduce him.* As both an actor and a public figure you are terrified, which is the main reason you decide to do it. And exactly what you hoped would happen happens: the first time you're naked onstage, you think to yourself, *Yep, that's my dick hanging out there onstage. Yep. Looks . . . looks kind of like a dick.* The fear turns out to be much ado about nothing. Well, not *nothing*, but less than a foot.

You have time to sneak in one more musical before *How I Met Your Mother* puts your theater career on a nine-year kibosh. You play both the Balladeer and Lee Harvey Oswald in Stephen Sondheim and John Weidman's *Assassins*. The production has actually been in the works for a few years, but massive terrorist attacks in Manhattan have a funny way of derailing musicals about people trying to assassinate the president. So the opening is delayed until spring 2004 . . . which happens to be just before the Republican National Convention . . . which makes publicity difficult, since with the *actual* president coming to town the city is none too keen on the idea of billboards and buses blaring the word

* That other man turns out be a young actor named Josh Radnor. To hang out with him some more, turn to page 133.

"Assassins" all over Midtown. Yet it's a great show, and the director, Joe Mantello, provides you with one of the most intense dramatic moments of your acting life: every night, after shooting JFK, you stand on stage and let the Zapruder film play onto your plain white T-shirt. To feel the weight, every night, of a thousand people reliving one of the darkest days in American history while staring *at your chest* . . . let's just say the palpable feeling of an audience's anguish invading your heart is something you'll never forget.

And then, at the end of a run in Jonathan Larson's quasi-one-man show *Tick, Tick . . . Boom!* in London at David Babani's brilliant Menier Chocolate Factory, you get a call that that TV pilot with the funny name you'd shot has been picked up by CBS, and you're due back in Hollywood. The rest is *HIMYM*story. You know from past experience that the rigors of a TV production schedule leave you no time to do long-term stage runs. Really, it's probably arrogant to think that you can do *any* kind of theater work.

If you're arrogant enough to think you can squeeze in one little piece of theater work around How I Met Your Mother, *turn to page 188. Warning: Patti LuPone is gonna be pissed.*

If not, go on to the next page.

If you're ready to take a break with a puzzle, turn to page 150.

Int.—Living room. The year 2030.

YOU: Gideon, Harper, I'm going to tell you an incredible story. The story of how I became a bro.

GIDEON: Are we being punished for something?

YOU: No.

HARPER: Yeah, is this going to take a while?

YOU: Yes. Twenty-five years ago, before I was Dad, I had this whole other life.

[The peppy theme song to How I Became a Bro *starts and we see images of you and your cast-mates.]*

It was way back in 2005. I was thirty-two, starting to make it (again) as an actor, and living in New York with your father. Then I had the crazy idea to move back to Los Angeles and give pilot season another shot. ("Pilot" is one of LA's four official seasons, the other three being "hiring," "awards," and "Botox.")

I thought it was time to dip a cautious toe back into the world of television. I'd somehow convinced myself that the ideal gig for me would be a supporting role in a one-hour drama. I remembered how much fun I'd had twelve years earlier appearing on (and "shadow-directing") *Murder, She Wrote,* and I envisioned something like that, only cooler and smarter. Something like *Six Feet Under* or *Twin Peaks,* only even better. *Seven Feet Under. Triplet Peaks.*

I started auditioning for various shows. Then I got an e-mail from my friend Megan Branman, who was casting a potential pilot for CBS. It was not a single-camera one-hour drama. It was a multicamera half-hour comedy. And it was called *How I Met Your Mother.* The title immediately raised all kinds of questions: Who was "I"? Who was "you"? Why would it take an entire half hour for this meeting to take place? And once they met wouldn't they have to keep changing the title to *How I Went on a First Date with Your Mother* or *How I Got to Third Base with Your Mother?*

Suffice it to say, kids, I had numerous concerns. But Megan was a friend, so in deference to her I read the script, and I liked it. It was funny, and unusually for a pilot it did not feel derivative of other shows. It had its own vibe; it was neither a traditional, family-friendly sitcom nor a "hip" sitcom trying too hard to be cool. But there was another problem. The character they wanted me to read for, Barney Stinson, was Falstaffian and Belushi-esque—a big, barrel-chested, beer-chugging, life-of-the-party guy. He wasn't like me at all.

Nevertheless I went in to meet with and audition for the creators, two former Letterman writers named Carter Bays and Craig Thomas. I considered it a foregone conclusion that I would never get cast and the show would never get picked up, and as a result I approached the audition with total nonchalance. There was a laser-tag scene and, throwing caution to the wind, I committed to it fully, rolling on the floor, making running sniper shots, and knocking over a chair while crouching behind it to hide from assassins. The first traces of what would become my character began to emerge. I was a proto-broan.

Carter and Craig laughed and said I was really funny, but a lot of other people had told me that at a lot of other tryouts recently and I never heard from them again. So I said, "Best of luck, nice to meet you," and left, thinking that was the end of it. But as soon as I left Megan came running out. She stopped me and, in front of the next guy slated to try out, said, "They love you, they want you, I think we're going to go to network!" Which felt great, but I felt really bad for the poor guy who was about to go in. Until I turned and saw it was . . . Benedict Cumberbatch.*

A week later I had a callback in front of the network suits in the dark windowless catacomby necropolis that is the CBS television building. Another would-be Barney was there. For the first time I met Jason Segel, called back along with another would-be Marshall. Alyson Hannigan was also there and I was happy to see her—she was my floppy-hatted friend from child-actor days. Still not really believing Barney Stinson was in my future, I auditioned with even more recklessness. By now I'd memorized the laser-tag scene, and this time at the end I did a fancy dive roll as I pulled my weapon out.

We filmed the pilot at the CBS Radford Stages in Studio City close to my house. I figured if I got the job, I could Segway to work. (I mean, I wouldn't, but I could.) The director was the incredible Pam Fryman, who would go on to helm nearly every episode of the series and become one of my closest friends and greatest mentors. And as I got to know Carter and Craig, I realized what lovely people they were. They were the antithesis of the stereotypical sitcom show-runners who shout at the writers and ramble on about their "vision" and demand that things be done their way. They were as inclusive and unprecious as could be.

There were no glitches, everybody got along, and we all be-

---

* It wasn't. But wouldn't that have been cool?

came fast friends. There wasn't an unpleasant person in sight. I was having the time of my life. And for all these reasons, I thought there was *no way* this weird little hybrid show with the ridiculous name would go.

But it went. Ridiculous name and all.

How I Became a Bro will return after this page break.

PLEASE STAND BY

We now return to *How I Became a Bro,*
already in progress.

Nine years of hilarity and hijinks ensued. Nine seasons—that's as long as *Seinfeld.* That's longer than the entire Bush administration, and arguably less destructive to the country. By the time it was over I had somehow, improbably, become a bro. I was an out, gay, monogamous family man who, in the eyes of millions of people, represented an archetype of raging hetero boorishness.

But it took a while. *HIMYM* never felt like a breakout hit. At the end of each of our first three seasons we were all pretty sure CBS would cancel us. It was only after we had four full seasons under our belt that we considered ourselves successful. I credit Les Moonves and Nina Tassler, the two top people at CBS, with believing in the show, and with never moving it to a different time slot. We aired on Mondays at either 8:00 or 8:30 for all nine seasons, and even in the age of the DVR and Netflix, that kind of programming consistency is vital. Look at *Community,* a fantastic show that never found the audience it deserved because NBC aired it in 437 different time slots.*

The greatest thing about the success of the show was that it meant we got to keep making it, which meant I got to spend almost a decade having the time of my friggin' life. If you can't tell by now, kids, I *loved* working on *HIMYM.* For starters, the workweek has gone down in the personal histories of every cast member as the greatest steady gig he or she has ever had. A lot of that was due to Carter and Craig's rare combination of humanity and competence. Some of it also had to do with the

---

* NBC actually invented and added a forty-ninth half-hour to their daily schedule just to air *Community.*

unique circumstances of our show. Most TV comedies are either multicamera (shot primarily in a few fixed sets and taped in front of a live audience, like *Friends* or *The Big Bang Theory*), or single-camera (shot in many locations with no live audience, like *Arrested Development* or *Parks and Recreation*). *How I Met Your Mother* was a multicamera show . . . except, unlike most other multicams, we didn't tape in front of a live audience, where you only have one day to shoot the entire episode. We had a laugh track. We could edit. We could retape. We could be flexible. We could play.

So here was my workweek:

MONDAY

I walked into a conference room around 9:00 a.m., said hi to everyone, got a copy of the script, sampled the lovely breakfast spread (oatmeal with blueberries was a favorite), sat down, did a table read—so-called because we're at a table, reading—heard the writers laughing at their own jokes, listened to network notes, and left before 11:00.

Then I enjoyed the rest of the day. Exercised, maybe caught a matinee. Took lunch at Soho House.

TUESDAY

I walked onto the set around 9:30, said hi to everyone, read through the now largely rewritten script, slowly wandered around the set rehearsing the scenes in order, broke at 12:30 for catered lunch, kibitzed, schmoozed, held a walk-through of the show so the writers can see what still needs work, and left before 2:00.

Then I enjoyed the rest of the day. Exercised, maybe took a light yoga class. Bikram if possible, Ashtanga if necessary.

WEDNESDAY

On a typical multicamera show, this is when the intense onstage rehearsal in preparation for the Friday taping begins. But not us. We just got in makeup and hair and began shooting. It was a twelve-hour day.

THURSDAY

Same as Wednesday. Twelve hours of taping, max.

FRIDAY

Same as Wednesday and Thursday. But keep in mind: if you weren't in the scene, you didn't have to be there. As one character in a five-person ensemble show, more often than not I got one of the three shooting days off. So I'd hit the beach. Visit the Getty. Hike the Santa Monica Mountains. That kind of thing.*

SATURDAY/SUNDAY

Please.

But as much as I loved the time I spent away from the show, I loved the time I spent *at* the show more. I got to spend day after week after month after year working and fooling around with four people you've come to know very well. That's right, kids—*How I Met Your Mother* is how I met your Aunt Cobie, Uncle Josh, Aunt Alyson, and Uncle Jason! (Although ironically it's not how I met your mother. You don't really have one.)

Cobie Smulders is an extraordinary person. She is a cool-ass

---

* Or, you know, wake up late, have lunch with friends, watch TV, and generally do nothing. That happened too.

chick, superfunny, supergenerous, and superhot without obsessing about it. Spending the last season planning our characters' wedding was true to life for me, because she's exactly the kind of woman I would want to marry if women weren't all gross and icky. Classic Cobie story: Joss Whedon was going to turn *Wonder Woman* into a movie and asked her if she'd be interested . . . and she said no. Who does that? Cobie Smulders. She was clear-sighted enough to know she didn't want her life trajectory to take her to a point where she had to constantly be aware of how she was looking for the paparazzi. She chose to actively avoid the A-list superstardom track, a choice most people would find insane, because most people aren't as smart or grounded as she is. Instead she got a nice little part in *The Avengers,* and now she'll get to be in seven *Avengers* movies and still be with her family and have a fairly regular life and go to the mall without hearing "Look, it's Doogie!" all the time.

(I mean, "Look, it's Wonder Woman!" "Doogie"?!? Ha! Don't know why I said that.)

Jason Segel and I hit it off immediately. We bonded over our many common interests, above all our deep Muppetophilia. I didn't think there was a bigger Henson fan than me until one day, halfway through the run, he quietly but proudly told me he was writing the new Muppet movie. He did, and not only was he the star, he almost single-hand-in-a-puppet-edly reinvented them for a whole new generation. I was extraordinarily jealous. He used to sit at the on-set piano and sing and play songs. He's a hopeless romantic and a dashing lothario.

I used to joke that Josh Radnor was on the wrong show. I mean that in the best way. He instinctively fought against the over-the-top pitfalls of a multicamera comedy. Double takes, mugging, and shtick aren't part of Josh's makeup. Popular music was not popular to him. When Katy Perry guest-starred on the show, he said he'd never heard a Katy Perry song. He meant it. I said,

"You've never heard 'I Kissed a Girl'? You can't escape it!" "Never heard of it." He's more of an NPR guy.*†† But ultimately he was on *exactly* the right show, because none of *HIMYM*'s lunacy and farce would have worked if it hadn't been playing against something or someone authentically based in reality, and that was Josh. That's why I also used to joke that *HIMYM* was always one Josh Radnor away from becoming a telenovela with all of us dressed as Bumblebee Man from *The Simpsons*.

Like I said before, I knew Aunt Alyson from my childhood acting days, long before *HIMYM*. I knew her for so long she already felt like family. There's something about her that's utterly ingratiating. She's able to ride a great line between serious and totally ridiculous. And she can be supersweet and at the same time supersexual. As anyone who's seen *American Pie* knows, no actor in history has ever been so disarming while discussing the vaginal self-insertion of woodwind instruments, and no, I'm not forgetting Betty White's famous monologue in *The Golden Girls*. Alyson had two babies over the run of the show—real ones, the kind that make real poop—so she was always sort of the mother figure among us. I think she was the heart of the show, whereas Josh was the brains, Jason the spirit, Cobie the soul, and I was the cock.

Which brings me to Barney Stinson, through whom I became a bro. Barney was my second long-term TV role. Doogie Howser was a great character, but he was the center of the chaos, the calm nucleus around which dozens of crazy electrons swirled. He wasn't very *fun*. Whereas Barney was a crazy insane person: two parts Larry from *Three's Company*, three parts Vince Vaughn from anything, a dash of David Beckham, and a heaping spoonful of Tom Leykis. (Look him up, kids.) The fun of Barney was that he

---

* Whereas I'm more of an NPH guy.

† Get it? "NPH"?

† I'll show myself out.

was incredibly damaged and no one quite knew why. He tried to maintain an aura of mystery about him. He did magic sometimes, and he had a mysterious job he refused to talk about, and he had huge daddy issues: for some reason he believed his real father was Bob Barker.

In time actors naturally take more and more ownership of their characters, and that certainly happened with Barney. From the outset I played a major part in shaping his wardrobe. My role model for his look was Dean Martin: well-tailored dark suit, light shirt, and a skinny-but-not-so-skinny-it-would-look-dated-in-syndication tie. So the clothes I wore on the show were by great designers like Dolce & Gabbana and Paul Smith. I wanted people watching old episodes to think, "Man, Barney still looks *sharp*."

I began taking ownership of Barney's psyche too. He was a damaged cat, no question about it, and as a friend of his I wanted him to grow and evolve. So I decided to start angling toward Cobie Smulders. Robin was the potential mother in the pilot, the girl of Ted's dreams, the one he thought he wanted to spend the rest of his life with. But I loved Robin. I don't mean Barney loved her; I mean me, Neil. I loved that she was a tough, cigar-smoking broad who wanted nothing to do with a relationship. That struck me as something Barney would dig. So in Seasons 1 and 2 Barney (with my full approval) began giving her extra-long looks or surreptitiously checking out her ass every time she left the bar. I wanted to see what the writers would do with that. And sure enough our characters wound up making out one episode. Our chemistry worked well, and I cherished every scene I got with her. And the years went by, and the plot thickened, and by the end lo and behold, the wedding anchoring the final season wasn't Ted's, but Barney's. And I couldn't be happier. I firmly believe marriage is a sacred union between a fictional man and a fictional woman.

The character took on a life of his own. Eventually Matt Kuhn, one of our writers and producers, was asked to write a Barney

Stinson book, which sold very well. And there's Barney's blog. I always wanted Barney to have a blog concurrent with the shows as they aired. And out of that arose a series of three successful *Bro Code* books, which I voiced for the audiobooks. I grew incredibly fond of Barney. And, as I hope the following testimonial shows, he grew pretty fond of me too.

GIDEON: Wait, wait! You never told us how *How I Met Your Mother* ended!

HARPER: Yeah! Did Uncle Josh meet the kids' mother?

GIDEON: Did you get married to Aunt Cobie?

HARPER: Was the final episode greeted with as much acclaim as the rest of the show?

GIDEON: Did it provide a resolution to the five characters' life situations that viewers universally found satisfying?

YOU: Kids, sometimes things don't end the way everybody wants them to. Sometimes they just kind of . . . end.

[Long, awkward pause.]

HARPER: That's how this chapter ends?

GIDEON: What a rip!

To hear from Barney Stinson, go on to the next page.

To kill someone, turn to page 165.

And now a few words from . . .

BARNEY STINSON

When Neil Patrick Harris asked me to pen a few words for his book, I suddenly felt all warm inside . . . like I was rocking a giant heart boner. And even though my daily agenda is crammed to the rim with cramming chicks to the rim (*What up?!*), I made time to jot down some awesomeness for my bro, NPH. Why? Because with his love of magic, penchant for fine suits, and dogged determination to have sex with as many women as he can, NPH is arguably one of my greatest success stories. Top fifteen for sure.

Once upon a time, Neil only knew one move to pick up chicks: pretend to be a doctor. Sure, posing as a physician is a great way to nail slutty nurses and hotties fresh out of a breast augmentation, but it doesn't work so well when you're, I don't know . . . *sixteen years old*!

Thankfully, Neil got his curly head out of his ass and started using my techniques. Slowly, he transitioned from an awkward, Gremlin-eared bed wetter who couldn't even parlay his *Teen Beat* cover into some PG "under-shirt over-bra" action, to the full-grown, well-manicured, chick-banging machine he is today. Seriously— you just *know* NPH is backstroking in vagina! God, that guy loves chicks!

And while I hesitate to take full credit, it's pretty clear that Neil has studiously followed in my bespoke, calfskin, cap-toe footsteps. If imitation is indeed the highest form of flattery, then NPH must flatt me very much.

Just look at the ways he's ripped me off:

	BARNEY STINSON	NEIL PATRICK HARRIS
Wears suits	✓	✓
Magician	✓	✓
Enormous penis	✓	✓
Blond hair	✓	✓
Has played a doctor	✓	✓
Number of sexual partners	Please	Please
Wealthy	✓	✓
Appeared on *The Price Is Right*	✓	✓
Dog lover	✓	✓
Published author	✓	✓
		(I've got 4 books to his 1, but who's counting?)*

Am I hurt that he has achieved fame and fortune by blatantly stealing my moves? Am I offended that his meteoric rise to stardom could only be achieved by standing on my well-toned shoulders? Am I meeting several times a week with a team of high-priced attorneys to consider legal action against him, his representation, and various studios both domestic and abroad for his brazen theft of my signature blend of witticism, comedic timing, and general awesomeness? No comment. But I will admit that I'm impressed with his creativity when it comes to seducing women.

As the author of *The Playbook: Suit Up. Score Chicks. Be Awesome*, I can literally say I wrote the book on how to bang women. But NPH—with his never-quenched thirst for the pootie—has thrown down the gauntlet with some truly masterly plays of his own:

---

* Actually this should count as another book for me too, so it's 5–1, Stinson.

"THE MAGIC MAN"

As NPH and I well know, nothing wets the panties faster than a guy who's into magic. So what did he do? He became so good at his craft he was able to trick the Academy of Magical Arts into naming him its president. That makes him head of the Magic Castle, the preeminent clubhouse for illusionists, manipulation artists, and close-up magicians in the world. With that sort of power, NPH practically has to beat the chicks away with a wand.

"THE THEATER KING"

Since the dawn of time, guys have been obsessed with cracking that most impenetrable sphere of babedom—theater chicks. This tantalizing world of young, impressionable wannabe starlets surrounded only by gay dudes lay untapped for millennia, despite countless attempts to gain entry (hello!).

• The Ancient Greeks created a "chorus" as an excuse to crowd a bunch of bros on stage. Tragically, nobody ever got past second base.

• The Japanese invented Kabuki: an art form in which guys dressed as women to get closer to theater chicks. This backfired in its own dramatic twist when they discovered that the "chicks" were simply other dudes trying the same play.

• *Cats.* I guess the plan was to squeeze a bunch of chicks into skintight cat costumes and pray for some sort of slutty Halloween miracle? After 7,485 unsuccessful shows, that sad but noble bunch of bros who had cat-suited up in search of tail finally gave up.

To ensnare those elusive theater chicks, NPH devised a simple yet deliciously diabolical plan: become a supertalented actor. He got so good, in fact, that he is now the de facto host of the Tony Awards. In this capacity, not only can he invoke Prima Nocta (the right to bang any actress on her "opening" night), he can also demand favors in exchange for awards. As impressive as this is, I'm a little upset he hasn't leveraged his power to stage a production of *Broklahoma!*—it's sitting right there, buddy.

"THE TWINS"

Neil took one of my oldest maxims ("Nothing attracts a hottie like a tottie") and began seducing chicks using a young child as a prop. But—as is so often the case with Neil Patrick Harris—it simply wasn't challenging enough. So what did he do? He teamed up with his wingman, David Burtka, and adopted twins! Genius! Now he and his best bro can troll for strange using the irresistible lure of *two* adorable infants! They even gave them names and clothes and everything! Legendary.

With the creation of these amazing plays, I'm forced to admit that the student has finally become the master. Neil is now the accepted worldwide leader in fooling women into having sex with him. Respect. But don't count Barney Stinson out. If NPH thinks he can use his forces of awesome to outduel me in a high-stakes match of chick-banging, then I only have one thing to say: "Challenge accepted!"

If, despite Barney's perpetual youth, you want to get older, turn to page 280.

If, despite Barney's lady-killer status, you want to get gay, turn to page 78.

DR. POURABLE'S DRINK-ALONG GROG

Whenever you need to relax after a long day of acting, awards-show hosting, or serving as guest judge at the Westminster Kennel Club Dog Show, you like to relax with a fine bespoke cocktail. Here's one of your favorites. This one has a lot of kick as a result of the jalapeño. While you definitely pick up on the cucumber and mint, the rum still shines. Velvet Falernum is one of your favorites, a tropical liqueur with notes of almond, clove, and allspice that help give this cocktail an easy-drinking, tiki-like component.

2 cucumber slices

4 mint sprigs

½ ounce simple syrup

2¼ ounces Flor de Caña Centenario 12-Year-Aged Rum

¾ ounce fresh lime juice

½ ounce Velvet Falernum

¼ ounce Cherry Heering

1 jalapeño slice (depending on your desired heat, you can leave or remove the seeds)

In a shaker, muddle 1 cucumber slice and 2 mint sprigs with the simple syrup. Add the rum, lime juice, Falernum, Cherry Heering, and jalapeño and shake. Fine-strain into a tiki filled with crushed ice. Garnish with the remaining cucumber slice and mint sprigs.

Return to the page from which you came.

Or, to star in the musical for which this drink was named, turn to page 181.

CRYPTIC CROSSWORD PUZZLE

The cryptic clues below all refer to your life. They are in random order. Solve them (the number tells you how many letters in the answer), and figure out where they fit in the grid on the opposite page. When you are done, the shaded letters will reveal a special word.

Sounds like an assortment of taxis in which you were the MC (7)

Decorate John's companion (7)

Wise-ass magician in the Ivy League (4)

Symmetries halved and reversed produce a ceremony (5)

Mixed, weighed, de-energized, played on Broadway (6)

Costar a large, fake amount of money? (7)

Collaborator with Apple by the other side of the road (10)

Kind of trooper preferred by Jefferson? (8)

Friend raised awkwardly and Southern (7)

You're this doctor, so doctor, broil her (8)

Up in the only actress who berated you (6)

Funny woman marvels in confusion (9)

He was against you, and it sounds like he's against everything (4)

He treats drunk whores (6)

Let show (4)

He gave you your big break in a domed office (6)

Musical to escort without air-conditioning (7)

For you he's an oldie but a goodie, almost (6)

She will be missed; a talk-show buddy (4)

Fancy award (4)

A friend and basket in Wisconsin (6)

Starts to build up romance to keep a lover (6)

Lothario! Unhinge 90 bras, boy! (13)

Idly wonders about your favorite place on earth (11)

Return to the page from which you came.

And now a word from your friend . . .

PEREZ HILTON

Dear NPH,

In the past, I was a douche. I'm not Oprah these days, nor am I trying to be, but I hope I am slightly less of a douche.

In the past, I said things and wrote things that hurt people. I don't know for sure if I ever caused you and your family pain. If I did, I'm sorry. Genuinely.

If I didn't cause you pain and you viewed me more like an annoying mosquito, then I'm sorry for that too. No one likes annoying mosquitoes!

In the past, I outed people, like yourself. I don't do that anymore.

Thankfully, I don't live in the past. My present is very different.

In addition to having a son and being a much happier and healthier person, I am thrilled to live in a present where you are a genuine inspiration to me and countless millions of people worldwide—gay *and* straight.

You are unapologetic about who you are—a dude who loves magic! Ha!

Kidding!

You are a successful and extremely talented actor, singer, father, and lover—who just so happens to be gay.

Your career has not suffered as a result of your coming out. In fact, I would argue that since you came out you are more successful than ever!

In the future, I only see your career trajectory continuing to go *up*!

In the future, I hope other actors follow your lead and see from your example the impact that living openly can have not just on one's own happiness but on the lives of others.

In the future, I hope I am more like you!

From the heart,
Perez Hilton

Return to page 171.

Sweeney Todd is one of the greatest and most satisfying experiences of your professional life. So when Stephen Sondheim calls you out of the blue to say he wants to discuss another possible project for you, you jump at the chance.

It's a beautiful day, so you decide to take a nice leisurely stroll to Sondheim's house in the jungle. You start wondering what he has in mind. You lose yourself in happy speculation.

Suddenly you notice the world slowly turning watery all around you. Looking around, you realize you have stumbled into a murky Amazonian river. You are being eaten by piranhas!

You desperately struggle to escape, but your efforts only cause the fish to sink their teeth in deeper. You look around for something to pull yourself out of the river with. A vine attached to a banyan tree dangles tantalizingly a few feet in front of you, but you can't quite reach it.

With your last breath you scream, "Help me, Stephen!" but your cry is quickly throttled by the angry piranhas gnawing at your throat. The last thing you see is Stephen Sondheim running to you wailing, "No, Neil! Not before we stage *Sweeney Todd 2: The Legend of Toby's Gold!*"

Your body is never found.

THE END

You and David are taking a hiking trip in northwest Ireland. You hike to the famous Giant's Causeway, which you reflect looks like something out of Myst before reflecting on how funny it is that to your twenty-first-century imagination, natural landmarks look like video games, not the other way around.

David has the intense desire to spend the night in a castle, which, of course, is *sooooo* David. He has an appreciation for certain finer things, like good food and good castles, and to be honest you're not averse to them either. But the place he has in mind, Ashford Castle, is an hour out of the way, and the rooms *start* at nearly 200 euros. You refuse on principle to devote that much time and effort to wasting that much money.

So you head to a nearby castle that's a little cheaper. When you get there you discover that as castles go, it's pretty much just a leftover turret. A turret trap, if you will.* You check in with a woman who has a lazy eye and a monotonous voice who looks like one of *Macbeth*'s witches. You will be the hotel's only guests. She casually asks if you want "to stay in the room where the suicides happened."

The story, she explains, is that a girl had once occupied the castle, a girl in love with a boy on the other side of the lake. She was forbidden to see him, and she died of pneumonia, and then her grieving mother jumped out the window, and now their two ghosts haunt the hotel. It's exactly the kind of tragedy that

---

* You will.

seems to happen only in old picturesque buildings that evolve into out-of-the-way hotels desperately looking for guests. You are none too impressed. You are a skeptic. You can do magic. You are from Hollywood. You are a fancy-pants person. Yes, you will stay in the g-damned suicide room.

Now, before going to Ireland you and David had stopped in Amsterdam, and lo and behold, you still have a leftover space cake. And you are slated to return to the States the next day. Well then, thinks you, what better place to eat an old, moldy space cake than at a haunted hotel in rural Ireland whose lobby is filled with taxidermied animals and the scent of decay.

Soon enough the hash, and whatever else may have coagulated its way onto the hash, kick in, and you suddenly become acutely aware the two of you are entirely alone at the very top of a giant turret. Even on a purely non-supernatural level, if a fire breaks out you're dead. But there is something in the air, you are sure, something . . . eerie. You decide to start just wandering around, Blair Witch–style, in the various unlocked and vacant rooms of the turret, because, again, this is a great idea for something to do in a haunted hotel in rural Ireland.

So you go around with a camcorder and record a bunch of truly freaky things: creepy taxidermied animals primarily, but also closet doors opening and shutting by themselves, and the sound of dripping water coming from no obvious faucet. Frightened, you scurry back to your room and are about to get into bed when you hear, above you, a thud and a long scrape. And then a pause, and another thud and long scrape. Over and over, like a kid playing ball, or a body landing on the stone ground and being dragged to her grave.

Yes, you're from Hollywood. And you're a magician. And a skeptic. You don't believe in ghosts, you don't believe in the afterlife, and you're nothing short of offended by charlatans who claim they can speak to your long-lost grandpa as soon as you fork over five hundred dollars. But there are no ladders going up the side, no way any human being could have snuck past you, and you would be lying if you said that at that moment, huddled in bed, tripping on hash, staring at the ceiling of a thousand-year-old turret and listening to the droning rhythm of thuds and scrapes echoing through the room, you weren't absolutely sure there was no g-g-g-ghost.

Then David says it must be the flagpole waving in the wind, and you each take a Valium and a half, and you're once again sure there's no such thing as g-g-g-ghosts, and go to bed.

The next morning as you say good-bye to the proprietress you recount your story, almost embarrassed. "We were really freaked out last night. We heard a thunk on the roof, like someone was dropping and rolling a ball in the attic. But there's no attic, haha. So it must have been the flag on the flagpole."

And the lady looks at us with her one good eye and says, "There's no flag on the top of the building. It must have been the daughter."

Freaky, right? Anyway, turn to page 280.
What? Sometimes in life you don't get a choice.

Tucked away in Hollywood is a mansion called the Magic Castle. It was once a private residence, but in the 1960s brothers Bill and Milt Larsen decided to turn it into a swanky club for magicians—the kind of place where prestidigitators, illusionists, and their invited guests can hang out, swap Houdini stories, and make one another disappear. Over the years they slowly kept adding new rooms and performance spaces until it grew into a major performance space, clubhouse, and fraternity.

It's the early nineties, and you desperately want into the junior program. (It's got to be the junior program. There are a lot of bars at the club, and there are no "backstage secrets" when it comes to the drinking laws: you ain't gettin' served.) But to get in, you have to audition. You put together a little act, try out, and are accepted. It's one of the greatest thrills of your life.

A few months later you're asked to present an award at one of their banquets. They (unnecessarily) lure you by saying, "If you present this award, we'll give you a lifetime membership at the castle." And you say, "Holy crap!" or words to that effect.

The next year you turn twenty-one and begin frequenting the grown-up club. There's a strict dress code: gentlemen must wear jackets and ties, women dresses or cocktail attire. It gives the place a very classy and retro feel, as if you're at a ritzy event in 1950. It instantly becomes one of your favorite hangouts. One of your favorite things is the piano. It's haunted by a ghost named Irma, and she'll play anything you want, but not like a jukebox: if you talk to her she'll answer your questions. Tell her what state you're from and she'll play the state song. Say "Beethoven's Seventh," and she'll play it. Want her to tinkle some Gaga? Done. It's fantastic.

Many years later, due to your relative notoriety, the president asks if you want to be on the board of directors. "It's easy," he says. "You just show up once a month and voice your opinions about how things are going." Well, that *does* sound easy, and when a magician tells you something it's not as if there's likely to be some kind of trick involved or anything. So you get on the ballot, and end up on the board. And after a term you're asked to be vice president, which you are repeatedly assured means absolutely nothing unless the president resigns for some reason. Then the president resigns for some reason.

Hail to the Chief.

You ascend to the presidency—god, does that phrase sound odd—in 2010, when the castle is facing some serious problems. The building is potentially going to be sold by the family to an outside party, which means there's a chance you could lose the clubhouse altogether. There are also several operational issues keeping the organization from running as smoothly as it should. And so you begin instituting systematic changes you're proud to say make the castle a much better place. You and your team beef up the quality of the entire experience, from the moment visitors call to make a reservation to the moment they leave. You bring in new valets, put new membership systems in place, and retrain the entire front-of-house restaurant staff. (Well, not personally. But you hire the right people for the job.) You also have to deal with the occasional e-mails from devoted members who, because they are there *a lot*, have no problem with taking time out of their and your day to inform you that the paint is chipping in a corner of the men's room, or that today's lamb chops were a bit undercooked.

Being the president of the Magic Castle is a passion project that puts you in an unusual role—that of producer. You're essentially the president of a company, and you see the job as an opportunity to learn how to manage people. And you quickly learn not to do it aggressively, because that tends to make people shut down, whereas a more positive approach makes people *want* to change. So you learn how to listen. (Even to Teller, which, considering he doesn't talk much, takes a great deal of concentration.) You never pretend you know more than the generations of older magicians who've been going to the castle for forty years, but at the same time you don't shy away from making changes you feel are necessary and appropriate. Some of your bolder decisions divide the membership in two, but in the Land of the Thin Saws, that's something you hope they're used to anyway.

If all this talk about magic is making you want to do some for real,
on live TV, in the middle of a freakin' awards show,
turn to page 238.

If all this talk about magic is making you thirsty,
turn to page 45.

If all this talk about magic is making you horny,
turn to page 168.

And now, more of the literary magical stylings of the actual NPH.

When you get really good at magic, you learn to use your skills at magic to cheat at cards. Really! You can magically control where the cards are in a deck. I'll show you exactly how that works.

Shuffle a full deck of cards, go through the deck and pull out the four aces. Put them on the table in front of you in a row, left to right. The order doesn't matter. Just make sure you have four aces, face up, on the table in front of you.

Good. Now turn the rest of the deck face down. I want you to deal a card, face down, on the first ace, then a card on the second, the third, and the fourth. Do that again—deal four cards face down, a card on each ace. And now a third card on top of each ace. When you're finished, put the rest of the deck aside. You won't need it again for this trick.

To verify: you should now have four packets of cards in a row in front of you. On the bottom of each packet is a face-up ace, and then three face-down cards on top of each ace.

Now, pick up the packet on the far left and, without turning or mixing it, drop it on top of the packet to the right of it. In other words, you are dropping four of the cards on top of four more cards.

Good. Now pick up the packet on the far right and do the same thing, dropping it on top of the packet to its left.

Let's check. You've now got two packets of cards on the table. Right?

Great. I want you to mix up the cards so that you know that you're making random choices. Pick up the packet on the left and give it an overhand shuffle. Or, if you don't want to shuffle it, just cut the cards and mix them up by pushing some cards in the middle of other cards. Don't turn more cards upside down; just mix up the order.

Now do the same thing to the other packet. But this time, before you put that packet down on the table, turn it upside down. Did you turn it upside down? Good. Now put it down.

We're going to reassemble the cards into one packet. Separate the packets a little bit, so you have a space between them. Now take one of the cards off the top of either packet, the left or the right, and drop it face down on the table between the other two packets. Now take the card on the top of the *other* packet and put it on top of that card. Keep doing this, alternating cards. One from the right, one from the left, one from the right, one from the left. Keep going until you have all the cards put back together again into one packet.

Pick up the big packet and cut it, completing the cut. Do that again, if you'd like.

Hold the cards in your hand. In case you're wondering, the technical term for this packet is a *mess*. You've turned various cards upside down, you've mixed them in your own way, you've put them all together again. Yep, it's a mess.

In fact, I'm going to show you how messy they are. Deal the cards out again into four rows. Deal the first four cards down onto the table, then four more cards on top of that. And then keep going, with all the cards. It will be like dealing out four hands of cards.

As you saw the cards go by, you probably noticed the mess. We turned over aces, and other cards, in a random order. I'm going to have you give them one more quick mix. Listen to these instructions, because this is where the magic comes in.

Pick up the packet on the far left, turn it over sideways like you're turning the page of a book, and drop it on top of the packet that's next to it, just to the right. It's just like closing the cover of a book.

Do that again. Pick up the double packet on the left, and turn those cards over, dropping them on top of the next packet to the right. Perfect. Now do that one more time. Take the big packet on the left, and just turn it over on top of the packet on the far right. Now you've just put all the packets together again by turning them over and over.

There's a technical term for that, too. It's called a *bigger mess*. Because some more cards have just turned upside down.

Now here's the amazing part. Just wave your hands over the packet of cards on the table. You might feel a little foolish doing it, but trust me. I'm a magician. That waving-the-hands part is very important. That's what accomplishes the magic! (That, and running around your house naked screaming "Ooga-booga." But that's only for advanced magicians, and you're not that good yet.)

Want to know where the aces are? Well, pick up the cards and spread them out. You'll see that all the cards have turned the right way again, *except for the four aces*.

It doesn't matter how you shuffled the cards, dealt the cards, or reversed the cards. All you had to do was wave your hands like that, and they magically went back in the right direction!

Yeah, right.

If you'd like to take part in another magic trick, turn to page 225.

If not, return to the chapter where you were before this one.

Unless you're hungry, in which case turn to page 111.

On the evening of September 22, 2012, you, Neil Patrick Harris, feel a sudden, overwhelming urge to commit murder.

It's not the first time you've felt it. Not at all. Truth be told, at no point in your life have you not sporadically been gripped by the need, the craving, the *hunger* to watch the life drain away from a man's face.

It has taken all the discipline and strength of will you could muster to stifle those cravings and channel those murderous impulses. But you have, and all that sublimated rage has paid off in the form of a successful acting career and a sterling reputation as a genial on-air presence and all-around nice guy.

But you, Neil Patrick Harris, are not an all-around nice guy. Deep in your soul you are little more than a craven hunter of human meat.

And tonight, as you drive home from the set of *How I Met Your Mother,* you are determined to finally give in to those dark instincts.

And that's when you see the hitchhiker.

The next morning you're sitting at the breakfast table.

"Did you see this?" asks David. "They found a headless body just off the road in Laurel Canyon this morning. Isn't that right on your way home from work?"

"Yes," you remark. "Freaky. Any suspects?"

"None," he says. "No fingerprints, no ID, nothing. And no sign of the head. By the way, where were you last night?"

"Oh, I was . . . bowling."

"Bowling?" says David, dubiously. "Since when do you bowl?"

"Since last night."

"Well, I suppose that *would* explain that new bowling ball bag I saw by the front door this morning."

"I suppose it would." You laugh. "By the way, you didn't, um . . . *open* that bag, did you? See its contents?"

"No," says David, "I didn't. But congratulations on your new hobby, Neil. Bowling. Maybe you'll earn yourself another trophy."

"I already have my trophy," you respond quietly, chuckling to yourself.

But David doesn't hear you. He has gone to the front door to unzip the bag and remove its contents . . .

. . . an ordinary bowling ball.

Then he returns to the kitchen, sneaks up behind you, and beats you to death with it.

"I hate bowling," says David. *"Almost as much as I hated that guy whose head I cut off in Laurel Canyon last night."*

THE END

You are gay.

You know that you are; you accept that you are; you like that you are; you're proud that you are. You are totally gay. And now you are totally gay and totally in love, and it's wonderful.

But love comes with a price; and while some say the hardest part of love is letting go, it is your humble opinion that sometimes the hardest part of love is exchanging frantic e-mails with your agent, manager, and publicist about the best way to word the press release that will announce your sexual orientation to millions of strangers. Which is exactly what you find yourself doing this fine morning in early November 2006.

It's now been over a decade since you first told a group of strangers at the Landmark Forum that you were "bisexual"—a half-truth, as it turns out; nine years since your first tentative hookups with your cast-mate on *Rent;* seven since you began having real gay relationships; and three since you met David. (And twenty-nine since you first fell in love with the score of *Annie,* which probably should have been the tell right there.) After a long internal journey, you now embrace being gay, recognizing it as a wonderful and integrally important component part of the totality that is you.

You are fully out . . . to yourself. But your status vis-à-vis the rest of humanity is more complicated. One day you tell your parents you are not bisexual, but gay. Your mom is cool and not surprised. It takes your dad a little more time to accept it. He has deep-seated Christian religious beliefs that you respect as part of *his* identity, and you understand that the truth you are asking him to accept is not easy. That's why seeing him and *feeling* him warm up to you and David and the children you will ultimately have together will be one of the greatest joys of your life.

As for your friends and colleagues, they know you're gay, especially now that you've met someone of whom you're so proud and who is so friggin' hot. When the creators of *How I Met Your Mother* hold a meet-and-greet before shooting the pilot, you bring David with you to the party. You are proud to be his partner, and besides the cast ought to know your status, especially since you're stepping into the role of a ladies' man. You and he go on dinner dates with other friends, and it's completely fine.

You've come a long way from the anonymous skulker trolling the AOL chat rooms. But at the same time you're not shouting *"I'm gay!"* into a megaphone from the middle of West Hollywood either. And why should you? There's a great deal of immodesty in assuming the entire world is desperate to know who and what you stick your wang into. You yourself aren't particularly interested most of the time. And you are not, by temperament, an activist. Despite your love for *Les Miz*, flag-waving on the barricade is not your style in real life.

But the awkwardness of the situation, the sheer *presence* of the unspoken truth, grows more palpable and, more important, begins to affect your relationship with David. It's increasingly untenable for him to continue the empty ritual of accompanying you to movie premieres and other Hollywood events, separating from you as you walk the red carpet and pose for pictures, then covertly rejoining you on the other side of the velvet rope. Untenable, and just plain disrespectful. But that's exactly what you end up doing for a time. Well versed in the ways of the tabloid press, you feel it necessary: you know all too well how actual fully developed human beings end up reduced to the conscribed two-dimensional public role assigned for them. You don't want David to just be known as your boyfriend, because he too is an actor looking for his own work and his own public identity as well and should no more be best known as "Neil Patrick Harris's partner" than you should be best known as his.

But with every new public appearance the pressure builds, the awkwardness grows, the unspokenness gets louder. The more you and David do the meet-me-at-the-end-of-the-press-line charade, the more the press starts talking. "Who's that guy? He's not his publicist. That's the third event I've seen him accompany Neil to. Is that someone he's dating?" Your publicist begins fielding a slow crescendo of calls asking about your sexuality indirectly, then directly. His response is always the same: "I make it a point not to comment on my clients' social lives."

Then in October 2006 you suddenly, from out of nowhere, find yourself bombarded with angry texts and calls from gay friends. "What is wrong with you?" "We heard you publicly denied you were gay." "What, are you ashamed?" "What the hell are you doing?" It turns out a certain website that will remain classless has been asking your publicist about you, and this time his response wasn't a variation on the theme of "No comment" but a definite quote "Neil is not of that persuasion."

"Not of that persuasion"? What the (literally) fuck?

On the one hand that's such strange wording, and so oddly timed, it's hard to believe it was something he would say. On the other hand it's such strange wording, and so oddly timed, it's hard to believe it was something he *didn't* say. When you call him he denies having said it, but that doesn't mean anything, because he is a publicist, a tribe for whom denying things is a way of life. And at this point it doesn't matter. However it happened, whatever he did or did not say, the quote is now on the internet, and the internet is where innuendo gains immortality. Once it's out there that you said it, you said it, even if you didn't say it.

So within a matter of days—hours, really—angry gay bloggers

who know you're gay, but up to this point had been respectful of your privacy, are up in arms. They take to the blogwaves (not a word but should be) to denounce you as a self-hating hypocrite, on a moral par with the closet cases in Washington who support antigay legislation.

Leading the charge is Mario Armando Lavandeira Jr., a/k/a Perez Hilton. At this point in his career, Perez is a crusading gay activist itching to out everybody in Hollywood. He deems it his responsibility as a journalist and openly gay man to speak the truth. To him, every gay actor has a responsibility to be open about who they are, and so when he knows a celebrity is gay—meaning he has talked to someone of the same sex who's slept with him or her—he has no problem with outing them.

For reflections from an older, wiser Perez Hilton,
turn to page 152.

To continue the happy, wonderful process of publicly
coming out, go on to the next page.

At the time, that is what Perez believes. You emphatically do *not* believe it. You believe the coming-out process is a highly individual one wrought with all kinds of neuroses and insecurities, and not something to be wrapped up in a one-outing-fits-all package. For many people, coming out requires a long incubation process, and *that's fine.* You were very lucky in that you fell into *Rent,* this huge hot tub of awesomeness and everyone being super-okay and loving you no matter what. You got to act and sing in that eight times a week. Between that show and *Cabaret* you'd been surrounded by awesome gay people who'd had boyfriends for twenty years and were playing the straightest guys ever. It was the perfect venue to take that first baby step and others followed, and that was the right way to go about it *for you.* But to a lot of actors who didn't get those chances, coming out can still seem a career killer, or at least jeopardizer. You respect their situations.

But Perez doesn't. And when he (falsely) hears you've claimed you weren't gay, he starts hounding you in his posts. "What are you thinking, Neil? Why would you say that? Why are you doing this?" The furor grows to the point where a lot of very close friends are very mad at you—too many for you to individually call and explain that you had in fact said no such thing. (Your gay attorney and gay agent are particularly incensed.)

Then Perez, in his indignation, pulls his coup de grâce: he asks for any man with definitive evidence of sleeping with you to come forward.

Eeeeeewwwwwww.

The boiling point is reached. It's time to make some kind of statement, to get ahead of the story before it seems like you're responding only because of some unearthed treasure trove of naked pictures or sworn affidavits. Or worst of all, naked affidavits.

If you choose not to come out, turn to page 101.

If you choose to come out in a rational, controlled way that allows your career to continue and thrive, turn to page 176.

If you choose to come out in a reckless, over-the-top way that justifiably destroys your career, turn to page 179.

Congratulations! If you are seeing these words while hearing them read out loud, you are attending a promotional event and reading along as I speak them. (No other pages lead to this page, and since everybody else reading this book will strictly follow instructions and only go to the pages to which they are directed, no one else could possibly know about it!)

As a reward for your participation in this reading and/or publicity appearance, please present this page at the conclusion of this event for signing. The signature will serve as notarized proof that your level of enthusiasm went above and beyond that of those who merely purchased this at a bookstore or, even lazier, one-clicked it online.

If you are reading this as an ebook, please feel free to present the screen with the below line on it to the author so he can sign it with a Sharpie.

_____

Neil Patrick Harris
a/k/a You

You call your manager, Booh Schut, and your agent, Steve Dottenville. You release the publicist who may or may not have gotten you into this mess to begin with, and in a spectacular display of irony, hire as your new flak none other than Simon Halls, David's ex-boyfriend. The man you once worried would help take down your career will now instead help you protect it.

And so now it's November 2, 2006, and here the four of you are spending three fitful hours exchanging ideas about the proper wording of your *mea gay-a*. The majority of it is crafted by Booh. Bless her heart, she's been at a silent meditation retreat where no one was allowed to speak for four days, and now she gets your frantic message and has to sneak outside the retreat and break her vow of silence to help draft your statement. Way to shake up the Zen, Neil. No silence, no meditation, and certainly not a treat.

You all know the statement needs to be universally positive, filled with confidence, in no way deflective or defensive or in response to anything. You also know that while some of the people who read it will know about the brouhaha, the vast majority won't, and it has to make sense for both sets of audiences, the irate and the oblivious. It has to be honest and true and heartfelt.

Thanks largely to Booh, it comes out exactly right.

The public eye has always been kind to me, and until recently I have been able to live a pretty normal life. Now it seems there is speculation and interest in my private life and relationships. So, rather than ignore those who choose to publish their opinions without actually talking to

*me, I am happy to dispel any rumors or misconceptions and am quite
proud to say that I am a very content gay man living my life to the
fullest and feel most fortunate to be working with wonderful people in
the business I love.*

It's your Gaytease-burg Address.

Writing the statement is step 1. Step 2 is figuring out where
to release it. Which trusted news source will be the conduit for
the earth-shattering news of your sexual preference? An LGBT
periodical feels too political, a TV network feels too solemn and
self-important, and *Popular Mechanics* just feels way off. You decide to release it to PeopleMagazine.com, because it has a wide
mass-market circulation, and to do it on a Friday night, which as everyone in Hollywood and Washington, D.C., knows is the best time
to announce things you don't want people talking about all week.

You click the Send button, and then wait.

Your announcement meets with several reactions. Kindness,
from many quarters. Lack of surprise, from others. (That does
make you feel emasculated, somehow, a little.) A fair amount of
"Oh, that's interesting. I'll file that away in my 'Things I Know
About Celebrities' file." But the biggest, and most gratifying, reaction is the deafening silence of hundreds of millions of Americans
thinking to themselves, *Who gives a shit?*

You had been genuinely afraid that after the announcement
people would hiss at you like a vampire when you walked down
the street. And as much as you'd told yourself you weren't worried about your career, the first thought you had as soon as you
pressed Send to *People* was, *I wonder what's going to happen to my
career.* But there is no hissing, no audition cancellations, no gossip
magazine covers, and least unhurtful of all, no Westboro Baptist
Church people picketing across the street. You don't know if the
apathy is directed at your sexuality or your career in general, but
at this moment you'll take either.

And so you officially become an out gay man in Hollywood. Which inevitably leads to the question "Is it your duty to be a role model?" You waver on this. You know there may be some people who look to you and your family as a source for pride, a reason to stand tall. And you're glad for that, because standing tall is what is most important. Yes, overt advocacy is vitally necessary in a bigoted world, and you do not shy away from it when appropriate. You are vacationing with David when you first encounter one of Dan Savage's "It Gets Better" videos, and it moves you so profoundly that, when Dan asks if you're willing to do one, you literally can't wait: you open your laptop, turn on FaceTime, and record yourself in one urgent take. Not polished, but raw, to reflect the sincerity of your message.

But you have seen instances when the hard-core vehemence of some gay-rights activists creates a backlash, making homophobes even more homophobic. For you it all goes back to the fundamental rule of creative endeavor, and life is if nothing else a creative endeavor: "Show, don't tell." Personal confidence, ease, conducting yourself publicly with grace and humility—these are the qualities you consider most effective. Directly *showing* family and neighbors and co-workers that you're proud of the way you live accomplishes something on a core level that intense advocacy sometimes can't. So for the most part your style is to lead by example, to show ordinary people—Oprah, say—around your home, to watch the twins play in the backyard and see what kind of family the four of you really are.

And let Oprah take it from there. That's pretty much your philosophy about most things: let Oprah handle it.

To dish about Oprah, along with the many other talk-show hosts whose shows you have appeared on, turn to page 215.

To take the next step toward building a family, turn to page 194.

It's just about 5:30 PST. You stand backstage awaiting your big moment.

It's taken you years to get to a place where you felt ready to share your truth with the world. But now that you are, you are going to do it *your* way. No more pretending. No more lying by omission. You are going to proudly let everybody know that you are gay, and you are going to do it your way . . .

"Ladies and gentlemen, welcome to the 2009 Academy Awards! Now, please welcome your host, Neil Patrick Harris!"

. . . by hijacking an awards show.

YOU: *Welcome to the Oscars on this beautiful night!*
   We're here to honor movies and we're doing it right!
   But before we continue I've got something to say:
   I'm Neil Patrick Harris and I'm gay!

LEATHER-CLAD CHORUS BOYS: *He's gay!*

The crowd starts squirming. Jack Nicholson smirks epically. The six actresses present who have not had Botox look shocked.

YOU: *To the billion people watching let me set things "straight":*
   I am a homosexual and man, is it great!
   I'm coming out, and isn't this the perfect way?
   I'm Neil Patrick Harris and I'm g-g-g-gay!

LEATHER-CLAD CHORUS BOYS: *G-g-gay!*

The unflappable Meryl Streep, attending her thirtieth consecutive Oscar ceremony, can be seen in the audience mouthing "Why? Whyyyyyyyy?!?" Tom Hanks—Tom friggin' Hanks—looks ready to kill somebody.

John Travolta looks confused.

YOU: *This is my town, and I'm coming out to it!*
             This is my moment and man, what a thrill!
             This is my world, and I'm gonna shout to it,
             "Hey, I'm as queer as a three-dollar bill!"

By the third chorus your career is over.

THE END

It's 2007, and America's television and movie writers are on strike. No one is making scripted entertainment anymore. Mirth is dead. A drama-hungry, comedy-thirsty nation slowly perishes of malhumorment.

How I Met Your Mother has stopped production, of course, and there's not a whole lot else happening to fill the void. You support the strike, but you're also suffering from creative atrophy, yearning to do good work with good people. One day you're in a cab in New York when you get a phone call.

"Hey, Neil, this is Joss Whedon, how are you? Listen, I know this is out of the blue, but I'm doing this online musical called *Dr. Horrible's Sing-Along Blog,* and I was wondering if—"

"I'm in."

"Wait a second. You haven't read the script, and it's a five-day shoot, and it will pay you nothing. Are you sure you—"

"I'm in."

Why hesitate? *It's Joss Whedon.* He's a genius, a visionary, a man who makes the average wordsmith seem a mere wordjones. His body of work is legendary.* *Buffy the Vampire Slayer* is one of your all-time favorite shows. So is *Firefly,* for which you had once auditioned; you were almost cast as the doctor, but negotiations fell through. But you happen to know Joss best from the semiregular readings of Shakespeare plays he hosts at his home in Santa

---

* You would have written "legen—wait for it—dary," but that line is proprietary to *How I Met Your Mother,* and besides, there's a writers' strike.

Monica. So many great actors and actresses gather to take part in these impromptu performances that you're just as likely to be cast as Spear Thrower #3 as Hamlet. But it makes no difference, because every time you go it's a rich and merry and culturally fulfilling experience and you leave thinking, *Here's a guy who's so creative, so prolific, so happy to embrace the nerd element to his world while still having a populist touch. I must work with this man.*

So you say it for the third time: you're in. And that simply, you begin work on what will become *Dr. Horrible's Sing-Along Blog*. And for all the blind faith you have going into the project, the reality turns out even better. First off it's shot entirely with Joss's money, meaning there are no movie executives on hand to meddle. It's just Joss, his two brothers Zack and Jed, and Jed's wife Maurissa. They've conceived the whole thing, and it's funny and sad and strange, and like any true work of art it's unlike anything you've ever seen before, yet feels immediately recognizable. All four have collaborated on the songs, which are soaring and impeccably crafted. Jed sings the vocals on the demo, and you end up listening to his version of each tune literally a thousand times, mostly at the gym. (Workouts are a great time to learn music, because your mind is grateful for the distraction: it's much more fun focusing on an internal rhyme than that thirty-fifth rep.) Even after the songs are pre-recorded you *still* keep listening to them because (a) they're so damn good, and (b) you want to get the lip sync exactly right. Some of the songs are hyperwordy. The toughest is "Brand New Day," which starts with a very fast patter lyric on a tight close-up.

This appeared as a moral dilemma 'cause at first
It was weird though I swore to eliminate the worst
Of the plague that devoured humanity it's true
I was vague on the how so how can it be that you
Have shown me the light . . .

The whole section needs to be filmed in one take, and it needs to look absolutely live. The slightest disjunction between lip and lyric would take the viewer completely out of the moment. And so you practice your mouth motion until one morning David tells you he caught your mouth lip-syncing in your sleep.

For time and budgetary reasons, *Dr. Horrible* is shot guerrilla-style, quickly and secretively, lending the whole endeavor a wonderful air of mischief. As a favor to Joss, Universal Studios lets you use its backlot, but that's as far as the studio involvement goes. In the intensely collaborative environment the limitations of schedule and money bring out everyone's ingenuity; constraints lead to solutions instead of frustrations. For example, the first three pages of the script are just Dr. Horrible monologuing into the camera, one continuous take, no edits. So for the sake of efficiency you take the script pages, rip them up into little pieces, and stick them all around the sides of the camera in different places, depending on where you think you will be looking. And that's exactly how that opening scene is shot. You feel a little guilty about it, but then you find out Spencer Tracy and Marlon Brando often did the same thing, and conclude (rightly) that it gives the scene the appropriate air of naturalism and (wrongly) that you are one of the greatest screen actors of all time.

Another number, "I Cannot Believe My Eyes," requires you to walk down the street lamenting your love for Penny, the girl from the Laundromat. That scene has to be shot at the end of the day, with time and sunlight dwindling. There's just one handheld camera, one sound guy holding a mic, and another guy off camera holding a boom box with the volume cranked up loud. You film it superfast in one continuous shot, again with no edits, and you wind up achieving the cinema-verité effect that, you all realize afterward, was exactly what the scene called for.

It's all massively fun and over far too quickly, and when it's done you think, *I cannot wait to see this!* But of course, that is precisely what you have to do, for three excruciating months. Never has the necessary work of post-production seemed so criminally glacial. But finally you and your costars, Nathan Fillion and Felicia Day, are summoned to a small office on the 20th Century-Fox lot to watch the whole thing. Giddiness and enchantment reign. *Dr. Horrible's Sing-Along Blog* is this delicious, flawless little thing.

After another seemingly interminable wait, the first of the three episodes is at last ready to be webcast. At 8 p.m. on July 15, 2008, you sit in front of the computer watching . . . and the viewer reaction is everything you'd hoped for. In general it is a very bad idea for an actor to obsess over online comments, for very obvious reasons, but you have to admit, when every single comment is positive, the practice has its charms. It makes you glad to see so many people embrace it so wholeheartedly, even those few taken a bit aback by the final episode's tragic, operatic conclusion, which you so admire. Even better, people grasp the possibilities represented by the way in which *Dr. Horrible* was made and distributed. They begin to think, *Wow, maybe there is a way we can get people to see our work without tons of corporate hoop-jumping or advertising mandates.* It makes such an impression with the television community, the Emmys create a new category seemingly just for it: Best Short-Format Live-Action Entertainment Program. And it wins.

But the real sign you've reached people deeply comes when the cast and creators are invited to do a panel at ComicCon. When you show up you're greeted by hundreds of people wearing Dr. Horrible costumes who proceed to ask you the kind of really obscure fanboy questions usually reserved for William Shatner and Mark Hamill. Later there's a special midnight screening that's so crowded the organizers have to dig up three additional DVD copies to play in *other* banquet halls as overflow screening rooms. As you and your cohorts sit in the back watching fans talk back to the film *Rocky Horror* style, you look at one another and think, *This thing is going to have legs.*

And it does. Years later you still listen to the cast album when you're feeling cranky, and it instantly puts a smile on your face. It all holds up, and knowing that every day new people are discovering it for the first time brings you great happiness.

As for the strike, it was ultimately resolved, and the TV writers returned to work—free once more to be their natural happy, care-free, well-adjusted selves.

To work with Joss Whedon again, turn to page 84.

For more fun on the interwebnet.com, turn to page 252.

Hungry? Turn to page 111.

To hear from your Dr. Horrible costar Nathan Fillion, go on to the next page.

And now a word from your friend . . .

NATHAN FILLION

Neil, I think you're competitive. No, I *know* you are. I've been friends with you since the '90s, but it wasn't until we made *Dr. Horrible* together that I found out about your . . . compulsion for victory.

We were on the Universal lot. We'd just shot the Wonderflonium Heist scene, and the whole thing was starting to feel big-time. I had just uploaded this new app called Ninja Ropes to my iPhone. I was eager for everyone to try this exciting game and show them how to finesse their little ninja-man from circle to circle. You were eager to try. Too eager, in retrospect. You asked me abruptly, "What's your best?" I told you 108 yards. Before the words had even finished leaving my mouth, you'd already turned and walked away. You were pulling out your phone, determined to beat 108.

I'd forgotten all about the incident and would never have remembered it had I not proceeded to top my own record—I got 119.7—and approached you about it during the Laundromat scene. That face a person gives when they're looking at you but the sun is in their eyes? That cross, stink-eye look? That's what you gave me. Then you exhaled like you were exercising restraint, pulled out your phone, and walked away. Again. Crazy? No. Awkward? Yep.

That year *Dr. Horrible* was nominated for an Emmy. A "Creative Arts Emmy." The ones they give the week before the *Emmy* Emmys. Our seats were taken by God knows who, who then refused to move for us. "Nice," was all you said. Not mean, just loud. Then in a bit of poetic justice, we wound up sitting directly in front of them and partially blocked their view.

As the nominees for each category were announced, you suggested we place a $20 bet on each award. "Call it and win," you said. "It'll be fun!" Soon, I was up $100. You turned to me and said, "If you get this next one, I'm going to punch you right in the face." Not mean, just loud. I laughed and looked at you. You looked back at me, but you weren't laughing. I recall being afraid. "Is he gonna smack me?" I wondered. I really didn't know. I remember wanting to go home early, lest you start smackin' anyway. But it worked: you got into my head. I couldn't pick a win after that moment. You ended up $60 on the night. More important, *Dr. Horrible* won an Emmy. Afterward we all went to dinner to celebrate the win.

I was sure to let the seats around you fill up before selecting one myself.

To watch the Emmys from a different perspective,
turn to page 259.

To hear from Joss Whedon, turn to page 84.

To win your first major competition, report to page 8.
Bring a pressed suit, your cutest smile,
and a $25 entry fee.

In the middle of your run in *How I Met Your Mother*, you try to squeeze in one little piece of theater work: a limited-run staged reading of Sondheim's *Company* at Lincoln Center. It ends up being an object lesson in why you should rarely mix business (TV) with pleasure (theater).

The reading features an all-star cast: Stephen Colbert, Martha Plimpton, Jon Cryer, Christina Hendricks, your old friend from the world of theater Patti LuPone, just an insane amount of talent. Everybody has a busy schedule, so director Lonny Price and choreographer Josh Rhodes block the whole thing with stand-ins and send out videotapes for you to study before the very abbreviated rehearsal period. It makes sense, since almost every actor in the show is essentially in their own solitary scenes. The only exception is *you*, because your character, Bobby, is the glue holding the show together and is more or less in *every* scene. Not fully appreciating this, and trusting in your own "vast" theatrical experience, you arrive at your first rehearsal ready to learn your lines and blocking, only to discover everybody else is already off-book. But the big network TV star is unprepared.

Somewhere, Kelsey Grammer is laughing.

You pride yourself on never being the least prepared guy in the room, but it quickly becomes apparent that that is exactly what you are. You spend the morning working with Colbert and Plimpton and Cryer, who have the stuff down *cold*. You don't even have it lukewarm. By the time you get to the dance number after lunch, you are descending into a shame spiral. *Oh crap, I don't know this scene, they're off book, I'm the weak link, they think I suck, and they're right.* After two days of this, the pressure really starts getting to you. *Sondheim . . . Lincoln Center . . . reviewers . . . all-star cast . . .* you start contemplating the doomsday scenario: teleprompters.

Somewhere, Kelsey Grammer is *dying* laughing.

Towards the frantic end of rehearsals you're doing a scene with Jon Cryer and Jennifer Laura Thompson. They're supposed to be stoned, and you're supposed to be laughing at them and moving things along with interstitial lines that you keep forgetting. Patti LuPone is watching all this. When it's over she tells Jon and Jennifer, "You guys are unbelievably funny." Then she looks at you and with a withering stare says, "You're getting there." And then she walks away. And that's when you lose it. You're so mad you're shaking. For about half an hour you are silent, stewing. Finally, when Patti notices and asks what's wrong, you—in front of everyone—stop and cry out, "I'm failing at this at every turn, and you're telling everyone else they're awesome and you're saying 'I'll get there,' but I'm not going to get there! It's not helpful! It's not funny!"

It's a pure projection of your own current inadequacy. You are flailing and you know it. And not surprisingly, Patti LuPone does not take kindly to your petulant tantrum. "Oh, no, this is on you," she retorts. "Don't put this on me, this is your thing, you—" whereupon she uses a colorful variety of Anglo-Saxon words before grabbing her script and storming out. You have been given the business by Patti LuPone. Nice. Well played, Neil.

Later that night you patch things up with Patti. But reconciling with your character Bobby takes a little longer. There are moments in the final dress rehearsal when you find yourself unable to even ad-lib your way to the next moment. You leave the other actors in the lurch while you stare existentially into an empty audience, reduced to uttering the most dreaded four-letter word in theater: "Line?" In fact the very first time you do the entire show from start to finish without stopping is the opening night performance in front of all the press. You end up putting the lines of your final scene on a little menu on the set just in case. Your performance is just okay, which is absolutely not okay. You feel like a failure. Thankfully you have three more performances to improve, which you do. Plus, a video crew films three of the four readings and edits together the most successful parts. An "all-star version" of *Company* is released in movie theaters nationwide.

God bless editing equipment.

If you want to reclaim your reputation in the Broadway community, turn to page 267.

If you feel horrible about what's happened, so much so that you want the world to know you as Horrible, turn to page 181.

If you would rather cheer yourself up by spending a week at Sir Elton John's home in Nice, turn to page 244.

As you get older you notice a surprising number of contemporaries who, when introduced to friends' children, demonstrate indifference at best, feral suspicion at worst. The most they can muster for the sake of politeness is a dutiful, vaguely distasteful pat on the top of the head. This always strikes you as bizarre. Not wanting children of your own you can understand, but not *liking* them? Not *getting* them? *What is the matter with these people?* you wonder. A lot, you usually end up finding out.

You know that not everyone had a childhood as happy as yours, or parents as loving. You were fortunate, and always in the back of your mind you had the hope and ambition that someday your own children would reflect on how fortunate they were too. But for a long time it was hard to imagine the circumstances by which such a family could be created. First of all, gay or straight, the risks of *any* celebrity parenthood to both parent and (especially) child are well known to anyone who has ever read a gossip site, watched *Mommie Dearest,* or attempted to keep up with a Kardashian. Gay celebrity parenthood kicks the degree of difficulty up a notch, especially when the gay celebrity parent in question is (a) coming to terms with his own sexuality, which is something you've done only recently, and (b) hell-bent on *not* being a single father. You envision yourself as a dad in a two-parent family, and of the men you've dated, none of them, even the one or two you cared about deeply, have felt like candidates to be The One You Want to Settle Down and Raise a Family With.

And then you meet David. Not only does he come from a

close-knit family that, like you, he longs to replicate, but—and how's this for a good sign—*he's already helped raise kids.* One of his previous boyfriends, an awesome guy named Lane, had told him on their very first date that he'd just started the surrogacy process and was expecting kids. As they kept dating and grew to be a couple David went through the whole surrogacy process with Lane, and when Lane had his genetic twins, David helped raise them as his significant other. In fact the four of them went through 9/11 together, which was a pretty intense bonding experience. Lane and David eventually parted on great terms (itself another good sign), but you are enamored by the fact that this guy you're falling for has already had a chapter like this in his life, and therefore is not unfamiliar with the day-to-day details of knowing what diapers to buy and how long to refrigerate the formula and what a baby's forehead should feel like. And all this makes you fall quicker and deeper in love with him, because you don't often meet a man this handsome who's also had this kind of experience.

Still, the idea of children seems abstract. You and David are actors living gypsy lives, never knowing where and for how long work will take you. The idea of raising a stable family seems lovely but impractical. The two of you sometimes engage in idle talk about having kids—extremely theoretical kids—at some point in the time frame of "someday."

But then circumstances quickly, terribly change. David is extremely close with his mother, Debbie, who is a phenomenal human being on every level. One day she visits the doctor for a random bruise on her leg. It turns out to be something that needs to be checked, and checked turns into tested, and tested turns into leukemia, which turns into *widespread* leukemia, which in rapid succession turns to hospitalization, chemotherapy, a respirator, and finally a coma. Then you face the nightmare conversation of deciding whether or not to pull the plug. Given her vegetative state, you do.

The entire process takes twenty-one days.

The profound sadness and immediacy of it all weighs heavily on both of you. But from it emerges a mutual recognition of the importance of doing things and making choices *now*, as opposed to "someday," because it is now painfully apparent that "someday" is not guaranteed. You had wanted to have kids in theory, but now this wonderful woman who would have been a doting grandmother, a constant presence of help and advice and love, is gone. You are thrown into turmoil, but from this turmoil emerges a sense of clarity and purpose. And one of these purposes, maybe the biggest one of all, is having children. If you're going to do it, what are you waiting for?

And now you sit in front of your house, staring at the stars, remembering Debbie, speculating about life and its meaning. *How I Met Your Mother* is just starting syndication, meaning that you'll be able to stay in one place with some financial stability for at least a couple of years.

"David," you say, "if we're going to have kids, shouldn't we do it now?"

He takes a deep breath, like the last breath you take before jumping off a bridge with a bungee around your ankle.

*If you change your mind about having kids,
turn to page 101.*

If you're ready for a family, go on to the next page.

B ut alas, try and try as you might, you and David simply cannot get pregnant.

You attempt everything. You stand on your heads, follow lunar cycles, try special diets, and have sexual relations in every conceivable position. Nothing. Is God punishing you for your lifestyle? Are you just naturally infertile? Impossible to know for sure. All that is certain is that neither of you is with child.

But your repeated failure brings up a larger point: over the millennia untold billions of horny, intoxicated people have woken up from a completely unplanned night to find themselves nine months away from having a completely unplanned child, and of those untold billions, *every single one* was a heterosexual. (They were that night, anyway.) Gay couples don't wake up pregnant. No homosexual in history has ever, as the result of a homosexual act, had an "oopsie!" baby. When gay couples have children it's invariably the result of a process that involves a lot of time, a lot of planning, a lot of money, and in many cases a lot of heartache. That is true for many heterosexual couples as well of course, but it is true for pretty much *all* gay couples. Every little miracle pushed around in a stroller by two moms or dads represents some type of prolonged adventure in either conception or adoption.

And so, abandoning traditional gay biology, you decide to make your way down the long, tedious, exhilarating, exhausting, enthralling, and maddening roller coaster known as Surrogacy.

Hang on to your hats and glasses, 'cause this here's the wildest ride in the Wilderness!

Your ride begins at Growing Generations, the same surrogacy company David's ex Lane had used. As someone obsessed with learning about secret behind-the-scenes tricks, you quickly find that the surrogacy process has you under its fickle spell. It's fascinating: so many preparations must be properly made to pull this magic trick off. You have to make sure the legal elements are right, the privacy elements are right, and above all that the two other key people in the equation—the egg-donor and the surrogate—are right. Otherwise no hat, and certainly no rabbit.

Who donates and who carries? Many people use friends or family for one or the other or both, which makes a lot of sense. But for the sake of simplicity you decide to keep things clean and unsentimental by hiring two carefully chosen strangers.

The last thing you want is to go through the emotional highs and lows of expecting a baby, only to be slapped with some sort of legal form at the last minute saying, "I've changed my mind, it's *my* child now." So both people you choose are very clear on that point and are in total agreement.

Or so you think.

Of the two, most people find it easier to settle on the surrogate. That's true for you and David. The company sets you up with an awesome, hilarious woman with a family of her own. She'd done a surrogacy for a same-sex couple before—twins, as it happens—and you and David like her and her family very much. That part of the process is relatively straightforward.

But choosing the donor . . . man, that's strange. Fun, but strange. Remember how, in spare moments of idle fantasy, you used to pore through books and websites listing thousands upon thousands of baby names and etymologies and variant spellings? Choosing a donor proves to be kind of like that, only instead of names it's women. Endless lists of prospective donors, along with small photographs and details about height, weight, job, siblings, and so on. For a substantial period of time, these lists are your assigned reading, their vital stats your syllabus. Some-times you imagine the whole thing is the kind of racket where if one day after looking through the binders you said, "Actually I'm kind of looking for someone who's a little more . . . *special,*" and dropped a wad of hundred-dollar bills on the floor, the guy behind the desk would say, "Well, we don't normally show people, but we do have *these,*" and reach back and pull out a binder full of glamorous blue-eyed Aryan blondes who cost five times as much per ovary. Because truth be told, after going through hundreds of these listings there is no denying that a striking number of less-than-striking women are eager to share their genes with the infertile. And, truth still being told, you and David are less inter-ested in them. Since you're going through all this added trouble to bring one or more bundles of joy into the world, you may as well make an effort to have them at least look presentable. But after a prolonged winnowing process and a whole lot of in-depth questionnaires, you end up choosing someone reasonably attrac-tive—but in a generic way, so that in your (admittedly uneducated) point of view, the unique physical traits of you or David would be imprinted onto the child.

Having watched *The Boys from Brazil* you are a little conflicted about this, but apparently not conflicted enough.

You start to get excited. You start to emotionally invest. You start to paint the guest bedroom blue and/or pink in the pigments of your imagination. Then, just before the egg is scheduled to be transferred, you get a call from the company saying the donor's father is refusing to let his daughter donate. To which you reply, "What?! He has no say in this. She's twenty-four, she's signed every paper, she's taking the shots, she's a grown woman, it's not her dad's damn decision!" But it turns out the dad is a medical lawyer and is unwilling to let his daughter go through the "risk" of the procedure—"risk" in this case being nothing more than going under general anesthesia. Maybe he has an ulterior moral or religious motive; you don't know. You do know that even though he has no legal leg to stand on, he may threaten to sue, and given how protective David and you are of your identities you don't want this dragged into court.

Because that's the other thing. Throughout this entire surrogacy process you are passionately maintaining strict secrecy. All it takes is one person to talk to someone in the press and suddenly your private quest to fulfill a dream becomes a public story about a gay celebrity couple looking to have kids. And if that were to happen it would take on a life of its own, and you'd be trailed everywhere you went. Maybe you're just being paranoid, or maybe you just get off on adding a little *Mission Impossible*-ness to everything. But whenever you go to the clinic you use aliases, and David arrives fifteen minutes before you, and when you get there you use a back entrance, meet him on the wrong floor, go down a staircase to a side door, and knock. Then the door opens up and you enter with the furtive stealth of two junkies about to purchase five kilos of heroin.

Oh, and for aliases you choose Jack and Sydney Bristow, 'cause why not.

To see what could happen if the press knew you were trying to have children, turn to page 207.

To continue the story, go on to the next page.

So now all that precaution and security seem to have been for naught. You're back to square one, older and wiser and sadder, the guest bedroom still its neutral, all-too-ironic eggshell. But Growing Generations feels bad about what happened. They start reaching out to their A-team—the past egg-donors who might be coaxed into doing so one more time. *Ova's Eleven*, if you will.*
And that is how you meet Ms. Right. She is a multiple egg-donor who truly loves helping couples have kids, and she's fifty times as gorgeous as the person you were going to use (take *that*, anonymous medical lawyer father!). Her pictures and video are very impressive, and her impressive track record of previous surrogate pregnancies clearly shows those are some Grade-A eggs right there.

So for the second time you enter into the sciency phase of the operation. The egg-donor and surrogate get on the same cycle, and they both start taking fertility shots to fill them with let's-have-a-baby juice. (Although maybe it should be called something different? "Let's-do-this serum," maybe? It's been a long time since you practiced medicine.) And then you go a-harvestin'. Harvesting eggs is like a Vegas crapshoot. You can put in and scrape and get 0, or put in and scrape and get 11. And you do this four times, and it's thousands of dollars every time.

The other end of the fertility equation is a lot cheaper, and in

---

* You needn't.

some ways a lot less technical. Quite simply, you and David each individually go into a private room in the clinic and hump a cup.

[NOTE: The following paragraph contains graphic details of masturbating into a cup. Parental discretion is advised. Which is pretty ironic if you think about it.]

It turns out that for all the miraculous scientific and technological advances behind the twenty-first-century surrogacy process, when it comes to the sperm-collection phase there is still no replacement for, or improvement upon, whackin' it. So you enter a very sterile medical-ish room with a stack of porn magazines and a binder of porn DVDs of every orientation and description. Whatever anyone might need to get the job done. You choose a perfectly functional piece of wank material for your chicken-choking purposes, featuring a strapping young man who . . . does something for you. And as you go about your business, you find two radically dissonant thoughts going through your mind: (1) *I'm about to ejaculate the actual sperm that will be used to father my child, so for reasons of karma I should fill my mind with extrahappy, extrasmart, extrawholesome thoughts;* and (2) *Damn, that guy's smokin' hot! He looks like David!* And to fulfill your dreams of parenthood, you must block out number 1 and focus entirely on number 2. Which yes, yes, yes, oh your god yes, you do.

A few days later the doctor tells you and David your sperm counts are both above average. (How did they count the sperm? Did they sit there staring at a petri dish in a magnifying glass shouting, "One, two, three . . ."? You don't know, but you're sure they know what they're doing.) The doctor also brings the happy news that your sperm testosterone counts, too, are both above average, although yours are a little higher.

"Wait, mine are higher?" you say.

"Yes," replies the doctor. "You're 62, he's 51."

"62 to 51?"

"Yes. They're both good."

"That's so interesting, because David is generally more sexual than I am."

"That doesn't make much of a diff—"

"So does that mean that I'm more 'masculine' than he is? Or not masculine, but . . . rugged? More of a he-man?"

"Okay, easy there, tiger," chides David, correctly.

The next steps are very technical and lab-oriented, but the ~~jism~~ gist of it is that through a series of tests the fertility doctors isolate your and David's best, healthiest individual sperm. "Neil," they say, "you have two A+'s, three A's, five B's, and a C. David, you have six A+'s, four A's, and three B's." Meaning David's sperm have better grades than yours. *So what?* you think. *His sperm are a bunch of apple-polishers. My little guys can outmacho his any day of the week and twice on Sundays.*

Then finally comes the momentous day when they mix one of your A's with an egg, and one of David's with an egg, and prepare two hot, fresh zygotic omelets, and implant them both in the surrogate and see if they cook.

You cross your fingers and wait. And wait. Wait for it. Wait for it. W—

If reading that last line made you think about Barney Stinson and you're suddenly anxious to hear from him, turn to page 145.

But you should probably stick around and go on to the next page. It's about to get really exciting.

Phone call! They take!

Both embryos take, and you're having twins—one biologically yours, one biologically David's, but in the most meaningful way, both equally both of yours. Looks like you'll be painting that guest bedroom after all. And the spare office too!

During the pregnancy you and the surrogate visit each other regularly. After a few months you head to the fertility doctor to find out the sexes of the babies. The timing of this revelation leads to some professional awkwardness. That very same day you're supposed to be filming a guest-spot on a Joss Whedon-directed episode of *Glee* where you will sing "Piano Man" at a bar with Matthew Morrison. The plan is to go the doctor with your surrogate at 8:00 a.m., find out the babies' sexes, and get to the set by 9:00. But David calls and says, "Sorry, I was wrong; her plane *lands* at 8:00 a.m. There's no way she'll be at the doctor before 9:15." Which means you're going to be very late for work, which is something you pride yourself in never ever being. So you call your pal Joss and say, "Joss, I have to tell you a secret that almost no one knows—we're pregnant, today's the day we find out the sexes, I hope you understand and I'm so so sorry but I *have* to be here for this." A few years later, you will use the opportunity of writing your memoir to publicly apologize to the cast and crew of *Glee* for pulling a Sheen and keeping them waiting 2½ hours.

And the sexes are . . . one of each! Again, you completely luck out. You couldn't ask for a better situation: had it been two boys you might have wanted to do it all over again so you could experience having a girl, and vice versa.

Now the anticipation really starts to build. The time alternates between going way too fast and way too slow. Finally it's October 2010, and the surrogate goes into labor in a small hospital in northern California . . . in a town called Paradise. (Seriously. In the future, if anyone asks you how to get to Paradise, tell them it's just east of Chico.) Security is still a paramount concern of yours, perhaps comically so. You actually hire a company whose specialty is whatever specialty guarding the newborn children of gay couples from paparazzi is considered. Your team cordons off a little section of the hospital without even telling the nurses what's going on. When they show up to work they must think there's been some lethal flu epidemic, because all of a sudden there's a big taped-off plastic barrier across the hall reading DO NOT ENTER. Anyone who wants to get close has to show a little badge and use a special entrance. You're afraid some nurse's assistant will take a camera-phone picture of the two-hour-old babies and a tabloid will pay $10,000 for it. Or, even worse, only $5,000.

Are you a little paranoid? Why, who's been saying that?!? Yes, no question about it, you're a little paranoid. But the experience you had with your half-coming-out/half-outing is still fresh in your mind. You figure it's better to be safe than sorry, to make sure your little family bubble is safe and secure, and you don't have to add *that* tension to the natural stress of witnessing your kids being born, instead of shrugging and not worrying about it and finding a picture of your twin newborns dangling from their umbilical cords on the tabloids with the caption "Stars—they're just like us!"

The surrogate will be having the babies through C-section, as her vagina has nothing to do with you.* You hope they will

---

* Actually, her previous birth had been a C-section, so it's deemed safer not to do it the other way. That's fine. You're quite fond of C-sections, often finding them the most melodic part of a song.

be born on the tenth, because that would make their birthdate 10/10/10, and you find something magnificent about that; 10/10/10 and 10/10/10, that's six perfect gymnastic scores right there. But David and the doctor both tell you, "Yeah yeah, that's great, Neil, mystical numerology and crap, but it's also important to keep the babies inside the womb *for as many days as possible*." They have a point, you suppose.

The two children you have been waiting for your whole adult life are born on October 12, 2010. The boy comes out first. The girl comes out a minute later and, to one-up her brother, immediately stops breathing.

You will never forget the emotional vertigo of that moment. You're sitting next to the delivery table wide-eyed, the room bright and antiseptically clean, everyone competently doing their job, because after all these people just sit around birthing babies all day long, right? And they bring out the first one, and he's amazingly beautiful in a gross purple gelatinous kind of way, and you cut the cord, and it all seems fine. And then the girl comes out and all of a sudden nobody's panicking but everybody's rushing en masse to some other piece of equipment, and while you don't know what's happening you detect a very strong energy shift from "Miracle of life" to "Uh-oh, this baby may die right now."

But you experience it for only forty-five seconds. Then you hear her cry. And suddenly there you are in this little hospital room in Paradise, David and you and these two little life-lumps with cute little smushed-up faces: Gideon Scott Burtka-Harris and Harper Grace Burtka-Harris.

Why do you choose those names? You've spent a lot of time scrolling through nomenclatural websites and concluded it's pretty hilarious what passes for actual viable names these days. America? Amerika? Mongolia? Really? Yes, you're looking for unique names, but not necessarily *countries*. You also want them to have an unambiguous spelling, to spare them the week of life *you've* wasted telling people "it's Neil with an 'i'." (Interesting side note: people named "Neal" are bad, bad people.) Most important, if less objective, you want names that won't automatically leave other people with an impression of who they are or what they are like. You feel like "Gideon" could be a scientist or an investment banker or a bassist, and that "Harper" could be a girly-girl cheerleader or a tomboy pro-volleyball player. They're both names that, at least to your ears, don't come with any kind of stereotype. As for the rest, "Scott" is your mother's maiden name, "Grace" you just like, and the last name is "Burtka-Harris" because if one or both of them ever do choose to be in the industry as actors, when they're listed alphabetically they'll be higher up on the list, and it's important to you that your children outrank other people's children in as many ways as possible.

Minus Harper's forty-five seconds of breathlessness, the whole thing goes off with neither a hitch nor a leak. You break your good news to the world in the same timeless way people have done it for thousands of years—via tweet. Two days later, the four of you fly back to LA on a little private plane (another pricey part of the master security plan). You are terrified that when you wake up there will be fifteen paparazzi outside your door clamoring for a picture or a slice of souvenir placenta. Nope. When you finally make it back home, the celebrity gay couple with its new surrogate twins finds no fewer than *zero* reporters waiting for it. You'd arranged for a security car to be driving in front, a dummy car to be driving in another direction, and a few other bits of trickery that appealed to your magician's nature, but all that proves utterly moot. The world is apathetic. It's wonderful news.

And so your lives as new parents begin. You hire a remarkable woman named Libby to be your baby nurse/sleep specialist. She tells you that with twins, the most important thing is to get them on the same sleep schedule. Not for their well-being: for yours. Because if they're out of sync with each other you will literally never sleep. One sleeps, one cries; one cries, one sleeps; repeat as necessary until both daddies are dead of exhaustion. So she helps you with that. Her swaddling lessons are particularly instructive. Swaddling and shushing, you discover; those are key.

Of course David has done all this before, so his abilities are tremendous. Even so, you find that everything they say about raising infants is totally true. You don't ever get enough sleep and you always feel supercranky and you don't ever get enough sleep and wait, did you say that already, yes you did, but you don't care you're just so bloody tired. As any parent could have told you—and many of them have, and do—your days and nights are spent sitting on a big giant exer-ball, holding one and/or another wailing and screaming baby, shushing in her or his ear for 1½ hours, shush, shushhhhhhhhh, for god's sake will you shushhhhhhh. It's a little embarrassing, at least in your own mind, to watch yourself living out the new-dad cliché you'd seen in a thousand bad sitcoms and movies, but the truth is undeniable. Clichés are clichés for a reason. And to top it all off, you and David can't breast-feed. You try and try, but after a week all you have is four grotesquely chafed nipples, and all they're oozing is blood. Clearly there's something wrong. The two of you haven't felt so inadequate since trying and failing to impregnate each other.

And now all of a sudden you're sitting at home writing this book and Gideon and Harper are 3½ and going to preschool. You're going to write that sentence again, this time in italics: *Gideon and Harper are 3½ and going to preschool.* You know intellectually that the earth has revolved around the sun 3½ times since that frantic day in Paradise, and as you scan your brain you vaguely remember living through a series of developmental milestones like sitting up and crawling and walking and talking. But you find it nearly impossible to furnish your memoir with in-depth anecdotes about those things, because in classic parent style the weeks and months and years have all accumulated in your memory in a kind of mental accordion folder that while neatly organized grows ever more compressed. Yes, they babble; yes, suddenly they're saying words; yes, suddenly they're saying complete sentences. But those stages all blend together. The individual memories are vivid, but they form a continuum, a kind of irreducible transcendent totality. You are living in a constant now in which Gideon and Harper are always glorious and fantastic, and the mere fact of their existence overwhelms you and strikes you as a miracle and a cosmic grace.

You wouldn't have believed it before, but everything everyone says is true. The cat's in the cradle and the silver spoon.

To further bask in the awesomeness of Gideon and Harper,
turn to page 276.

To watch Bret Michaels of Poison get whacked upside the head,
turn to page 211.

A cordon of police cars follow behind you. Ahead, a highway overpass rapidly fills with people waving and holding posters like STAY STRONG, BARNEY and RUN, NPH, RUN! A half-dozen helicopters circle above you, shooting real-time footage telecast live around the world to over 500 million people.

And all the while, you sit in the passenger seat of the white Ford Bronco that David is driving.

How could I have been so wrong? you wonder. You didn't think anybody would care that you and David were trying to have children through surrogacy. Why should they? It's 2010. Gay couples have kids all the time. So you'd been going to the clinic together using your actual names, taking absolutely no security or privacy precautions. Four days ago, as you left, David thought he spotted a photographer taking a picture of the two of you. "Damn, that's going to be in the papers," he said. "No it won't." you replied. "Believe me, nobody cares about two happily partnered men trying to have children."

The next morning your story dominated international headlines. "HARRIS, BURTKA ATTEMPTING TO HAVE NON-BIOLOGICAL CHILD," blared *The Wall Street Journal*. "NPH, PARTNER IN SICKO BABY QUEST," screamed the *New York Post*. "美國男同志演員有孩子," blasted the *Beijing Times-Picayune*.

The three days that follow are a nightmarish whirlwind. The paparazzi stalk you mercilessly. Your deal to star in the upcoming action movie *Hetero Man* completely falls through. Gay activists hold you as an example of everything deeply right with Hollywood, fundamentalists as an example of everything deeply wrong with Hollywood, and gay fundamentalists, as always, remain deeply in the closet.

No one is talking about anything else—not global warming, not terrorism, not even the latest bit of Kardashiana. All seven billion people on planet Earth are united in their single-minded obsession with the possibility of you spawning.

You and David somehow escape the media crush in the middle of the night and hide out with friends. In the morning you hop back into the white Ford Bronco. You are spotted, and now every major network is covering the slow-speed chase down the California highway.

Suddenly your phone rings. Who is it? Fox News? *Out*? TM friggin' Z? You just changed your number twenty-four hours ago, and now already the vultures in the press have gotten hold of it? How dare they?

"How dare you?" you scream into the phone.

"I'm sorry, um, Mr. Harris? This is the clinic. I was just calling to tell you the news that both embryos took. You're going to be having twins."

And all at once, everything is wonderful, and nothing else matters.

You and David look at each other and smile for a moment in sheer bliss.

Then David realizes he probably should be watching the road. He turns his head forward just in time to see the eighteen-wheeler barreling towa—

THE END

Fundamentally interwoven in your genetic makeup is the ability and desire to play the role of Kermit the Frog or P. T. Barnum—the impresario, the circus ringmaster, the one who welcomes other people in and lets them know what they're in for and then keeps checking on them to make sure everything's okay. And over time, hosting awards shows becomes, to the extent any particular thing is your thing, your thing.

You've hosted the Creative Arts Emmys, the TV Land Awards on Nickelodeon, and the Video Game Awards on Spike, and done several guest spots on the Oscars and the Grammys. But the awards shows you're best known for are the Emmys (which you've done twice, in 2009 and 2013) and the Tonys (four times and counting). Your affinity for hosting awards shows has become such a well-known proclivity that at the 2013 Emmys you appeared in a pre-recorded sketch in which your *HIMYM* cast-mates diagnosed you with EHD—Excessive Hosting Disorder.

Like all good comedy, it's funny because it's true.

If you would like to host the 2009 Tonys and watch a hair-metal hero almost die of blunt-force trauma, go on to the next page.

If you would like to host the 2011 Tonys and sing a legen—wait for it—dary opening song called "Broadway Is Not Just for Gays Anymore," turn to page 227.

If you would like to host the 2013 Tonys and pull off an extraordinary theatrical coup involving 121 actors in which you literally jump through a hoop and then disappear from the stage to reappear in the middle of the audience five seconds later, turn to page 238.

If you would like to host the 2013 Emmys and wrangle together a half-dozen other awards-show hosts to perform with you in an evening whose overall theme turns out to be the icy hand of death, turn to page 259.

It's the 2009 Tony Awards and you are over the moon. It's your first time presiding over one of the four "major" awards shows. You're on a mission. You're not just going to host this awards show—you're going to revolutionize the way it's done. No, more than that; you're going to change the world.

Like you said, first-time host.

But the co-executive producers, Ricky Kirshner and Glenn Weiss, pitch you an idea for a giant opening number that *doesn't* involve you. Instead, cast members from different nominated musicals will all sing excerpts from their songs, one following the other in seamless choreography. It will be the biggest opening number in the show's history, and only at the very end will you come out. You know what? This *is* your first major awards show, and you *are* a little nervous, and maybe *not* bearing the burden of the opening song on your shoulders would be just fine.

So now the ceremony has begun, and you are standing off stage left, looking at a monitor and watching this truly grand piece of musical stagecraft unfold at Radio City Music Hall. This happens to be the year the jukebox show *Rock of Ages* is on Broadway, and its section of the medley features about a half-dozen performers and, making a cameo appearance, the rock band Poison. They, like everyone else performing in the opening medley, had heard this mantra repeated a hundred times over the course of the week: Giant pieces of scenery will be descending from the rafters throughout the number, so for safety's sake, as soon as you're finished, go upstage quickly. Yet despite this warning, at the appointed time, Poison's lead singer Bret Michaels turns back to give the crowd one last unrehearsed I-love-you-Cleveland hand gesture. As he turns upstage, with comic timing worthy of Buster Keaton, a giant backdrop comes down right on his forehead and flips him onto his back.

"Oh!" you immediately scream. You also realize that that backdrop isn't done going down yet. It's heading all the way to the floor, with Bret Michaels's cranium beneath it. You are running through the likely scenario that Bret Michaels is now dead, his skull crushed, and the first line of your first Tony Awards hosting job will be, "Ladies and gentlemen, I'm sorry to say this, but there's been a terrible accident. Bret Michaels . . . is gone." How should you say it? With what combination of authority and sadness? Should you take off your glasses like Cronkite after JFK? Too much? Too soon?

These are the hypotheticals you feel obliged as a professional to weigh in your mind at this potentially bleak moment in American history. Fortunately, you soon see that Bret is more or less okay. The cast of *Shrek* is tending to him, presumably in response to someone shouting, "Is there a cast of a Dreamworks-based musical in the house?!?"

You frantically ponder how to acknowledge what just happened as you walk to begin your opening monologue. Because you can't *not* acknowledge it. It happened right in the middle of the stage; there was an audible gasp from the crowd; it would be disingenuous to pretend it hadn't taken place. This is your big moment, your baptism by fire. A theater-award-loving nation hangs on your every word. Are you up to the task of the off-the-cuff zing?

After a couple of jokes you quip, "By the way, Bret Michaels just gave head-banging a whole new meaning."

Zing accomplished! Well, partly. Bret later threatens to sue you for the aforementioned zing. But eventually he thinks better of it, as—you will hope five years later—he will think better of suing you for recounting the anecdote in a book.

It's an early object lesson in the proper use of ad-libs. As host you have the opportunity, and sometimes the duty, to adjust on the fly, but you must do so with judgment. While it's often sorely tempting to reappear after some particularly crazy or rambling acceptance speech and snarkily ask, "Wow, was that crazy or *what*?!", it's rarely a good idea. It will probably either come off as mean, sour the mood in the room, or lengthen an already over-long telecast.

But in this case the joke strikes the right note. And you will return to the theme at the end of the night. In lieu of an opening number, you have told Glenn and Ricky you want to do a *closing* number. Your idea is to musically recap all that had transpired over the course of that very evening, almost like a magic trick. Although Glenn and Ricky reluctantly agree to your idea, they are dubious. Not only is there a high degree of difficulty involved in writing and learning the song over the course of a night, but their instincts are that it's all for naught, since people stop watching awards telecasts the moment the last award is presented. They're not alone in this opinion. A few weeks ago you spent a few min-utes chatting with a previous Tony host, Nathan Lane. You went to see him in *Waiting for Godot,* and in his dressing room after-ward you filled his ears with warranted praise for his amazing performance. He responded by letting you know he'd heard you wanted to do a closing number at the Tonys and "that's a really bad idea, Neil, 'cause after the last award people stop giving a crap and you're wasting your time and believe me I know." When you respectfully tried to parry with "Well, that's why I'm trying it, because I think it will be a fun, unique signature piece that breaks tradition," he glared at you, closed his eyes with a slow blink, and oozed, as only Nathan Lane could, "Well, good luck with *that.*"

Mr. Sunshine, that Nathan Lane.

But you have two secret weapons in your arsenal: the genius

songwriters Marc Shaiman and Scott Wittman. They shine to your idea, and immediately focus on "Tonight" from *West Side Story* as the ideal musical jumping-off point. "Tonight, tonight, the Tonys were tonight . . ." You can hear the thing practically writing itself.*As for the lyrics, you realize the shrewdest thing to do is write them in advance based on what you feel is *likely* to happen. The three of you write lyrics for the favorites and lyrics for the second choices, get the awesome director/choreographer Rob Ashford to work out a little bit of movement for you, and trust that if something out-of-the-ordinary happens—like an underdog winning, or Bret Michaels getting bonked in the forehead with a backdrop—you'll be able to quickly bang out a couplet to replace a weaker joke, rehearse it backstage during the last twenty minutes of the show, and sing it off teleprompter. And sure enough, it goes like gangbusters, and you're able to add,

> "*What class, what drive,*
> *Now Angela [Lansbury]'s won five,*
> *And she hooked up with Poison backstage.*"

All in all, a great night for you, and a horrible one for Bret Michaels.

If you'd like to host the Tonys again, turn to page 227.

If you'd like to be hosted by Katy Perry, turn to page 255.

---

* Note: the thing did *not* write itself. Marc and Scott wrote it. Songs very rarely write themselves. They're lazy like that.

[You sit behind a desk. After a few seconds of upbeat music, you turn to the camera.]

YOU: Welcome back to *The NPH Show*! I'm your host, Neil Patrick Harris. My guest tonight is an actor, performer, and insanely handsome man currently starring in *Neil Patrick Harris: Choose Your Own Autobiography*, playing the title role of "you." Please welcome Neil Patrick Harris!

[You walk onto the page and wave to the reader. Then you go over to yourself, shake your own hand, and take a seat.]

YOU: Look at you! You look great!

YOU 2:   Thanks! So do you!

YOU: Now, Neil, you and I go back a long way, but if I'm not mistaken this is the first time you've appeared on *The NPH Show*, right?

YOU 2:   That's right, although in my defense this show is a purely literary construct.

YOU: Fair enough. Still, it's safe to say it's probably the only talk show you *haven't* been on before, right?

YOU 2:   As Ed McMahon used to say, you are correct, sir! I've been on just about every TV gabfest there is, from Letterman to Leno to Kimmel to Fallon to Conan to Stewart to Colbert, right on through to RuPaul, Megan

Mullally, and Ellen DeGeneres, usually multiple times.

YOU: Clearly they love having you. You're a good guest. What's your secret?

YOU 2: *[Stretching out on couch]* Well, I would say informality. Looking and feeling relaxed.

YOU: And what about banter? I would imagine that you're good at—

YOU 2: —getting into a rhythm where you're sort of—

YOU: —in sync with the other person and there's—

YOU 2: —no awkward silences, exactly.

YOU: Which show have you enjoyed the most?

YOU 2: That's a hard one. Fallon is fun. We play games; I rocked a magic trick once. He just makes you feel relaxed and comfortable, like you're two old friends hanging out. I'm looking forward to doing his show to promote my book because when I'm on I'm going to read a little excerpt—this one right now, probably—and then when I'm done I'm going to reach over and French-kiss him.

YOU: That'll make for great TV. Let's talk about some of the giants of the late-night world, because you mentioned Ed McMahon before, and I don't think people realize you've been doing the circuit for so long you actually did Carson.

YOU 2: Yes, *three times* back in the early '90s. What a rush that was for a sixteen-year-old kid. I even got to do a magic trick with him.

YOU: I'm intrigued. Do you have a clip?

YOU 2: No, this is a book, Neil.

YOU: Oh, right. Let's talk about the other godfather of late night, Letterman. You go way back with him too, right?

YOU 2:   I've done his show ten times. The first was in 1994. I played a game where he and I tried to bowl and knock over random things in the NBC hallways. I also had a running gag that I'd get electrocuted every time I touched his microphone. I *love* David Letterman. He's like a father figure to me. Only a sexy father. So suave; so rakishly handsome. And a generous kisser, a generous lover. You might expect him to be more selfish in bed, but no. He's very thoughtful, always tending to my needs first, and next time I'm on his show, I'm gonna find some organic way to tell him how much I appreciate that.

YOU: Oprah Winfrey.

YOU 2:   Funny story about her, Neil, and please stop me if you know it—

YOU: Of course *I* know it, but go ahead.

YOU 2:   For the longest time—and here's the insecurity talking—I thought that for all I'd achieved in the business I still hadn't truly "made it" because I was Oprah-less. In fact I carried this silly anti-Oprah grudge because during the Doogie years Fred Savage and I appeared at a benefit for her, and afterward she ran up to Fred and told him how awesome he was, but barely said a word to me. It was silly. *Extremely* silly. She had no reason to know who I was. But two decades later, after David and I had our kids, her people called saying she wanted to come to our house and hang out with us, which under normal circumstances I might find weird, but of course Oprah is not normal circumstances. And I can guarantee you, by the time she arrived, our house had never been cleaner. I'm talking *immaculate*.

YOU: Any other interviewers you particularly admire?

YOU 2:   Howard. I *looovve* Howard Stern. He is the best in-
         terviewer in the business. I bought Sirius Radio be-
         cause of him; I only wish he were broadcasting live
         24/7. He approaches his subjects almost the way a
         psychiatrist approaches his patients. If he sees there's
         something they don't want to talk about, that's what
         he asks about. Which is human nature and a riveting
         interview technique, and *exactly* why I was so terrified
         the first time I appeared on his show. All I could imag-
         ine is that he'd have his numerous callers say awful
         things about my sexual proclivities and ask whether
         or not I love fisting. But I decided to face my fears, and
         he couldn't have been nicer. We played "Fuck Marry
         Kill," took some calls, and had a lovely chat. I've done
         his show again since then, and I hope I get to do it
         once more for the book tour. Maybe I'll get to throw
         bologna slices on a stripper's ass. Or finger-bang Rich-
         ard Christy.

YOU: Awesome! Maybe I'll be there for that as well. We
         have to take a break. Can you stick around for another
         chapter?

YOU 2:   I can, but other people might not want to, so let's give
         them a chance to change channels.

If you want to read the rest of your interview with yourself,
turn to page 221.

If you want to hear from a close friend of Howard's (and yours),
go on to the next page.

If you've had enough of this meta-self-indulgence and would like
to mix yourself a drink, turn to page 149.

And now a word from your friend . . .

KELLY RIPA

One of my job perks is that occasionally I get to meet people I've admired for years. And every so often we become friends. Such was the case with you and me.

We first met when you were a guest on my chat show a thousand years ago. The producers and I know a great talker when we see one, so it wasn't long before our show was reaching out to you to cohost with me from time to time. From there our relationship just blossomed. We became very close, as did our families, and so we took it to the next level . . . Thanksgiving dinner.

As you know, my kids are obsessed with you in general and your sleight-of-hand tricks in particular, so it was a real treat when, after a delicious and relaxing meal, we all settled into the living room to sit by the fire and be entertained by the magical stylings of NPH.

What took place next is the stuff of family arguments, paranoia, folklore, and urban myth.

I know you know what happened, and how it happened (how, Neil, *how?!?*), but let me explain how it looked from *our* point of view. You asked Mark for a one-dollar bill, then asked me to write down the serial number. You took the dollar from Mark, tore it up in a zillion pieces, and burned them in the fireplace. By the way, Neil, the trick could have ended there. The kids had never seen anyone take money from their dad, tear it into a zillion pieces, and then burn it. They'd never been so dazzled in their lives.

But of course, it didn't end there. Now you reached into the flower arrangement I had specially made just for Thanksgiving, complete with a cornucopia feature and fresh apples. (Look, Thanksgiving happens once a year. Give me a break.) You grabbed an apple from the center of the arrangement, broke it in half, and pulled out a soaking-wet dollar bill with, of course, the matching serial number!!!

How did you do it? We watched you burn that dollar. And that apple dollar was wet. Soaking wet. Like it spent its entire life in that apple. And while we're on the apple, how did you get to my cornucopia?

I was freaked out, but Mark was *beyond* freaked out. You remember how, at this point, he tried to put out the fire and piece together the burned-beyond-recognition dollar-bill fragments so he could figure out the trick, right? Well, to this day he's certain you had broken into our house a week earlier and spent a week living there without our knowledge just to gain access to that cornucopia. He also accuses me of aiding and abetting, whatever that means. And that's why he still follows you around every time you come over, by the way. He's convinced a trick might unfold all around him.

Anyway, that's my "you" story. You can finish interviewing yourself about your talk-show appearances on the next page now. Or you can hang out with other magic types like yourself on page 159.

See you soon!

YOU: We're back to *The NPH Show.* I'm here with Neil Pat-
           rick Harris, or "NPH," as his fans call him.

YOU 2:   Here's a little bit of trivia: I'm known as Neil *Patrick*
           Harris only because when I first joined the union, an-
           other actor already had the name Neil Harris.

YOU: That's right. That's how a lot of famous people wind
           up known by three names.

YOU 2:   Either that, or they're assassins.

YOU: Zing!

YOU: You mentioned earlier doing a magic trick on Carson.
           That's become one of your signature talk-show moves,
           the magic trick.

YOU 2:   Yes, I've been doing them off and on ever since. I did
           one on Arsenio that worked very well. I produced a
           white dove out of a balloon I popped. Arsenio did
           most of the work and I took all the credit. That's how
           magic works.

YOU: When it works.

YOU 2:   Tell me about it!

YOU: No, you're the guest. You tell *me* about it.

YOU 2:   Oh, right. Well, one time on *Ellen* I brought out a big
           giant guillotine head-chopper onstage. (Ed Alonzo
           helped track it down for me.) As we'd rehearsed, I put
           my head inside it casually, like I was just demonstrat-
           ing, and then she said "Oh, what's this?" and pulled
           at a rope, at which point the blade dropped and cut

my head off. It fell into a basket, while my body lay there motionless, and Ellen drily turned to the camera and says, "*Harold and Kumar: Escape from Guantánamo Bay* is in theaters everywhere this Friday." Well, the next day Ellen had to go on her show and explain that what had happened was a trick. She had received dozens of worried and angry e-mails from children and parents. "I'm seven years old, why would you try to kill Neil Patrick Harris?" "My kids watch this show—you think it's funny to hack some guy's head off in the middle of everything?!" So she had to apologize on my behalf, and show footage of me getting out of the prop to prove that she hadn't murdered me in the middle of the show.

YOU :   Yikes! Was that the only time you tried magic on *Ellen*?

YOU 2:   No. Another time Ed and I—he's my partner in crime for all these kinds of things—conceived this great trick. I would take a lightbulb, put it inside a small Ziploc bag, hold the bag in my fingers, and then, using just my mind, the lightbulb would start to glow. Then I would concentrate even further, count to three, and the lightbulb would shatter inside the bag. Ed and I rehearsed it, it goes great. But you have to hold the bag at a specific angle and, evidently, practice more than I did. So during the show, which thank god was taped and not airing live, I did the whole setup, put the lightbulb in the bag, made it glow, concentrated further, one two three . . . nothing. Nothing happened. And the audience is squirming, and so is Ellen, and I say, "Oh, well, that didn't work." We completed the rest of the interview with me feeling sheepish and mortified. So afterward I talked to the segment producer, who kindly said, "Don't worry. We're post-taping this.

We can just reset it and do it again." So they reset
the mechanism that's supposed to make the lightbulb
break while I came back out and explained to the audience we were going to restart at an editing point and
reshoot the end of the trick. Take two: I do the whole
setup, put the lightbulb in the bag, it glows, I concentrate further, one two three . . . nothing. Again. I'm
oh-for-two. At this point even *I'm* finding humor in the
depth of my failure. So with the indulgence of Ellen,
her crew, and the audience, we did it a *third* time. I do
the whole setup, put the lightbulb in the bag, it glows,
I concentrate further, one two three . . . and the bulb
finally shatters! The audience goes ballistic like I'd
made the Statue of Liberty vanish and reappear. It was
very skillfully edited, but if you ever watch it you'll be
surprised just how enthusiastically the audience re-
sponds to a broken lightbulb.

YOU: I/you have to ask you/me: Has being on so many of
these shows given you any desire to host one your/
myself?

YOU 2: Well, I'm hosting one now.

YOU: Right, but for real, not as a written gimmick for an
alter ego.

YOU 2: I see. Well, you know, I've already cohosted about a
dozen *Live with Kelly*s, and discovered it's much more
of a high-wire act than just making an appearance.
It's fifteen minutes of talking about current events,
followed by sit-down interviews with three guests in
whom you may or may not be genuinely interested.

YOU: [*Checking watch*] Mmm-hmmm.

YOU 2: But the saving grace is working with Kelly. I cannot
say enough good things about her. She's one of the
smartest, funniest, nicest, most genuine people you

could ever meet, which is clear when you watch her on air but even more so when you get to know her as a human being. And having such a fun, convivial time with her, I have to admit the idea of doing a show like that, where you're essentially paid to be yourself for a few hours a day, does have its appeal.

YOU: So is an *NPH Show* something your fans can look forward to in the future?

YOU 2: The future? What do you think I'm appearing on *right now*?!?

YOU: [*Realizing*] Whoa. We just blew our mind.

YOU 2: I'll say.

YOU: Well, we're almost out of space. *Neil Patrick Harris: Choose Your Own Autobiography* is available online and at bookstores. Neil Patrick Harris, thanks for stopping by your show.

YOU 2: Thanks for having me, me!

[The NPH Show *theme song plays both of yous out of the chapter.*]

To flip the channel and find yourself on How I Met Your Mother, *turn to page 133.*

To flip the channel and find yourself hosting an awards show, turn to page 210.

To flip the channel and find yourself in one of a dozen made-for-TV movies, turn to page 89.

And now, one more magic trick from Mr. Neil Patrick Harris.

I hope you've enjoyed my mystical stylings. I will leave you with an encore. This time no cards are needed—only you and your beautiful, beautiful hands.

Hold your right hand in front of your face, with your palm facing you and all your fingers out straight, just as if you were going to read your palm. Your thumb should be pointing to the right. Now with your left hand, point to your right pinky.

In a moment, I'm going to ask you to make five "moves" from the pinky. A move means that you're moving your left pointer finger right or left, to the one next to the one that you're on right now. You can only move one space (digit), but you can move up and back, right and left, as many times as you want. And remember: even though we have a different name for it, the thumb is one of your fingers, so you can move on or off the thumb.

Remember, move only one space, but you can go back and forth, in either direction, to a finger next to it.

Okay, do that with me now. Make one move. Now two. Three. Four. Five. Good. Wherever you've ended up, keep your left finger there.

Of course, since all of you moved in your own way, you've chosen different fingers. But I can tell you personally that you didn't end up back on your little finger. And you didn't end up on your thumb. So I want you to fold those fingers in. So now you've just got three fingers pointed, and one of them is the one you've selected.

Let's stop using the little finger and thumb, and confine all our moves to these remaining three fingers. I want you to now move once. Just once, to the finger next to the one you've selected.

Have you done that?

Good. I can tell that you didn't end up on the ring finger. That's the one next to the little finger. So fold that one in as well. That leaves these two fingers, and you're on one of them. Aren't you?

So I want you to make one last move, to the finger next to it. Do that now.

Excellent. Because after that little demonstration of free will, you might be surprised to find that I knew exactly what you were going to do. It's almost like you thought you had free will, but I was secretly inside your head, making you do exactly what I wanted.

You've stopped on your index finger, your first finger. That was your final choice.

I'm right, aren't I?

Mmmmmmmagic!

[Vanishes in puff of smoke]

Sorry. The magic show is over. Please exit through the rear doors and emerge on page 133.

Although if you're still interested in doing more magic as Neil Patrick Harris, only this time on talk shows, feel free to take the secret exit leading to page 215.

In 2011 Glenn and Ricky bring you back to host the Tonys for the second time. The ceremony is being held at the Beacon Theatre because a new Cirque du Soleil show has rented out Radio City for the entire summer. On the one hand it's a bummer because the Beacon's a much smaller venue. On the other hand it feels more like you're doing the show in a real Broadway house rather than a cavernous spectacle room. What's lost in grandeur is gained in intimacy.

It's the year of *The Book of Mormon.* Satire and lightheartedness are in the air. You are keen to do an opening number, so you hire David (DJ) Javerbaum and Adam Schlesinger, the songwriters of the 2008 Broadway musical *Cry-Baby.* DJ is the former head writer and executive producer of *The Daily Show with Jon Stewart,* so he represents exactly the kind of smart, sharp comedy you want. Not only for this lyric, but on *any* future project requiring editorial supervision.*

Anyway, at the initial meeting DJ pitches a couple of ideas for songs, including one called "Broadway Is Not Just for Gays Anymore." You're worried that it may be a one-joke idea, but the more you talk about it, the more it seems like a solid opener, especially as a prelude to a night likely to be dominated by *The Book of Mormon.* And you're just the man to sing it. Coming from you, its message of heterosexual inclusion will feel friendly and welcoming. But you have to fight to do the song. The American Theatre

---

* A choose-your-own-autobiography, for example.

Wing and the Broadway League, the two organizations in charge of the ceremony, are—understandably, given the classiness of the night and the median age of the attendees—worried about having an entire opening song about homosexuality. One executive in particular screams and yells at the very notion and swears you will have to perform it over his dead body, which would of course make the choreography very difficult.

Ultimately they trust you. You know the song will only pack the desired punch if nobody knows it's coming, so you're very hush-hush. You practice it in closed rehearsal spaces and have all the dancers sign confidentiality clauses. And then you take it to Gideon-and-Harper-are-about-to-be-born levels of secrecy. The song has to be orchestrated and pre-recorded with musicians in a studio, any one of whom could blog or tweet or Facebook the number "out of the closet." So you ask DJ to write dummy lyrics for the entire song. For example, the line

Attention every breeder, you're invited to the theater!
It's not just for gays anymore!

becomes

I'm proud to be your greeter for the very best in theater!
Tonight at the Tony Awards!

It's as lame as a two-legged goat. If any of the musicians leak anything, it will be along the lines of "Just recorded Neil's opening number and man, is it going to suck." Which is fine.

Another funny story about the lyrics: The last line is supposed to be

Come in and be inspired!
There's no sodomy required!

A great capper. But CBS is adamant that you can't end the number like this. They make us come up with a new ender, which they approve:

Come in and be inspired!
There's no same-sex love required!

It's as lame as a one-legged goat. (And really, why is "same-sex love" less offensive or scandalous than "sodomy"? "Sodomy" is a neutral term describing a physical act, a scientifically accurate word. "Same-sex love" opens the whole thing up to the possibility that gay couples might actually *love* each other. Shouldn't *that* notion be more offensive to whatever fine upstanding Bible-thumpers happen to accidentally tune in to the Tonys for a moment while switching over to *The 700 Club?*)

So you approach Glenn at dress rehearsal and innocently ask, "If I accidentally say 'sodomy' instead of 'same-sex love,' what would happen? Would you have to bleep me or something?" And he says, "Well, no, it's not a curse word. We wouldn't be fined for it or anything." "Okay. Good to know," you say, and drift back to DJ.

"You know what? I think that when we do this live, I may accidentally say 'sodomy.' What do you think will happen?"

"I guess we'll find out," he says.

So when the big moment comes at the climax of the song, sure enough, oops darnit!, you make the mistake. And the first person you see backstage is Jack Sussman, who is the head of CBS Special Programming, and man, does he look pissed. He has to get on the Batphone—seriously, a special red phone—to explain to his bosses what just happened. But to his credit, Jack stands up for you, and that song is remembered not as another "wardrobe malfunction," but as one of the great moments in Tony history. The broadcast ends up winning five Emmys—one for DJ and Adam, one for Dave Boone and Paul Greenberg, who wrote the rest of the show, one for Glenn Weiss's directing, one for you for hosting, and one for the show itself.

And it's fun to win an Emmy for the Tonys, especially because you can't win a Tony for the Emmys. Or an Oscar for the Grammys. Or a Nobel for the Sexiest Man Alives.

If you'd like to host the Tonys a third and fourth time, turn to page 238.

If sodomy genuinely is required, turn to page 78.

And now a word from your friend . . .

SETH MACFARLANE

The first time I met you, I was covered in my buddy's brain and skull fragments.

It was Guadalcanal, 1942. We were losing the battle, losing the island, and my buddy had just lost eight pounds of head-meat that he'd never put back on. Suddenly, out of nowhere came a hot-tempered corporal with an M2 Carbine in one hand and a towel in the other—*you*. You tossed me the towel and said, "Wipe that Iowa off your face" (we called my buddy "Iowa," 'cause he was from Iowa) "and let's go kick Tojo in the balls."

As I watched you pocket Iowa's last letter home to his best gal and charge out of the foxhole, I called after you, "I think we're under orders to hold our positions, Corporal . . . is it Corporal Neil? Corporal Patrick? Harris?"

"It's all three, bitch! And sorry, I can't hear you. My ears are full of revenge!"

I had no choice but to follow as you stormed uphill, into the teeth of the dug-in breastwork. And what I saw as I followed is something I'll never forget: you were a death machine. Just an unstoppable one-person barrage of hot lead, cold steel, and ethnic slurs (it was a different time, and we were at war). At one point you pulled out a man's still-beating heart and squeezed the contents into a tureen ("I'm gonna pour your blood on my cornflakes!"). As you kicked the squozen heart-husk over toward the buzzards that had begun to follow you, I thought, *I could really see this guy hosting the Tonys.*

By the time you'd killed your way to the top of that bloody hill, I'd forgotten all about poor dead Ohio ('cause my buddy, I'm just now realizing, was from Ohio, not Iowa; I always get those two mixed up), and could only think about you as this reaper of destruction, and the trail of carrion you were leaving in your wake. "Who is that guy? Where is he from? Will he someday play a kid doctor on TV?" Those were the questions I asked myself.

But then I was hit. I was hit bad and went down on top of a pile of about fourteen guys that you had just killed. Some of them had voided their bowels when they died, so it was really kind of a problem. You bent over me and tried to fish out the shells with an MRE pop-top, and as I felt the life draining from my body, this is the conversation we had:

ME: It's . . . too late for me, Neil. I'm a . . . goner. . . .

YOU: Don't talk like that, private! You're gonna live! We're gonna get you outta here and you're gonna make it and maybe someday you'll go on to produce three animated sitcoms, and two of them will be reasonably successful!

ME: Will they . . . win lots of . . . Emmys . . . and be critically . . . acclaimed?

YOU: Let's just . . . let's just get you outta here, buddy.

I woke up two weeks later in a military hospital in Honolulu, only to find out that what I'd witnessed was you, Neil Patrick Harris, mistakenly fighting your way up a hill of our own guys. Even my own wound was from your gun. I found a note crammed in my pocket that said, "Ooops! Sowwy! —NPH," with a little frowny-face on it. You'd written it on the back of Ohio's last letter home, which was not a very cool thing to do.

All of which is to say that you may be charming, funny, charismatic, and insanely talented, but you're really kind of a dick.

To do damage to a different kind of company, turn to page 188.

To hear from one of your costars in Seth MacFarlane's film A Million Ways to Die in the West, *turn to page 264.*

You have a very healthy inner child, and for many years it's been asking your outer adult to get more work in kids' entertainment. But your outer adult needs no prodding; it's always consciously tried to maintain a presence among multiple demographics, and no demo is more important, or adorable, than children. So the two yous form an uneasy professional alliance, and it quickly pays dividends in the form of voice-over work. Your mellifluous—or cackling, if needed—intonations can soon be heard in audiobooks, animated kids' shows, and even video game adaptations of *Batman* and *Spider-Man*. (By the way, why is Spider-Man hyphenated and Batman not? These are the questions that keep you up at night.) Before you know it you land a big-screen role in *Cloudy with a Chance of Meatballs*. You voice a mentally deficient monkey who speaks only in one- or two-word sentences that are processed through a Speak-and-Spell attached to his chest. It's the role your larynx was born to play!

It's a unique skill, voice-over work. It's all about inflectional variation. You're in a little booth with a whole bunch of audio engineers and moviemakers on the other side. When they push a button you can hear them, but otherwise you can't hear anything. There's a pattern to the proceedings: you say your line, then wait in silence and watch a half-dozen people huddle up and talk about you. Then after about fifteen seconds the engineer says, "Great, do it again but this time you're happier." So when you record *Cloudy with a Chance*, you end up having conversations like:

YOU: Gummy bear!

(Pause; huddle.)

ENGINEER: Great! Now like it's the most delicious gummy bear ever!

YOU: Guuuummmmmy beeeeaaar.

(Pause; huddle.)

ENGINEER: Great! Now say it like you're afraid of the gummy bear.

YOU: G-g-g-g-g-gummy b-b-b-ear!

(Extralong pause; huddle.)

YOU: Did I do something wrong?

ENGINEER: No, Phil was just telling us about this hot chick he's banging.

The video-game voicing is particularly bizarre, because you're recording not only the dialogue but the interstitial scenes. You need to read and/or come up with fifteen different little lines for when, say, the player goes to the bathroom. "So are we gonna do this or what?!?" "Gotta tinkle, tough guy?!?" By variation 15, you are absolutely out of ideas about how to taunt incontinent gamers. Then it's on to variations 1–100 on the sound of getting punched in the face.

YOU: Oof.

(Pause; huddle.)

ENGINEER:	Great! Now a harder punch.
YOU:	Ooooof!!

(Pause; huddle.)

ENGINEER:	Great! Now harder, right in the sternum.
YOU:	OOOOOOOFFFFF!

(Extralong pause; huddle.)

YOU:	Did I do something wrong?
ENGINEER:	No, Phil was showing us a nasty text he just got from that chick he banged.

But you've always enjoyed the technical aspects of putting creative projects together. The greater the challenge, the greater the appeal. So when executive producer Jordan Kerner asks you to read the script for a movie called *The Smurfs*, you don't need much convincing. The idea of interacting with computer-generated creatures has tremendous appeal to you. Plus you like the idea of creating a family movie that grown-ups would also like, so they won't start going crazy when they hear it blaring from the backseat of their SUV for the fourth straight time. And above all, you're flattered that, given what everyone knows about your personal life, a big company like Sony wants you to star in a potential blockbuster movie.

Because that's what it is, a potential blockbuster. You know very well that the chance to star in a giant "tentpole" movie doesn't come along every day. When choosing actors, studio heads and casting directors look at lists showing how your most recent movies have done financially. If you want to be in the next David Fincher movie (and you are), it helps to show that your last three films have grossed over $800 million. So *The Smurfs* is not only a job, but an investment. And sure enough it ends up breaking your streak of big-budget disappointments. It makes over $550 million worldwide, opens number one at the box office in France, Germany, Mexico, and Brazil, and spawns a sequel that takes in over $347 million. That's a lot of green . . . from a lot of blue!*

For a kids' movie, *The Smurfs* is pretty intense. The interaction with the technology requires laser precision. On one typical day of shooting, you sit in an otherwise empty living-room set. The director, Raja Gosnell, says, "Okay, the Smurfs are going to come in and jump up on the couch, and then one's going to jump down onto the chair, and you're going to pick him up in your hand and set him over on the other chair and then talk to everyone in their different places." The crew sets up little gelatinous figures that are the actual size of the Smurfs. Then right before you film, you look in the eyes of the little figurine you're "talking" to, and they put a dot at the end of your eyeline so that when they add the Smurf later you'll appear to be staring right at it. When Raja yells, "Action!" you talk to a dot representing Papa Smurf, then "follow" him to your cupped hand, which he will eventually be standing on. All the while you wear an earpiece to hear the voice-over actors doing their dialogue in a different room.

And that's just dialogue and blocking. There are other, more elaborate scenes, like the one where the Smurfs tickle you. That one's kind of embarrassing because, of course, *no one* is actually tickling you. You're just wearing a T-shirt with lots of monofilament strips attached to it being pulled by effects guys. It's a slow, technical process, but it's much freer than voice-over work in one respect: the animation hasn't been done yet, so you have the ability to actually affect how things will be drawn. For example, the

---

* Thanks to eight-year-old Timmy Weissbard of Seattle, the winner of the "Write a Joke for Neil Patrick Harris's Book!" kids' competition, for that joke. (Yes, that was the best joke you received.)

script calls for you to order the Smurfs into a suitcase, but you ad-lib a mime of one slipping and falling and you picking him up and throwing him in, and they wind up animating in that joke to match your motion. It's neat to do stuff like that, to work with talented costars like Jayma Mays and Hank Azaria and (in the case of *Smurfs 2*) Brendan Gleeson. That one's more fun to shoot because you get to do effects. You wear a body harness in front of a giant green-screen soundstage as they hoist you on cables and you do front flips and back flips and spins. You've never felt more like an acrobat, even that time in Berlin when you felt up an acrobat.

To innocently hang out with your kids,
turn to page 276.

To not-so-innocently feel up an acrobat that time in Berlin,
turn to page 78.

To hear from Amy Sedaris, a friend you made on the set of the movie
The Best and the Brightest, *a small independent film that is otherwise*
not mentioned anywhere in this book, turn to page 119.

After hosting the Tonys again in 2012, the producers ask you back the next year for a fourth (but hopefully not final) time. The show is moving back to Radio City Music Hall, and you feel it's important to acknowledge the change of venue, the fact that the awards are back in their traditional battleship-sized home. So one day while driving you come up with the idea of a song called "Bigger." You hear it as kind of like an Irish drinking song with an oompah, South Parky chorus that would just be "It's bigger, it's bigger, it's something something something," and then you do a bunch of fast talking, and then more "it's bigger, it's bigger," and you keep adding more people and more business and more craziness onstage until by the end the stage is filled with everybody—not just the casts of the nominated shows, but the Statue of Liberty, the Naked Cowboy, the awkward Elmo who haunts Times Square, *everybody*. And those are the vague marching orders you give Lin-Manuel Miranda, the star and songwriter of *In the Heights,* and Tom Kitt, the composer of *Next to Normal.* Basically you give them the title—"Bigger"—and a directive—"bigger." And they proceed to crush it, to write an opening number whose scale, size, and sheer biggitude outbig all previous biggings. There's no bigness like this bigness like no bigness you know.

But the title is a hubristic affront to the awards-show gods, and sure enough simply coordinating the rehearsal schedule proves a monumental task. The song features 121 people, including the partial casts of no fewer than nine Broadway shows. Couple that with Actors' Equity's strict policy limiting the number of hours actors can work, and you end up with an insanely compressed amount of time. Prior to the last frantic weekend, there is *only one day* when the entire cast is available. Thankfully, the brilliant director/choreographer Rob Ashford has the creative imagination to meld the varied theater throngs into a seamless vision of Broadway splendor, but to bring it to life every second counts. When you arrive at rehearsal you're told, "Hi, we literally have eleven minutes to do this, so let's go, we're gonna start here, here's the cast of *Kinky Boots,* they move here, you do this, then you stand here, sing the lyric, take four steps there, they go off, enter the cast of *Motown,* you meet them, you move here, great, let's try it. 5, 6, 7, 8, now here's when 75 more people will be coming on, some orphans, a coupla tap-dancing kids, the gang from *Pippin*—hey, that reminds me, how'd you feel about jumping through a hoop?"

That's right. You literally jump through a hoop. The universal metaphor for ridiculous tricks becomes your reality.

And still you want bigger. You're drunk on bigness. You demand ever greater biggitude. So you throw in some actual magic. Recruiting your usual partner in magical crime Ed Alonzo, you jump a bunch of steps and get into a big giant box wheeled onto the center of the stage. On cue, a rope is pulled, the four sides flop down accordion-style, and you're gone. You practice the trick over and over but it takes you forever to escape and you keep missing the musical cue. But you keep at it and, thank God, when you do it live, it works like a son of a bitch. The walls open and you're gone and, lo and behold, the camera spins around to find you walking up the aisle, at a seemingly impossible distance from the stage, gallivanting with a bunch of *Newsies.*

How did you do it? You're not going to tell you. Magicians never share their secrets, even with themselves.

But the hardest thing to pull off is the lyric. Lin-Manuel is such a master wordsmith, his flow so exuberantly dense, that as the broadcast nears you keep asking him to *remove* prepositions, articles, and any other not-strictly-necessary words just so you can take breaths. Thus,

Well, if it isn't Pippin!

becomes

[Gasp for air] It's Pippin!

The lyrical climax is a feat of verbal dexterity so difficult you can do it only by just staring at the teleprompter and not moving. You plant yourself while everyone dances around you and just think, *Dear god, please get all these words right.* And you do.

And the words are worth it.

*There's a kid in the middle of nowhere, who's sitting there living for
Tony performances,
Singin' and flippin' along with the Pippins and Wickeds and Kinkys,
Matildas and Mormonses.
So we might reassure that kid
And do something to spur that kid
'Cause I promise you all of us up here tonight we were that kid . . .
And now we're bigger!*

That's Lin-Manuel in his soul. That's exactly what he believes. Listening to that, you get the same goose-bumpy feeling when you watched him in *In the Heights.* Those words and the way he pops his rhythms are sublime.

You use his lyrical genius in the closing number too. It's the fourth time you're doing one of these end-of-the-show recap numbers and you're out of ideas. Then Glenn the director suggests Lin write a rap to Jay-Z's "Empire State of Mind." Someone proposes getting 452-time Tony-winner Audra McDonald to do the Alicia Keys sections of the song with you. Lin prepares the choruses in advance, but he and his frequent writing partner Tommy Kail write the verses during the show.

As often happens, you find yourself rooting for certain people to win solely because you have a great joke ready for them. Lin is particularly rooting for winners with exactly three syllables in their names, because it fits nicely with the "Yellow cab / gypsy cab / dollar cab" rhythm in Jay-Z's original. So he's happy when Tracy Letts and Judith Light win. But when Courtney B. Vance gets a Tony he informs you, "As far as you're concerned, he's Courtney Vance. No B."

And you're ecstatic when the award for best play goes to Christopher Durang, because it gives you an excuse to include

The '80s came back with a bang, not 'cause Cyndi Lauper sang,
It's because the best play was by Durang, Durang.

Fantastic opening number,* fantastic closing number, and that's not even mentioning making out with Sandy the dog from *Annie* on national television. It's your favorite awards show. By far. So far.

To host the Emmys later this same year, turn to page 259.

To hear from the man who hosted the Oscars earlier this same year, turn to page 231.

---

* And the next year, Lin and Tom win a well-deserved Emmy. It's the third straight year one of your Tony songs wins an Emmy. You're either hiring, or sleeping with, all the right people.

S esame Street is one of the greatest and most satisfying experiences of your professional life. So when Big Bird calls you out of the blue to say he wants to discuss another possible project for you, you jump at the chance.

It's a beautiful day, so you decide to take a nice leisurely stroll to Big Bird's house in the mountains. You start wondering what he has in mind. You lose yourself in happy speculation.

Suddenly you notice the world slowly, inexplicably turning white all around you. Looking up, you realize you have stumbled onto a steep alpine mountain. You are in an avalanche!

You desperately struggle to escape, but your efforts only cause you to sink deeper. You look around for something to pull yourself out of the avalanche with. A cord attached to an ice-tree dangles tantalizingly a few feet in front of you, but you can't quite reach it.

With your last breath you scream, "Help me, Big Bird!" but your cry is quickly throttled by the densely packed snow filling your throat. The last thing you see is Big Bird running to you wailing, "No, Neil! Not before we shoot *Sesame Street 2: Days of Grover Past!*"

Your body is never found.

THE END

It's a typical day. After a quick jaunt on the jetty boat to the restaurant overlooking St. Tropez—where you and a dozen beautiful young people savor a lunch of locally caught fish, ripe tomatoes the size of your head, and $400 bottles of *txakolina* (a delightfully refreshing dry Basque wine)—you reboard the 150-foot yacht for a sunny, champagne-filled cruise back to the colossal mansion on the hill with the commanding views of both the French Riviera and the Alps. Then, after a dip in the massive marbled azure infinity pool commanding the front terrace, you walk past the entire bedroom that's been converted into a storage room for china, pause to admire a coffee table whose smooth glass top is supported by a life-sized female mannequin in bondage on all fours, then make a quick pit stop in the gilt-and-marble bathroom before finally climbing the set of Carrara marble stairs for cocktails and dinner with Bono.

No, seriously.

You are really doing this.

You are doing this, and all kinds of indescribable other things like this, and you're doing them for an entire week, and you'll probably be doing them for one week a year *every year for the rest of your life.*

You shit you not.

You are doing this because you and your partner David (Burtka) have become very close friends with Sir Elton John and his partner David (Furnish), and you now have a visa to Elton-world, which depending on how one looks at it is either realer or more fantastic than Disney World, but inarguably spanglier.

As you ascend the staircase, you reflect on your history with the man. You first meet him in 2009. You're backstage at the Tony Awards, and there's a guy sitting in a chair, and he reaches out his hands to you, and Oh your god it's Sir Elton John. He kisses you on the lips and tells you he's glad you're hosting, that he had a thing for you when you were on *Doogie Howser,* and that you should hang out sometime. You say that sounds amazing, walk away, and squee.*

Then a few months later, at the banquet for *Time*'s 100 Most Influential People of the Year, one of whom you inexplicably are, you feel a tap on your shoulder. It's David Furnish stopping by to say hello. And inviting you over to his table with Elton. And giving you a card with their phone numbers and e-mail addresses on it. But when the squeeing subsides, you and (your) David get into the same prolonged discussion of etiquette you've had before: when one gay couple asks another out for dinner, is it the same as a date? If so, does it seem desperate to call them that night? Do you wait a day? Three days? Oh, and what if the other couple *is David Furnish and Elton John*? What would you even say when you called back? "Hi, one of the greatest songwriters of the twentieth century, it's Neil and David from the *Time* magazine gala! Wassssuppp?!? You down for Applebee's?" In the end you're so paralyzed by insecurity you never call them.

For the cardinal sin of not once but twice forsaking the amiable overtures of Elton and David, you deserve never to be graced by their majestic presence again. But fate is inexplicably kind. Two years later, while your twins are in utero, you and

---

* "Squee." 1 (*verb*): To emit an onomatopoetic girlish swooning sound out of pure fanboy adulation. 2 (*noun*): the sound itself.

David B. decide to take one last couple's vacation to the Greek island of Mykonos. It's a fantastic place with spectacular sights, including a nude beach ambitiously but more or less accurately called Super Paradise. You very much want to go *au naturel* but feel insecure about being nude on a beach among hundreds of smart-phone-bearing tourists. (Posed, well-framed paparazzi photographs of your face and clothed body are one thing; candid, weird-angled pictures of Neildini and his two spherical assistants are another entirely.)

So you put on short shorts and find a couple of discreetly placed chairs and begin drinking to still your beating, dick-pic-fearing heart when David says, "Hey, look over there! Is that David Furnish?"

Yep. That's David Furnish.

"Yep, that's David Furnish."

"Go talk to him!"

"I'm not going to go talk to David Furnish at the gay nude beach in Mykonos! I don't even know him!"

"He gave you his card! He wanted to hang out!"

"We're on a gay nude beach in Greece. Everybody already *is* 'hanging out.'"

David does not find this funny.

"Neil, go talk to David Furnish *now!*"

So you begrudgingly get up and go over and say hello, and David and his friends couldn't be nicer, and invite you and David to join their little group. Elton isn't with them, but that night you and David B. are sitting at Mykonos's famous ~~Applebee's~~ Nobu Matsuhisa restaurant with David Furnish and a dozen gorgeous guys whom it is entirely possible he and Elton packed in their luggage. (That is a joke. Sir Elton never travels with luggage.)

As the meal and the drinks come and go, the two Davids hit it off particularly well. Must be a "David" thing, you suppose. David B. is as excited as you are about your imminent fatherhood, and as their conversation turns slightly personal and the booze starts kicking in he decides to violate your pact of strict confidentiality. He leans over and says, "Neil and I have a secret to tell you. We're expecting twins through surrogacy, in the middle of October."

At which point David F. blanches, looks around furtively to make sure no one else is listening, and says, "That's unbelievable, because I have a secret for you: Elton and I are expecting a child in late December through surrogacy!"

Your jaws nearly fall into your *txakolina*. What are the odds? What are the chances of two male-male celebrity couples randomly bumping into one another in Mykonos—granted, Mykonos *is* the most likely place for two celebrity gay couples to randomly bump into each other, but it's still pretty unlikely—and discovering they're *both* simultaneously going through the exact same process of hope, disappointment, breakthrough, setback, paranoia, and anticipation known as surrogacy?

From that moment, you were fast friends, you reflect while toweling off from your dip in the pool and pondering whether to take a quick drive to Monte Carlo in one of the convertibles Elton and David keep on hand for their guests' disposal. The shared uniqueness of your circumstances serves as a bond. Within a week Elton is flying the two of you on his private plane to San Diego and back to attend one of his concerts. And a few weeks later, he invites you to spend a week at his house in Nice for the first time. And here you are. And holy shit.

You reach the place by climbing a curving road up Mont Boron surrounded by pine trees until you reach a big set of metal gates. They open, and you behold emerald green lawns, a flower garden radiating every color of the rainbow, and a magnificent pool fronting a villa one can only assume Elton time-shares with God. It's got a gym and a massage therapist and spectacular gardens and a tennis court and a delightful staff and when you wake up in the morning all your laundry is washed and folded and put away more neatly than you could ever possibly do yourself. And tasteful? You want tasteful? *The entire place was designed by Gianni Versace.* Everything, from the layout of the house down to the design of the toilet-paper-holder thingies. It's a world beyond the beyond, one of the most extraordinary and exclusive destinations to which any human could ever dream of getting invited.

You quickly learn that the only time you are expected to be anywhere is dinner. Guests assemble in semiformal attire, at seven o'clock. Elton shows up in whatever specific diamond-and jewel-encrusted clothing he's chosen for the night. Could be diamond-studded shoes. Could be a watch with sixteen rubies floating in it. Also, his suit might be purple, or yellow, or orange. It would not shock you at all to learn he has infrared clothing.

Caviar is served, because why does caviar exist if not to be served at the cocktail hour of a party in Nice, and then you go in for dinner. On any given night your fellow guests might be Tim Rice or Elvis Costello or Gwen Stefani and Gavin Rossdale or any of dozens of endlessly fascinating people. This evening the dinner guests happen to include Bono and his wife, Alison (Mrs. Bono?), and The Edge and his wife, Morleigh (Mrs. The?). Bono is an incredibly charismatic, interesting, and interested person, and yes, he *does* keep the sunglasses on indoors. You hit it off splendidly; he's very much a classic Irish storyteller in the style of James Joyce, or Denis Leary. Later, you will all go to a private VIP room at the Monte Carlo Casino and hang out with Prince Albert and his fiancée and Liza Minnelli, who will sing for you.

That last bit may have been slightly exaggerated but still, not bad for a Tuesday.

When living in Elton's world, your natural tendency to observe yourself living your life kicks into hyperdrive. Take last night. Elton decided he wanted to get dinner at La Petite Maison, one of the best restaurants in all of France, and therefore the world.

So his drivers and security people prepared two 1955 convertible Bentleys to chauffeur you and David B. in one car, Elton and David F. in another. And you cruised downhill through the streets of Nice as the perfect sun set over the perfect sea and people stared and waved, and all you could think was, *I'm in a James Bond movie. I'm in a James Bond movie. Any moment an agent from Spectre is going to start shooting at me from a passing Rolls-Royce. But that's okay because then my car will release oil from its trunk and make the Spectre car crash.*

It's funny to watch yourself grow quickly and eerily adjusted to your surroundings. On the first morning you timidly ask Laurent and George, the two wonderful assistants whose job it is to provide guests with whatever they need, "George? Laurent? Would it be possible to have a cappu—?" A hot frothy cup sits steaming in front of you before you can even say "-ccino". Then Laurent says he's ready to prepare you whatever breakfast your heart desires, and the very idea that your heart could desire a breakfast nearly moves you to tears. Yet within forty-eight hours this insane, impossible idea that you can have whatever you want to eat at any time becomes so second nature to you that you find yourself barking orders like: "George! Laurent! Ripe blueberries, please!" and "George! Laurent! My 85 percent pure dark Guatemalan hot chocolate has lost its heat! *Qu'est-ce que se passe?*"

And at the center of this world sits this incredible force of nature named Elton John. You have seen him walk through a Dolce & Gabbana store that's been opened just for him, saying, "We'll take this one and this one and those five over there and Neil, pick out whatever you like." (This puts you in an awkward if enviable position: Do you pick out the $7,000 super-kick-ass dinner jacket? Or do you not because you don't want to be that guy buying the most expensive thing, even though he said to pick whatever you want and it doesn't really mean anything to him financially? Best play it safe and get the medium-priced thing, which in this case is a mere $800. Man, are some ethical dilemmas more fun than others or *what?*)

What is easy to overlook is that the man is so fundamentally *nice*. He did not grow up rich; he spent most of his childhood living in a lower-middle-class semidetached house. And despite the superficial pomp and circumstances he retains a deep-seated humility. He's *genuinely* liked by almost everyone he encounters. He's very well informed, spending much of his morning reading every newspaper under the sun. (This works out great, since so much of your time with him is spent under the sun.) Plus he's hilarious. He has a habit of walking around singing songs, his own and others, and replacing the lyrics with filthy words. "Can You Feel the Love Tonight?" for example. There are several variations of this lyric that he likes to sing, soulfully. It is never not funny. And David Furnish is every bit as full and extraordinary a human being. He's an accomplished film producer who has devoted his life to his family and to leading the Elton John AIDS Foundation, which has raised over $200 million to support HIV/AIDS programs in more than fifty countries. He showers you and your David with respect and guidance every time you visit.

Despite their lifestyle, there is nothing remotely snobbish about them. One year they show up at your nice-but-not-Nice-nice house in LA for the Super Bowl. Several security personnel hover outside on the street, but inside your two guests make themselves perfectly at home, friendly, gracious. Elton lolls around in a tracksuit watching the game, talking about the players, yukking it up with your buddies. When he and David leave, your friends have to stop and take a moment and pinch themselves. One of them jokes, "That was an amazing Elton John impersonator you hired."

It's this very normalcy and personal ease that makes it so strangely *not* strange to spend family time with them, to watch the four kids play with one another in the garden (they have a second child in 2013), or to see them reading bedtime stories to their kids just as you do to yours. Elton keeps photo albums full of Polaroids of every guest who's ever stayed with him. One day you look through a bunch of previous albums. In years past they were full of half-naked people doing or about to do very naughty things, but the recent albums are far more G-rated because they are *literally* full of kids, theirs and yours and many others. Elton has become a bona fide family man.

A family man who, when you mention you need a backpack for a quick trip, gives you a $3,000 Yves St. Laurent bag to keep.

Which is why, even though it feels like destiny that your David spotted Elton's David on Mykonos at precisely the same imminently momentous occasion in all four of your lives, and you hope and believe those lives will remain intertwined forever; and even though there could be no more pleasant experience in the entire world than spending a week at Elton John's "summer house" on the French Riviera; despite all that, it is probably good for your soul when those weeklong trips are over, and the none-too-friendly clerk at the airport, who cares not even *un peu* in whose house you have been vacationing, orders you to slap down $150 for each piece of oversize luggage.

It's a bracing but necessary swift slap in the face.

Time to go back to reality.

To tweet about how awesome Sir Elton John is, go on to the next page.

To live a life in which you never meet Sir Elton John,
turn to page 19.

To spend more time with Sir Elton John, go back to the top of this chapter
and reread it. Continue as needed. Don't be ashamed.
Why would you want to leave?

Neil Patrick Harris
@ActuallyNPH

Tweets

You first hear about Twitter from Felicia Day, your *Dr. Horrible* costar. "You've got to try Twitter," she said. "Sounds stupid," you say.

about 3 hours ago

You're not sure about social media. AOL chat rooms helped you come out. But Facebook? "Neil! It's Jeremy from PE class! Let's do lunch!" #worst

about 3 hours ago

But Twitter quickly goes from want to need so you cave in, thinking it will just be a thing to send your friends funny pictures.

about 3 hours ago

But within a week, with no promotion, you have 30,000 followers. Soon, everywhere you go, you tweet about it. #YouWinFelicia

about 3 hours ago

 You learn your lesson on Twitter early on when an aging soap star is slated to play Robin's father on HIMYM.

about 3 hours ago

 The night before taping the star backs out 'cause "he didn't have enough lines" and "the part wasn't big enough." He screws the cast over, and you're furious:

about 3 hours ago

 ███████████ *is a d-bag. The actor, (Robin's dad) agreed to a cameo, then last night bailed, saying the part wasn't 'substantial' enough.*

about 3 hours ago

 Turns out the soap's on CBS, and within 7 minutes your publicist calls and says take it down. "No," you say. "Yes!" he says. And he's right.

about 3 hours ago

Sure enough, it turns into a moderately big story you bear the brunt of. Lesson: don't ever call anyone a d-bag on Twitter. Even d-bags.

about 3 hours ago

 You even launch an offshoot account, @NPHFoodPorn, strictly to show pics of great meals. (Some non-foodie fans find them odious.)

about 3 hours ago

 Now you love Twitter. You like the brevity. 140 characters, that's it. It keeps you from ranting.

about 3 hours ago

 You like giving shout-outs to friends and crafting bite-sized tweets and purposely only following exactly 69 people. #heh #heh

about 3 hours ago

Turn to page 285.

*Unless you prefer the number 233,
in which case turn to that page.*

It's the night before Super Bowl XLVI (spoiler alert: Giants 21, Patriots 17), and you are in the host city of Indianapolis, attending something officially known as The DirecTV Super Saturday Night Hosted by Mark Cuban's HDNet and Peyton Manning, although in reality it's a Katy Perry concert.

Earlier this afternoon you'd participated in The DirecTV Sixth Annual Celebrity Beach Bowl, playing flag football with Joe Manganiello and Kate Upton and Artie Lange and other equally random people on a gigantic artificial beach built underneath a gigantic heated tent that was erected in the outfield of the local triple-AAA ballpark and then filled with 700 tons of sand, a few artificial palm trees, a full concert stage, and many other wonders dreamed up by the good people in the publicity department of DirecTV.

Now it's early evening, and Katy Perry has taken the stage with a gaggle of gay dancers (and yes, "gaggle" is the proper term for a group of gay dancers). You've worked with Katy before* and had a great time, and now you and David are in the VIP section trying to enjoy her concert. But it's a little crowded and hard to see, so you leave that area and join the rest of the concertgoers nearby so you can really soak up Katy in all her big-bosomed blue-haired glory when *boom!*

Someone kicks you in the ass. Like, *hard.*

---

* On *How I Met Your Mother,* episode 127: "Oh Honey." She played Zoey's dumb cousin, and did so with the skilled comic chops of someone who in reality is as smart as a whip.

You stumble forward a few steps, then turn around to see the culprit. It's a twentysomething girl with a beer in her hand. She has a sullen, vapid expression on her face, and she's standing next to her equally sullen and vapid twentysomething friend.

You shout, "Did you just *kick* me?"

She ignores you, even though you're five feet away and closing in rapidly.

"Excuse me," you repeat, "but did you just, like physically kick me in the ass?"

In the half second you wait for her response you silently reflect on the irony that while people threaten to "kick someone's ass" all the time, rarely is the act *literally* done.

"Yeah, whatever," she goes. (She is the kind of person who "goes" things rather than "says" them.)

"No, *not* whatever," you say. "You don't just kick somebody. Don't *ever* kick me! What the fuck is wrong with you?"

And she goes, "I don't care, you're a faggot so it doesn't matter what you say."

Wow. Just, wow.

David's fists start clenching. He gets up in the girl's face. "What'd you call him? What'd you call him?" You hold him back. It's such an intense experience, not only because in and of itself it's crazy, but because it makes you understand how lucky you are as a gay man to be living in Hollywood. You're exposed to all kinds of tabloid gossip and internet slander living in LA, but in general you no longer have to worry about total strangers kicking you in the ass and calling you a faggot. This is extreme homophobia, and it justifies an equally extreme response. Someone's calling you a faggot? Well, you know exactly what you have to do:

Calmly notify the proper authorities.

You walk to the nearest security guys and say, "Hey, that girl over there just physically accosted me and called me a faggot.

Can you get her kicked out of here?" They are happy to oblige. So
you point her out and stand behind her as the men approach. She
ignores them, then tries to disappear into the crowd, then screams
"Get your hands off me!" as they physically escort her out. Oh,
and best of all, best of *all,* you find out later they ended up putting her in jail for the night for resisting arrest outside the venue.

Let that be a lesson, homophobes, you think proudly. *You wanna
try to bully me? Prepare to get calmly notified the shit out of.*

The DirecTV people get wind of the situation. They feel so
bad they take you to Katy's private VIP section, just offstage. You
enjoy the rest of the concert and hang out backstage with Katy
and her gaggle. Look, there's Peyton Manning! He walks up to
you and says, "Hey, I'm having a party at my apartment. You
wanna stop by?"

Sure, you'll stop by. It's Peyton F'ing Manning. (The "F" is for
football.)

As a courtesy you tell Katy where you're going, and politely invite her to come with you, figuring (a) Peyton wouldn't mind, and
(b) no way will Katy Perry want to come. But she says, "Sure, let's
go." And you and David get in the car, wondering, "Is Katy Perry
really, legitimately, going to meet us at a party at Peyton Manning's house? Because it seems like the amount of pure random-
ness that would open a hole in the space-time continuum right in
the middle of Peyton Manning's apartment."

But you get there, and soon enough Katy shows up, only it's
not just Katy: *it's her entire gaggle of gays.* And now the party
consists of Peyton and his wife, the small remaining group of
(presumably) straight local businessmen and their wives, and
you and your (presumably) gay husband, and Katy Perry and
her entourage of ten bright, colorful, hilarious, wonderful people,
dressed at least to the nines if not the tens, joking and laughing and drinking and generally acting like you would expect the
ten-gay-man entourage of Katy Perry to act at a party at 2:00 a.m.

They take over the place. Their energy fills the room. Dance music starts blaring, loud.

But it's cool, and it's fun, and Peyton and his wife are awesome, and everyone gets along, and you all end up staying till four 'cause you're having such a blast. And then the next day you watch the Super Bowl from Bob Kraft's suite alongside Michael Douglas and Pat Riley.

So all in all it's a good weekend, except for the one thing.

For a 100 percent gay-friendly vacation, turn to page 285.

For a 100 percent straight-friendly musical number, turn to page 227.

In either case, feel free to stick around the end of this chapter for a few minutes and schmooze with Michael Douglas. Did you know he produced One Flew over the Cuckoo's Nest? *It's true! Ask him about it.*

In 2009 you host the Emmys for the first time to widely favorable reviews. You have solid jokes, a wickedly witty and on-point opening number courtesy of your old partners-in-crime Marc Shaiman and Scott Wittman, and a whole lot of goodwill. Last year's ceremony was infamously cohosted by five reality-show stars—Heidi Klum, Jeff Probst, Tom Bergeron, Howie Mandel, and Ryan Seacrest. Individually, any one of them might have been fine, but as a quintet they were, in the words of the *Los Angeles Times,* a "historical disaster." (Really? Come on. Chernobyl was a historical disaster. The 2008 Emmys were a less-than-fully-realized awards show.) As a result, the bar has been set at ground level. You leap over it, then sit back and let critics call you a high-jumper.

But four years later the Emmys ask you back again, and this time the reviews afterward are more mixed. All right, not mixed; negative. All right, not afterward; *during.* Steven Levitan, the creator of *Modern Family,* calls them "the saddest Emmys ever" *while accepting his Emmy.* That's not good. In fact, if anything, it's ungood.

What goes wrong? In a word, *death.* A lot of famous television figures have passed away over the previous twelve months. This is not in itself uncommon. Over the years it's become quite customary for TV stars to end their careers by dying. Usually these deaths are noted in a single "In Memoriam" montage, but this year Ken Ehrlich, a really nice guy and a show business veteran, decides to give lengthy, star-studded tributes to *five* different recently departed figures. Edie Falco remembers James Gandolfini; Rob Reiner salutes Jean Stapleton; and most controversially Jane Lynch pays tribute to Cory Monteith, the *Glee* star who had just died of a heroin overdose. To her credit, Jane speaks very honestly about the senselessness of Cory's death, and insists that we run an antidrug public-service announcement immediately after. But many people still deem it wrong to single him out for remembrance. (The late Jack Klugman's family is angry *he* wasn't singled out for commemoration, and you can't really blame them.) The larger point is, at five different times over the course of the night, the show goes to commercial with the stench of death—tragic early death, in Gandolfini's and Monteith's cases—in the air. You voiced concerns about this beforehand, but they were not heeded. Sure enough, from a hosting standpoint, their deaths spell *your* death.

And that's not to mention Carrie Underwood's mournful version of "Yesterday" marking the fiftieth anniversary of JFK's assassination. Or your buddy Elton John's sad ballad in honor of Liberace. Or the Emmy for Outstanding Writing for a Drama Series being presented posthumously to the writer Henry Bromell. By the end of the night, you're surprised the Grim Reaper himself hasn't started escorting the winners offstage and into eternity. Afterward Steven Levitan elaborates on his onstage comments: "Poor Neil Patrick Harris, who was so brilliant, had to keep digging himself out of the holes dug by these sad moments, time and time again. It was very difficult." Yes. Yes it was.

Aside from all that there's *still* an "In Memoriam" section, and a few days before air the producer shows it to you, because he's very proud of what he's done with it. Instead of just cutting or dissolving from one face to the next, he's *morphed* them into each other. That thing they do in Michael Jackson's "Black or White" video? That's what he's done with two dozen dead members of the Academy of Television Arts and Sciences.

Oh, dear lord.

It takes an extraordinary amount of begging and cajoling by you and the writers to persuade him to replace it with a more conventional montage, and thank god. As deathly as the show turns out to be, that would have been deathlier. It would have forever banished the "In Memoriam" video to the realm of an "In Memoriam" video.

There are also more than the usual amount of booking issues. You can't always get who you want, as the Rolling Stones nearly said. Booking is always an issue with awards shows; a lot of ideas rely entirely on the participation of specific people, and if they are unwilling or unable to be involved you're screwed. In some cases, that's probably for the best. There's an attempt to arrange a running bit throughout the broadcast of an "Emmy kiss-cam" that will feature random celebrities kissing backstage. It's another idea you're skeptical about, and apparently so is everyone else: No one is willing to do it. No one. Not even *actual married couples*. You mercifully kill the Emmy kiss-cam a few days before the broadcast.

But in some cases it's more heartbreaking. Ken had talked to the White House about the possibility of getting President Obama to appear on the show. It's a great idea. Although you don't keep up with politics, you've heard that Obama is considered powerful in certain circles. So you and the writers come up with a pretaped bit involving TV presidents—Tony Goldwyn (*Scandal*), Billy Campbell (Lincoln in *Killing Lincoln*), Julia Louis-Dreyfus (*Veep*—she is "just" the vice president, which was the joke), and Jay Pharoah (*SNL*'s kick-ass Obama impressionist). You will intercut among them as they say things as if they had actual authority, and then at the end Obama will appear and essentially remind them who the real president is.

You get the draft out to the actors, and immediately the attrition begins. You lose Billy Campbell right away—he's in Canada shooting. Scheduling also proves too much of an issue for Julia.

You write a new draft replacing her with Martin Sheen as President Bartlet from *The West Wing*, but when Sheen says he wants Aaron Sorkin to rewrite his parts, it's another fond farewell.

A revised draft with only Tony, Jay, and Obama goes to the White House. They approve, with the caveat that we add a mention or two of the Affordable Care Act rollout that is happening around the same time. This is problematic. To have the president appear merely in his capacity as president is one thing, but having him soft-sell policy initiatives is quite another. You pretape Tony's and Jay's parts and schedule a taping at the White House, but you feel conflicted. As it happens you are not nearly as conflicted as Syria, which that week explodes into a full-on international humanitarian crisis, taking with it any chance the president would want to participate in your silly little Emmy bit.

Oh, plus there's no opening number.

To pull off one of the more extraordinary musical numbers ever on live TV, turn to page 238.

To continue hosting the Emmys, go on to the next page.

A few months earlier you'd opened the Tonys with "Bigger," one of the more extraordinary musical numbers ever pulled off on live TV. You don't want to compete with that, so for the first time at a major awards show you eschew* an opening number. (Instead you include a number in the middle of the show. It's called "The Number in the Middle of the Show," and that's exactly what it is, an absurd uptempo sparkly dancy thing, costarring your buddies Nathan Fillion and Sarah Silverman, that provides a nice little boost of midfuneral energy.)

Your opening is a pretaped bit in which you sit in a chair and binge-watch every episode of every nominated show, followed by an opening monologue that's "interrupted" by previous Emmy hosts—Jimmy Kimmel, Jane Lynch, Jimmy Fallon, and Conan O'Brien. It turns out their interruption has been orchestrated by Kevin Spacey as Frank Underwood. The bit is good, but it's not jumping-through-a-hoop-then-disappearing-from-the-stage good.

After a show like this, you make an effort to learn lessons so that you can do better in the future. You make that effort for approximately twelve hours, until you get the news that the ratings for the Emmys were the *highest* in eight years. At which point you realize that the true lesson is the usual lesson, which is that there is no lesson.

To spend more time with Nathan Fillion, turn to page 181.

To spend more time with Sir Elton John, turn to page 244.

* Gesundheit.

And now a word from your friend . . .

SARAH SILVERMAN

We met backstage at something about six years ago. What was it? The shitty Creative Arts Emmys before the real Emmys? I don't remember. I just remember exchanging mild but genuine dick sucks (on my end anyway). Through the years after that we would see each other, schmooze with each other, and move on. Then eventually, mostly through David, we exchanged info and took that next step from fake show-biz friendship toward *real* show-biz friendship.

When you and David saw I had nowhere to go one Christmas Eve (it was really no tragedy—I'm a stay-home-on-holidays kind of Jew anyway), you would *not* have it. I went to your beautiful, warm, art-filled home, ate special veggie food David made for me, which was probably the best food I've ever had, and was allowed to go home—after a long night of food, laughing, and games—only after accepting a giant bag filled with presents. One, a brush, is still my brush. My one brush.

Then you and I were both cast in Seth MacFarlane's comedy western *A Million Ways to Die in the West*. I was so happy I had a friend in the cast. You remember, we were shooting the movie in this small town in New Mexico known for its turquoise jewelry, crystals, and dreamcatchers, where there's almost no place to get food after 9:00 p.m. I hadn't had a social night out in two weeks until the night I e-mailed you and asked if you wanted to get dinner. You texted me you were downstairs in my hotel lobby getting a drink. I quickly took a puffsky as I'm wont to do before a fun dinner out, then ran down to meet you.

We walked to the only place open, a pizza place called The Upper Crust (not the one in Boston). It was empty and the burnouts working there were jazzed to see us, which was nice. We ordered pizzas and you got a beer, because you're a man, and sat at a table outside. We gabbed and laughed and were having a great old time until you looked down at your phone and saw that David was calling. As I overheard (listened in) on your conversation I began to feel an *intense* pain in my side that went up to my shoulder. So while you were having a conversation with David, I had one with myself consisting of gentle but desperate assurances that I was fine and not dying and please don't blow your first night out with another human being in two weeks on some phantom pain.

Meanwhile, poor David was at his wit's end, alone with the twins, one of whom would *not* go to bed. David was trying his best to be loving but stern, but he is weak with the kids, as I would undoubtedly be if I had them. I can't take kids' tears. Somewhere in my screwed-up head I feel like they're crying about the Holocaust or Darfur and it seems so wrong to ignore.

You were the perfect husband—feeling terrible and guilty that you weren't there to help and instead having a great night with your superfunny comedian friend, Sarah. But even as I registered this, the world got really far away and I felt a familiar feeling. I knew I was going to faint. It's something I've always done infrequently—maybe once a year or so—but when it happens there's nothing I can do about it, and it was coming. You saw it on my face before I could even say anything.

"Are you about to pass out?"

I remained calm, and would have laughed if I weren't so totally outside of my body already. I managed to say, "I am fine. I faint sometimes. I will be 100 percent fine. I need to lie on the ground with my feet up is all. If the guys from the restaurant look over, tell them I tweaked my back and I'm just lying flat for a second."

And down I went.

It happened a couple times, and both times you held my hand and were so loving. Little gestures like that mean so much. I had accepted already that this was wildly embarrassing for both of us and apologized while floating in and out. I remember saying, "I didn't want David to have all the attention." You laughed and said, "Now I don't have to feel bad that I was out having a good time without him! This sucks!"

When I returned to my body, you walked me home and safely to my little room. I ate some olives I had bought and the salt brought me fully back.

And that's that. The moral is, never leave home without Neil Patrick Harris and/or olives.

To appear in a musical number with Sarah, turn to page 259.

Everything you've learned and achieved as an actor, performer, entertainer, and host culminates in 2014 when you play the title role in the Broadway revival of the rock musical *Hedwig and the Angry Inch*, which after nine years on *HIMYM* you instinctively refer to as *HATAI*.

The producer of the show, David Binder, had approached you as early as 2007 about portraying Hedwig, the tragic, triumphant, transsexual German-American rock star. You've been a fan and admirer of the piece ever since you saw its legen—wait for it—dary run at the Off-Broadway Jane Street Theater in 1998, which starred its creator, John Cameron Mitchell, singing with a band led by the show's songwriter, Stephen Trask. Both that production and the subsequent movie version had achieved cult status, but the creative team had long and correctly felt *Hedwig* deserved a broad(way)-er audience. They were seeking a more mainstream star, you were their first choice, and they were willing to wait a few years—until Ted Mosby finally met his soulmate—to snap you up.

But *why*, exactly, would you want to take on that role? Two major aspects of both Hedwig and *Hedwig* seemed to go against your performance grain. Hedwig is feminine, alluring, a convincing-enough woman for her innocent male teenage protégé to fall in love with, and you are . . . not. In fact over the years you've gone out of your way to eliminate any traces of femininity from your behavior. It's what's enabled you to credibly play Barney Stinson on *HIMYM*. So how are you going to pull off the part of a man who's had his part pulled off?*

Then there's the rock 'n' rolliness of it. The music in *Hedwig* is 100 percent straight-up rock 'n' roll, and that too has never been your style, either vocally or personally. Your musical tastes run more toward show tunes and the big band era, and though you've done a lot of singing onstage it's never been in the rock idiom. The closest you've come was *Rent*, but that eclectic score was more of a rock/show-tunes hybrid. Will you be able to get your voice to sound genuinely rock 'n' roll? And if so, will you have the discipline and endurance to keep it that way for a four-month run?

These are challenges, but the challenges are exactly what make it so appealing. The challenges, coupled with the fact that the show and the character are just so good, so rich, so human, so vital. She is a truly larger-than-life figure, and she'd better be, because the entire show is pretty much her. She's onstage for the entirety of the show; she has all the dialogue and almost all the singing, and not a small amount of dancing, either. She has to be a dazzling spellbinder displaying complete control of the band behind her, the audience in front of her, the story within her . . . everything, except the potent emotions and resentments that flare up and eventually burst through in a climax filled with rage, forgiveness, and catharsis. It's a live high-wire act with a great degree of difficulty. And yet with its emphasis on risk and physicality and showmanship (not to mention costume and hair changes) it is the logical end point of the progression of live high-wire acts you've done up to now: *Rent* and *Cabaret* and *Assassins* and "Not Just for Gays Anymore" and "Bigger." After all, the premise of the show is that you're giving a concert to a large

---

* *Note:* It is scientifically impossible to talk about *Hedwig and the Angry Inch* for five minutes without making a double entendre about penises.

group of theatergoers. In a sense, *Hedwig* would be the ultimate host job.

You're so in.

And thus begins a rehearsal period unlike any you have ever had, and probably unlike any you ever will have. This is no mere matter of learning blocking and memorizing lyrics. This requires total absorption and transformation, and it starts with your body. Starting six weeks before the end of the TV show, your diet and exercise routine changes completely. To make yourself more slender and wispy you do copious amounts of cardio and quasi-yogic stretching exercises, and substitute late-night sushi binges with regularly scheduled bottles of liquid kale. As a result you lose twenty-two pounds, develop an eight-pack, and have the most vivid, drool-inducing food dreams of your life.

And then there's the vocal training. At the start of rehearsals Stephen Trask compiles a playlist of songs by artists who inspired him and John when they wrote the show. He also gives you a videotape of some live rock performances to marinate your eyes, ears, and soul in. You begin working intensively with Liz Caplan. Officially Liz is *Hedwig*'s "vocal supervisor," but for you a better title would be "personal voice hero." With a rigorous and meticulous regimen, she begins shaping and strengthening your voice into a rock 'n' roll instrument—one up for the challenge of singing 100 minutes of emotive, frenzied music seven times a week.

Eventually Stephen and the director, Michael Mayer, send you out to perform as a rock singer. You end up fronting a couple of impromptu concerts at various Lower East Side bars, arriving unannounced, accompanied by Tits of Clay, the amazing band that Stephen pulled together for the show. The gigs go well, and they have the desired effect: you begin to understand and feel the mythic, sexual power wielded by the rock 'n' roll front man.

But you need to be a front *woman,* and your feminization is an ongoing process. You dye (head) and shave (body) your hair. The visionary costume designer Arianne Phillips fits you with a pair of custom heels, and from then on you and Michael Mayer and the routinely brilliant choreographer Spencer Liff devote countless hours to developing Hedwig's gestures, postures, and movements. For you the rigors of this are as much psychic as physical. Strutting around in a huge blonde wig and bra with your wrist cocked and your hips swaying does not come naturally to you. It feels a little weird. But that is the joy of it: the total commitment, the complete immersion into the role, the gradual replacement of self-conscious awkwardness with (literally) balls-out confidence.

Previews begin in March 2014, and soon a regular preshow routine develops. For an 8 o'clock curtain, you arrive at the Belasco Theatre around 5:30, relax, eat half a sandwich, answer a few e-mails, and try to relax. Then at around six o'clock you work with Liz for half an hour, either live or by FaceTime. She leads you in a series of focused vocal and physical drills that are effective, essential, and, from the point of view of an outsider, pretty funny. In one you sing an arpeggio on the sound "Heeeeee!" while biting on your pinky, then stop, say the word "Ping!", clear one nostril, then the other, and repeat the arpeggio a half note higher. In another you sing Mozartian-style trills with a ripped paper towel wrapped around your tongue. "Yegeeooweeooweeoooooowah," you intone in all twelve keys, up and down, doing it so often that the word "Yegeeooweeooweeoooooowah" begins to sound stupid.

At 6:30 you sit down for your session with the youthful Mike Potter, the makeup mastermind who did the designs for the original production and the movie. For forty-five minutes you lie *Sweeney Todd*–victim style on a fully reclined barber's chair while Mike and his nymphlike assistant Nicole lovingly subject your skin to a series of viscous substances including, but not limited to:

- Elmer's glue—applied to the eyebrows to keep them down.
- Orange concealer—to hide residual stubble shadow.
- Blush—to contour the jawline.
- Rouge—to give your cheeks a severe, pseudo-trashy look. (To achieve the necessary angularity, Mike places a piece of paper from the top of the ear to the corner of the lip and applies the rouge above it. The piece of paper is a folded page from *Guns & Ammo* magazine, which adds extra irony.)
- Fake eyelashes. (You like to fan them with an old-style Japanese fan to get them to dry faster.)
- And of course, glitter up the yin-yang.

The makeup mirror is decorated with photos of various rock 'n' roll idols (Bowie, Iggy, Lou Reed), along with a couple of random stock photos depicting life in East Germany back in the '70s. There's one picture of a forlorn young man sitting on the radiator watching a lousy TV show that you find endlessly fascinating, as it makes you imagine what Hedwig must have looked like as a young boy.

Mike usually has '80s music blasting during the makeup application. When he leaves you switch to dance music and do some exercises to get your blood pumping. Sit-ups always get you going. Then your invaluable dresser Danny starts helping you into your Hedwig outfit. Now, the character's "angry inch" is of course the "one-inch mound of flesh where [her] penis used to be." Given this, and that Hedwig wears tight pants, the first thing you do is get fully naked and put on a specially created undergarment that lifts your testicles above your wang and hides your Neil Jr. in a small little flap. The end result is the "Barbie-doll crotch" referred to in the show. If all goes well, it will be an inch that for you on-stage will *not* feel angry, and only occasionally itchy.

But wait, there's more, because Arianne Phillips has provided you with fishnet stockings, a bra with a mic inside, a black camisole, a sexy patchwork denim jumpsuit designed to resemble the Berlin Wall, giant glittery gold fuck-me boots, a green-and-gold neckerchief, and, courtesy of hair-mistress Perfidia, a gigantic blonde wig—the first of a half dozen you'll be wearing between now and 9:40.

Then, finally a walk backstage, past the five-piece band and supporting cast led by the incomparable Lena Hall (who plays Yitzhak), to upstage left, where you receive one final strap-on: you are strapped onto a flying harness from which you will momentarily make your first appearance onstage, descending from behind the proscenium like a sneering angel.

This is followed by 100 minutes of cooing, screaming, charming, grinding, sobbing, shredding, flirting, grieving, taunting, climbing the walls, licking the floor, gnashing your teeth, batting your eyes, spitting on a random audience member and lip-kissing another, baring yourself in every way, breaking yourself down, building yourself back up, and bowing.

And then, if it's Saturday or Sunday, hopping into the shower, removing all your makeup, and doing the whole thing over again an hour later.

It is nerve-racking, and to make things even harder on yourself you keep an active side schedule of promotional appearances and other work, and to truly abuse yourself you specifically ask the producers not to hire an understudy. You want to walk the tightrope day after day for four months, because what makes it nerve-racking is what makes it positively exhilarating. The reason for taking big risks is that they can bring big rewards, and night after night (and Sunday afternoons) you reap them. You are the center of a perfectly crafted 100-minute communion between actor and character, writer and interpreter, and entertainer and audience. You walk offstage after every performance sore, exhausted, and alive to the core of your being. It is the most satisfying and complete role you ever play.

But *Hedwig*'s rewards extend beyond the dramatic. It gets you in shape. It raises your stature on Broadway. It makes you feel good about your decision to rededicate yourself to theater and helps justify your post-*HIMYM* decision to relocate your family permanently to New York, in a new town house in the same great Harlem neighborhood you'd lived in part-time for years. And the critical, commercial, and audience response is overwhelmingly positive. In the wake of great reviews and a massive promotional blitz the show sells out every performance, and within weeks of opening night you find yourself nominated for the entire gamut of theater awards . . . including the one you hosted with supreme biggiosity the previous year.

You are not one to belittle the importance of winning a Tony.* But you had no idea how nervous the desire to win one would make you. Knowing that the Tony-nominating voters were in the audience one week, and that the Tony-*awarding* voters were officially in the audience a few weeks later, but unofficially could be there at any time, lends a tense background feedback hum to your performances. It's true what they say—it's an honor just to be nominated. But darned if you aren't nervous as hell by the time Tony weekend rolls around. It's a spectacularly busy forty-eight hours. You are both nominated for an award and performing a song at the ceremony, and you squeeze in Tony rehearsals in the morning and early afternoon before heading off to do your usual two *Hedwig* shows. Then on Sunday you have an early-morning Tony dress rehearsal and a *Hedwig* matinee, after which you quickly don your tux, rush to Radio City, smile for the camera people, appear with Hugh Jackman in the opening number, frantically Hedwigize backstage, perform the song "Sugar Daddy"—during which you stroll through the audience, perform a lap dance on

---

* Come to think of it, you are the *last* person to belittle the importance of winning a Tony.

Sting, lick Samuel L. Jackson's glasses, and rub your junk in Orlando Bloom's face 'cause, I mean, you can—then frantically de-Hedwigize backstage and return to your seat to wait for Audra McDonald, who that night becomes the most Tony-winning actress of all time, to say who won the 2014 Tony Award for Best Actor in a Musical.

And the winner is . . . you!

You kiss David and walk onto the stage, basking in a standing ovation. A wave of gratitude and humility sweeps over you. You accept Audra's warm embrace and shiny trophy and begin:

> *A year ago I was hosting the Tonys. This is crazy-pants. . . . Playing Hedwig is an absolute joy. It is a role I was terrified of and taking it on has changed me and challenged me, and it's exhausting and it's so fun to perform it and I love doing it. . . . I'm such a fan of the show and John Cameron Mitchell and Stephen Trask, you've created a character that is so beautiful and songs that are so amazing to sing . . .*

Then, after thanking Michael Mayer, Liz Caplan, your spectacular personal dresser Danny Paul, the rest of your support team,* the three other members of Team Burtka-Harris, and the three original Ruidosan members of Team NPH, you do something you know better than anybody can be murder on an awards show—you go long and talk over the exit music. But you can't help it. The poignancy of the moment requires one final callback.

> *Lastly, I would just like to say thank you to the people who inspire us creatively like teachers: Churchill Cook, Danny Flores, Diane*

---

* Although you egregiously forget to mention two people on said support team: your brilliant publicist Shea Martin and your even brillianter assistant Zoë Chapin. Both extraordinary human beings, ridiculously hard workers, and lifelong friends. Your excluding them from your acceptance speech will haunt you for many lifetimes or, at least, weeks.

Keeson . . . these are teachers in small-town New Mexico who showed that when sports was the only option, creativity had a place in the world. And without them I would never be able to do any of this.

Lena wins for Best Featured Actress and most important, the show itself wins for Best Revival. Both awards are deserved, and both help rid you of any lingering suspicion that your Tony was given more as a token of appreciation for your work bolstering the theater than genuine recognition of a quality performance.

When your run ends in August you are good and weary. The show goes on, with the terrific Andrew Rannells taking your place, but you decide to take a brief respite from theater while you attend to a few other items of business, like promoting your upcoming bizarrely premised memoir. But the *Hedwig* experience never leaves you, any more than the experience of playing Toto as a ten-year-old in the Ruidoso High production of *The Wizard of Oz* could ever leave you. Looking back on your life, you realize one is only the natural outgrowth of the other. The boy enthralled by the way makeup could transform him from human to canine is now the man enthralled by the way makeup can transform him from Neil to Hedwig. It is still thrilling. It is still all about preparation, precision, commitment, and artifice. And, three decades later, it still draws you to the stage like a moth to the f(l)ame.

The only difference is that now, when Heineken Light calls offering you a whole bunch of money to endorse their beer, you don't have to turn them down on account of being underage.

You're ready for your closing number. Turn to page 288.

Your four-year-old twins, Gideon and Harper, share a number of relatively unusual characteristics. For example, they are the best kids in the whole wide world, yes they are.

Gideon is a boy. More accurately, he is a boy boy. He likes to play with pretend guns, which you've been told is normal. He is crazy about knights and swords and enjoys pretending he's galloping on his horse. Last Christmas you got him a drum set and he loved it. He also likes anything nautical and is especially obsessed with anchors, dating from the time when your friend Diana Jenkins let him pull up the anchor on her yacht. But his interests evolve rapidly. As you sit re-editing this manuscript, you realize that in the last few months he's entered his construction phase. He loves trucks, diggers, and cement mixers and walks around in a hard hat. By the time this book is published it is entirely possible he'll have moved on to online poker.

He is quiet, cerebral, a natural problem-solver. His vocabulary is amazing. At three years old he uses words like "gargantuan" and "barbarian." If you ask him if he wants something, he'll say, "I'd like that, perhaps." He likes making up stories about, oh, robots caught in a ditch but then the ditch has a spacecraft in it so he escapes in the spacecraft and flies into the mouth of a giant corn dog. That type of thing. (That plot still makes a lot more sense than *Purple People Eater*.) He is a lot like you. If you had to wager, you'd guess he is your biological son. But you don't have to wager, and it doesn't matter.

Harper is a girl. More accurately, she is a girl girl. She loves princesses. She is tender and kind. Last Christmas you got her a dollhouse and she loved it. She loves animals with an all-encompassing "Awwww, look at that ant, it's so sweet!" kind of love. She likes to put costumes and wigs on Watson, your big Labradoodle, and parade him around the house. (Watson is cool with it. Fred, your cairn terrier, is less so, and is not shy about yapping his disapproval.) She loves to play with her stuffed animals. Kitty Kitty is her pink cat. Pinky the Elephant is her security blanket. You repeatedly try to explain to her that Pinky is in fact a lifeless object incapable of independent thought, much less protection, but she refuses to listen. Instead she puts on "Let It Go" from *Frozen* and lets loose on the kitchen counter.

Harper has a big personality. If she doesn't get what she wants she can scream at the top of her lungs with a ferocity that suggests a future career in musical theater. When she is three, you catch her singing Miley Cyrus's "Wrecking Ball," a song nobody should sing until they're at least dead. She is also precocious. Sometimes you and David worry that you're raising a stripper because she has such an affinity for taking her clothes off. And what a shameless flirt! She has a boyfriend in her preschool class whom she is going to marry. As a two-year-old she climbs up a slide at a park in Harlem, waves to the basketball players at the nearby court, and shouts, "Hey boys, look at me!" She is sassy, extroverted, and nurturing. If you had to wager, you'd guess she is David's biological daughter. But you don't have to wager, and it doesn't matter.

Like many twins they always have each other's back and miss each other terribly when they're apart. They love to play games together and play robot or veterinarian or, when they're feeling fancy, robot veterinarian. One Saturday morning you're asleep when you hear a ruckus downstairs. (Parents are the only people who ever hear ruckuses.) You investigate and uncover a saltwater apocalypse: Gideon and Harper have opened the top of your fish tank, reached in, and tossed most of the coral out, and are now throwing things in—paper clips, pencils, chicken bones, whatever's around. They're not trying to hurt the fish; they're trying to feed them. But when you try telling that to the fish, they just don't want to hear it.

From the beginning they've been gourmets. This is largely due to the influence of their Daddy. (To the kids, David is "Daddy" and you're "Papa." You find it a more convenient system of nomenclature than "Daddy 1" and "Daddy 2," or "Sinners A and B.") David is a formally trained chef, and he does not let any junk food pass their lips. As soon as they're able to eat solid food, he goes to the market, buys fresh produce, and purees it himself. Every day. Then when they're ready for real food, he makes them *real* food. Curried carrots. Zucchini with *herbes de Provence.* As one-year-olds they wolfed down prosciutto, truffled cheese, and sushi. They love bold flavors. Harper's current favorite foods include lox and asparagus. Gideon frequently devours two sashimi platters at one sitting. Seriously. Two entire sashimi platters. And he's rail-thin. There may very well be a wormhole to another dimension somewhere in his digestive tract, because it is otherwise physically impossible to explain how so much food can disappear into such a little body.

They are not allowed to watch TV during the week. However, so as not to totally alienate them from the medium that has been so kind to Papa over the years, they are allowed *unlimited* TV time on the weekends, so long as it's kid-friendly. They enjoy this indulgence immensely. Harper will sometimes binge-watch three consecutive Disney movies. You don't see too much harm in this, although occasionally you worry it will give her the wrong idea about how much spontaneous singing and dancing takes place in castles and aquariums.

They are your children, Gideon and Harper, the ones you worked so hard to get, the ones you waited for so long, and you love them madly, crazily, bottomlessly. When you're home you spend as much time with them as you can, and every evening you and David read them good-night stories, then let them repeat them to you in their new and much improved way. But the realities of your job(s) require you to be away from them far more than you'd like. It's hard to conceive what parenthood was like before modern video technology. When you're gone you FaceTime them at least once a day (at bedtime). And you miss them like hell. And you and David tell them that Papa is gone doing things to help the family, which is true, but does nothing to allay the missing-like-hell. So you fly home as soon as you can, and savor as many moments of the terrible twos and the throttling threes as you can, because every moment is awesome.

One day their preschool teacher asks the students what they want to be when they grow up. Harper says, "A princess." Gideon says, "A doughnut."

Awesome.

To take your kids on a fun trip to Disney World, turn to page 285.

For a happy ending, turn to page 288. A real happy ending. Not a metaphorical "happy ending," sicko.

Although if you want that, that's back on page 78.

Y ou are, like, crazy loved.

On March 30, 2013, you receive an unmarked package containing a shovel, a flashlight, a key, Tums, Advil, and a bag of jelly beans, along with a note that reads, "Be ready to leave at 7:15 p.m." An hour later you arrive at your friends Dilson and Walter's house for what turns out to be a surprise party. The crowd sings "Happy Birthday." It's a surprise indeed, since your fortieth birthday isn't for another two months. Still, it's a very thoughtful and nice thing for David to have organized.

Over the course of the party you get drunk. You also receive forty mysterious white envelopes from random partygoers, bartenders, and even the DJ. At 2:30 a.m., you open them on your kitchen floor. Each envelope contains a jigsaw-puzzle piece. When put together they make a picture that says, "Life is a garden. Dig it." Evidently you are supposed to use the shovel and flashlight and dig up something in your garden. But where are you supposed to . . . wait a second, why is there a circular sign reading SCAN ME in your garden? Are you supposed to dig there? Yes, you are. What is it? It's a lockbox. Where's the key? Right, you got it before. Let's see what's in the box . . . an iPad mini! Thank you, David, what a great gift! Wait, if you point the mini at the SCAN ME sign, what happens? Holy crap, there's a video! It's David in a black-and-white parody of the opening of the old TV series *This Is Your Life*:

This is David Burtka, bidding you welcome to This Is Your Life.
Neil Patrick Harris, this is your life. Get ready to travel through time

into your distant past, and into the darkest recesses of your soul . . .
tomorrow, we begin our return to the past. And it's a long way from
here. Good luck.

Your mind-hole is blown.

The next morning another video awaits on your iPad. It's from your luminous friend Kate Jennings Grant, telling you to report to Whole Foods, where a vehicle waits for you. What kind of vehicle? She sings "Ride Sally Ride" as a clue. And where are you supposed to drive it? To the cabana where you got drunk on rosé with her last year . . . in Las Vegas.

What the?

You go to Whole Foods. There's a Mustang (Sally) waiting with part of a United States map inside. Four hours later you and David are in Vegas. You pull up to the spectacular Cosmopolitan resort and wander toward the pool. In the cabana you find wine, the key to a suite, and a certificate for a ninety-minute massage. The masseur hands you another card to scan. Now Kelly Ripa is telling you to go to the place where you skipped out on a tab four years earlier. It's Robuchon at the MGM Grand, one of the best restaurants in the world. You and David proceed to share a 581-course meal. At dessert the waiter hands you (surprise!) another card to scan. It's your hilarious buddy Lex Medlin telling you to report tomorrow morning to the place where he once dared you to eat something for $100. He's referring to Krispy Kreme at Circus Circus.

Thus ends day 2 of what will be an eight-day cross-country adventure organized and recorded for posterity by the wonderful David Burtka. For an entire week you travel around by bus, car, and private plane, receiving scannable cards from random people, watching old friends tell you where to go next, solving ingenious clues and having the best fortieth birthday it is conceivable to have. You train with Cirque du Soleil performers in Vegas. You visit your family in New Mexico. You go to San Antonio for a thrilling afternoon at the Ropes Course Canopy Challenge. You jet to Disney World and spend the night in the private suite at the top of the Cinderella Castle. (By the way, there's a private suite at the top of the Cinderella Castle.) All the while, waiters are dropping off clues in lieu of bills (how cool is that?), and you're decoding letter-shifted cryptograms to find driving destinations (how cool is *that*?), getting "pulled over" by fake cops who instead of a ticket give you a clue sending you to a free meal at your favorite Albuquerque restaurant, Frontier *(how cool is that?!?)*, and taking an emotional journey through forty years of memories and friendship, without the counterpoint of which the physical journey would be merely a fun vacation and not the incredible act of love and devotion it is.

At Frontier, a stranger asks for your autograph. Then he gives you a note: "John Wayne, draw!" What could that possibl— Oh, of course, that painting on the wall of John Wayne pointing a gun. Only what's that someone put on the gun? Another circular scanning card.

In your hotel in San Antonio you receive four glasses along with instructions on how much water to place in each one. When you strike them in the order provided in the clue, you hear the opening notes of "It's a Small World." Guess you're going to Disney World.

From there you fly a private plane to New York. At the Mondrian Hotel you find a piece of paper with Japanese writing taped to the mirror. The Japanese-speaking concierge reads it and tells you that you have an 8:30 reservation at Masa, which is one of the greatest sushi restaurants in the world. Fish line up to die at Masa. *That's* how good it is.

On the eighth and final day of your adventure of (at least the first half of) a lifetime, you are sent to three different New York City venues where you have performed. In front of each one is an envelope with a key. When you have all three, you're told to go to your favorite pre-theater bar. You order a tequila and are given a triple lockbox. Inside are the final pieces of the U.S. map you've been gathering throughout your trip. You assemble them all and see nothing. Then you turn them upside down. The back forms the mask logo from your favorite current off-Broadway show, *Sleep No More*. It says, "Be there at 7 p.m." That's in half an hour. You race there just in time to attend a performance . . . only tonight the show has been entirely reconceived to be about *you*, Neil Patrick Harris, right down to a re-creation of your childhood bedroom. An actress playing your mother tucks childhood "you" into bed and tells you a story.

> *There was once a little boy. He was my little prince. Everything was exciting and mysterious to him. Everything was possible. He loved playing with soldiers and cowboys. He took piano lessons too. I remember once he had a piano recital. I would nag him to practice over and over but he never listened. I never heard him play the whole piece. And then, the night of the recital, he walked right up to the piano and played it perfectly. Something about having an audience there made him come alive. You look just like him. Like the man I hoped he'd become.*

Your mind is melting. Your "mom" opens the door to send you on your way, and standing on the other side is a ten-year-old blond boy—a younger you—beckoning you to follow him as he takes off running down a hallway. So you are now Adult Neil chasing Childhood Neil away from the past, and through the shadowy corridors of the future. You eventually wind up in a darkened room. The lights kick on. And there your journey ends . . . with another fantastic surprise party filled with all your friends from New York.

And by your side, as he has been the whole time, is David Michael Burtka. The man who planned, produced, and organized the whole thing with the insight of someone who genuinely knows you better than you know yourself, and the wholehearted commitment of someone who quite possibly loves you better than you love yourself.

But also quite possibly, not as much as you love him.

THE END

You're on the Peter Pan's Flight ride at Disney World. You are forty years old going on five. Wheeeeeeeeeeee!

This is not your first time flying through the air with Hook, Smee, and Princess Tiger Lily. Oh no. When you were a child, your parents took you and your brother out of school for a week every year and drove you a thousand miles cross-country Griswold-style to vacation at Disneyland. You stayed at Howard Johnson's. (Having not yet at that point stayed at Elton John's, you considered it paradise.) And you fell utterly, *spiritually,* in love with the park. There is no bit of Disney magic that doesn't enchant you. The precision and brilliance of their parks reflect a true and deep understanding of the nature of entertainment. It's the same reason why later in your life you will fall in love with Las Vegas; it's little more than a giant theme park whose theme is theme parks. From the first day of your first trip, you consider yourself a citizen of the Magic Kingdom, despite your inherent distrust of their monarchical form of government.

As you grow up, your love for Disney and theme parks in general will not go unrequited. During the *Doogie* days, the Disney-MGM Studios flies you out with your friends and family and gives you free meals, VIP tours, and the works in exchange for appearing in a parade and doing a couple of interviews. It's called the Star Today program, and it's epic. You're still a kid, and you find being at the Disney-MGM Studios far more thrilling than being at *actual* studios.

But it is Disney with whom you end up forging a happy

(though not dopey or grumpy) relationship. You work with them in numerous capacities over the decades—everything from promotional appearances to hosting the star-studded launch of their latest cruise ship. And now, as in your childhood, you are once again a regular yearly visitor to the Magic Kingdom—only this time, they invite *you*. Every December you and your family travel to Orlando to participate in the annual Candlelight Processional. Thrice nightly for three nights, you recount the story of the first Christmas to a large audience at the American Pavilion in Epcot's World Showcase, accompanied by a full orchestra, two full-sized children's choirs, the entire Walt Disney World choir, and the Voices of Liberty, a professional, hyper-enunciated, ethereally-ten-part-harmonized a cappella group. You solemnly walk out to the lectern, intone "Let's begin," then serve as narrator and emcee for a fifty-minute ceremony of songs and Bible readings. (Spoiler alert: Christ the Savior is born.)

It's a thrill. First of all you're hosting, so it's physically impossible for you not to be enjoying yourself. But it feels particularly satisfying to read this biblical story to an audience that for the most part is well aware of your status as an openly gay man. You stand before thousands of people from all over the country and the world, some of whom no doubt have presupposed opinions about your "lifestyle," but who all nevertheless respectfully listen to your telling of the story of the birth of Jesus. You've never gotten any backlash, and neither has Disney, and neither, as far as you know, has Jesus.

Plus the gig comes with perks. During the day, you and your family have the time of your lives. You have your own guide; you don't wait in line for anything; your wish is Disney's command. Wanna see a fireworks show? We'll put you on a barge. Wanna see this parade? Here's a double-decker bus. Wanna go underneath the American Adventure ride and see how the pneumatics work? Be our guest. Turkey legs? Here are photos of the turkeys—choose your favorite! It's a very nice deal, especially for your kids. Gideon and Harper get to experience all of the good stuff and none of the bad.

And now for your hundredth time and their very first, you are boarding Peter Pan's Flight in Fantasyland. It's one of the few original Disney attractions still in operation, and of course you—savvy, sophisticated you—know all its secrets. You're familiar with how Omnimovers work, you've seen how Audio-Animatronic figures are programmed, you've studied the circuitry, you know where the speakers are. And knowing all this makes you greater appreciate the artistry, and you find yourself admiring the thousand little details that go into the ride. But some of the wonder, you admit to yourself, is gone.

Until you gaze at your two-year-old son sitting on your lap, and his twin sister, sitting on the lap of the man you love so much, and this five-minute climate-controlled adventure that you've grown a little jaded about is once more a spellbinding enchantment, because you're seeing it anew through their eyes. Gideon gapes at Captain Hook. Harper gasps at Peter soaring through the sky. They both squeal with delight as the crocodile does his dirty work. You experience *them* experiencing pure magic, unadulterated by cynicism or irony or self-consciousness. And as the ride makes its full circle, so do you, until Peter Pan has done it again, and you are once more a child, taking it all in, amazed, overwhelmed, enchanted.

Then it's over, and Gideon and Harper, these two little organic walking talking miracles that are somehow yours, are cheering at the end for the ride they called "Boat." "More, more!" they shout.

And so you cry your eyes out.

And you ride it again.

Go on to the next page.

[You speak the first two lines in rhythm.]

You started out your story as a child in Ruidoso.
You hoped for fame and glory, though your odds, at best,
were so-so.

[You start singing. Light music begins.]

Down life's long path you went, your
Route unplanned, your travels stressful.
You chose your own adventure . . .
And your choices were successful!

[Big brassy show music kicks in. A DOZEN HOT DANCERS join
you and dance with you all over the page.]

YOU MADE IT!
You made the trip from the past
All the way to the present!
YOU MADE IT!
Your journey's over at last,
And it wasn't unpleasant!

You turned a lot of pages.
You acted many ages.

You went through, and performed upon,
One hundred different stages!

[You jump through the fiery hoop below.]

[You hold for applause, then resume singing.]

YOU MADE IT!
You made your story a book,
And then sat down and read it!
YOU MADE IT!
You made the proofreader look
For one final ~~eddit!~~ *"edit."*

The only thing left pending
Is this, the happy ending—
Which everyone appearing in
The book will be attending!

[EVERYBODY mentioned in the book comes out and bows. Then they sing to you.]

You played Doogie Howser and met someone's mother!
You hosted four Tonys and hoisted another!
You acted with Smurfs and got high with two stoners!
You came to discover that men gave you boners!

[DAVID joins you onstage and kisses you.]

And now there you are, with the family you've started!

[GIDEON and HARPER join you. The four of you form a gorgeous tableau.]

You'll share new adventures for now still uncharted!
You've spun out a tale, and the tale is still spinning!
Your real happy ending is only beginning!

[Big key change. You and the CHORUS sing together as you take your final bow. Fireworks explode on the page.]

YOU MADE IT!
You reached the ending to start
Yet another transition!
YOU MADE IT!
But every moment's a part,
And you have to audition.

So go ahead and play some more pretend!
'Cause you made it!
You made it!
You made it to . . .

[You feel a tap on your shoulder. It's your twelve-year-old self as the narrator in How the West Was Really Won *at Ruidoso Middle School. He hands you his corncob pipe.]*

YOUNG YOU: Have fun, Neil.

NOW YOU: I already have.

[You blow into the pipe. Baby powder emerges, filling the page with sweet-smelling smoke. After a second it disappears . . . and so have both of you.]

. . . THE END!!!

To live your life again, turn to page 1.

THANKS TO:

Zoë Chapin—the trustiest sidekick around

David "DJ" Javerbaum—a collaborator so good he should be a collabo-*greater*

Jim Steinmeyer—the master of magical methods

Suzanne O'Neill—the editor-at-large-and-in-charge

Laura Nolan—the classy catalyst for this creation

Shea Martin—pal and practically perfect person

Sheila Harris—the encyclopedic memory of facts and dates

WITH A LITTLE HELP FROM YOUR FRIENDS . . .

Steven Bochco—the man who gave me my medical license

Nathan Fillion—a really good bad good guy

Adam Frager—cocktail alchemist and mixologist extraordinaire

Whoopi Goldberg—Clara's heart and Neil's mentor

Antony Hare—The illest-rator around

Jon Hurwitz and Hayden Schlossberg—writers of the Harold and Kumar chapter (and movies); channelers of my very bad self

Perez Hilton—nemesis turned fremesis

Penn Jillette—the man who made me gay

Matt Kuhn—writer of the Barney Stinson chapter; alter ego of my alter ego

Seth MacFarlane—the war buddy I never knew I had

Kelly Ripa—dear friend and mystified apple-eater

Amy Sedaris—she just loves beavers

Sarah Silverman—my all-time favorite fainter

Stephen Sondheim—nothing will ever harm him, not while I'm around

PHOTOGRAPH CREDITS

From *Clara's Heart*: Michael Ochs Archives (Getty Images)

From *Doogie Howser, M.D.*: ABC Photo Archives (Disney ABC Television Group via Getty Images)

From *The Tonight Show*: NBC (NBC Universal via Getty Images)

With Stephen Dorff: Ron Galella, Ltd (Ron Galella Collection via Getty Images)

From *How I Met Your Mother*: Pamela Fryman

From *Rent, Proof, Cabaret, Assassins,* and *Hedwig and the Angry Inch*: Joan Marcus

From the 2013 Tonys: Andrew H. Walker (Getty Images Entertainment)

All other photographs are from the author's collection.

SONG CREDITS

Lyrics to "Bigger," from the 2013 Tony Awards, words and music by Lin-Manuel Miranda and Tom Kitt; Tony Award® Productions © 2013; Tony Award® is a registered trademark of the American Theatre Wing, used with permission.

Adapted lyrics to "Empire State of Mind," from the 2013 Tony Awards, lyrics by Lin-Manuel Miranda and Tommy Kail; Tony Award® Productions © 2013; Tony Award® is a registered trademark of the American Theatre Wing, used with permission.

Lyrics to "The Judge's Return," from *Sweeney Todd,* words and music by Stephen Sondheim, © 1979 RILTING MUSIC, INC. All Rights Administered by WB MUSIC CORP. All Rights Reserved. Used by Permission. Reprinted by Permission of Hal Leonard Corporation.

Lyrics to "Brand New Day," from *Dr. Horrible's Sing-Along Blog,* words and music by Jed Whedon and Joss Whedon, © TIME SCIENCE BLOOD CLUB, LLC.